Pathway to a Better Life in Haiti

Praise for this book

'Based on personal experiences and interactions with powerful women and valued colleagues, *Pathway to a Better Life in Haiti* offers an incisive and honest account of the pioneering efforts of Fonkoze to address extreme poverty in Haiti. Werlin's deep knowledge of the organisation's ever-evolving approach conveys the importance of listening, learning, and changing course accordingly. A must read for anyone interested in the practice of poverty alleviation!'

> Dr Keetie Roelen, Senior Research Fellow in Poverty and Social Protection and
> Co-Deputy Director at the Centre for the Study of Global Development (CSGD)
> in the Faculty of Wellbeing, Education and Language Studies (WELS)
> at the Open University, UK

'Steven Werlin's *Pathway to a Better Life in Haiti* offers a profoundly human and hopeful portrayal of how Fonkoze's graduation approach transforms lives amid extreme poverty. With clarity and compassion, Werlin's storytelling gives voice to those rising from entrenched poverty, revealing their courage and resilience—making this book an inspiring call to action.'

> Aude de Montesquiou, VP Economic Inclusion, Trickle up and Senior Advisor at
> BRAC Institute for Governance and Development and the World Bank

'In *Pathway to a Better Life in Haiti*, Steven Werlin chronicles a great Haitian success story: the inception and seventeen-year refinement of Fonkoze's CLM program, which has provided a staircase out of ultra-poverty for ten thousand families, and counting. Werlin reminds us that supporting the most vulnerable on their journey out of ultra-poverty is not quick or easy work, yet Fonkoze has shown that if we accompany those we aim to serve while empowering them to facilitate their own transformation, the results can be stunning.

At a time when new thinking and more sustainable approaches are needed globally, this important work should be included in conversations around poverty, as it provides a blueprint for those in the development community seeking to support vulnerable populations facing the most dire circumstances.'

> Gerald Oriol, Jr., Haiti's Former Secretary of State for the Integration of Persons
> with Disabilities, and Executive Director of Fondation J'Aime Haïti

'Steven Werlin is a gifted writer who gives voice to these women and their families as they struggle to escape poverty. I encourage you to read this book — it will leave you deeply grateful for all that you have.'

> Anne Hastings, Vice President of the Board of Directors of the University
> of Fondwa USA, Inc

Pathway to a Better Life in Haiti

Fonkoze's graduation approach
for poverty alleviation

Steven Werlin

Practical
ACTION
PUBLISHING

Practical Action Publishing Ltd
25 Albert Street, Rugby,
Warwickshire, CV21 2SD, UK
www.practicalactionpublishing.com
© Steven Werlin, 2025

A catalogue record for this book is available from the British Library.

A catalogue record for this book has been requested from the Library of Congress.

ISBN 978-1-78853-410-9 Paperback
ISBN 978-1-78853-446-8 Electronic book

Citation: Werlin, S. (2025) *Pathway to a Better Life in Haiti: Fonkoze's graduation approach for poverty alleviation*, Rugby, UK: Practical Action Publishing http://doi.org/10.3362/9781788534468

Since 1974, Practical Action Publishing has published and disseminated books and information in support of international development work throughout the world.

Practical Action Publishing is a trading name of Practical Action Publishing Ltd (Company Reg. No. 1159018), the wholly owned publishing company of Practical Action. Practical Action Publishing trades only in support of its parent charity objectives and any profits are covenanted back to Practical Action (Charity Reg. No. 247257, Group VAT Registration No. 880 9924 76).

The manufacturer's authorised representative in the EU for product safety is Lightning Source France, 1 Av. Johannes Gutenberg, 78310 Maurepas, France. compliance@lightningsource.fr

Cover design by: Katarzyna Markowska, Practical Action Publishing
Typeset by vPrompt eServices, India

Contents

Acknowledgements   vii
Foreword   ix

1. To eliminate poverty   1

2. Defining poverty   7

3. A little history   13

4. Selection: making lists   23

5. Selection: with lists in hand   33

6. Joining CLM   41

7. Getting started   51

8. Home visits   59

9. The stipend   77

10. Building wealth   83

11. Saving   93

12. Committees   105

13. Health and safety   113

14. Building a home   119

15. Healthcare   131

16. Graduation   143

17. Success   151

18. Changed lives   159

19. Perspectives   165

References   169

Acknowledgements

By happy accident, I completed the first draft of this book on 8th June 2024, my father's 91st birthday. I had been thinking about all the people who have made my work possible over the years, but his birthday brought before me the obvious fact that no one has done more to make what I do possible than my two parents. They set me on my own pathway to a better life and have accompanied me all along its twisting, turning way. I have reason to be grateful to them and for them every day of my life, and I dedicate this book to them.

I wrote most of this book on my balcony in Mibalè, over the course of five or six years, and it would have been impossible without a lot of help. I depended, first and foremost, on my colleagues at Fonkoze, especially my two bosses, Gauthier Dieudonne and Hébert Artus, their boss Carine Roenen, and the families that they and I have had the privilege of working with. But without feedback and encouragement from Anne Hastings, Leigh Carter, David Shiner, Kevin Topper, Matt Balitsaris, and Margaret Dulaney the work of writing would have been neither possible nor hardly even desirable. Suggestions from Nina Ryan, who edited the earliest versions of the first parts of this book, were also indispensable.

Foreword

By Aude de Montesquiou and Syed Hashemi

Conventional development thinking is dominated by Northern perspectives, often muting Southern voices and appropriating their ideas. In Bangladesh, the radical vision of confronting power structures that is inherent in the initial microfinance model eventually shifted towards emphases on sustainability and financial sector deepening, losing some of its transformative potential. Many innovative grassroots programmes promising greater democratic control by the poor never scaled up due to the South's inability to strongly articulate and promote alternative visions globally.

This book presents a counterexample. Chemen Lavi Miyò (CLM) is a programme developed by Haitians for Haitians, following the pioneering work of BRAC in Bangladesh. In this foreword, we provide some background on how a Southern-developed approach gained global recognition as a legitimate contribution to the development discourse to eliminate extreme poverty.

From 2005 to 2014, CGAP (the Consultative Group to Assist the Poor) and the Ford Foundation worked with local organizations to develop 10 pilot projects in eight countries. The authors of a *Development in Practice* article (Hashemi and de Montesquiou, 2024) were leading this effort at CGAP, and we summarize that article in this Foreword. We offer insights into the adoption and expansion of BRAC's programme for families in ultra-poverty and how BRAC's model evolved from a local intervention into a global framework for poverty reduction and economic inclusion. We discuss how the process of scaling took place and analyse the broader policy implications of this Southern-led development model.

Neoliberal economics in the 1980s increased vulnerabilities for massive segments of the population in the Global South. The *World Development Report 1990* called for state support for the poor, positing 'safety nets' as part of a global poverty reduction strategy. Throughout the 1990s, safety nets were seen as residual state responsibilities rather than integrated elements of development strategies, with beneficiaries viewed as passive recipients. The 1997 financial crisis in Asia and subsequent crises in Latin America and the former Soviet Union renewed interest in social protection, broadening ideas about its goals.

From its inception, BRAC strongly believed in poverty alleviation, equity, and social justice through the agency of the poor and marginalized.

Its approach was based on immersion among the poor, understanding their lived realities, and continuous learning and improving. BRAC's innovations stemmed from this pedagogical approach.

Recognizing that its microfinance programmes were not impactful for the poorest, BRAC developed the TUP, or Targeting the Ultra Poor, model in 2002. This closely monitored, tightly sequenced, multisectoral initiative aimed to improve the conditions of the poorest and reduce the probability of their backsliding into poverty. The programme reached over 2 million households, with 100,000 female heads of households accepted into it each year. Randomized controlled trials revealed sizeable economic impacts sustained many years after participants entered the programme. This same realization, that standard microfinance does not serve families in the deepest poverty, would eventually lead to Fonkoze's adoption in Haiti of the programme this book describes.

TUP was built on years of interactions with, and learning from, the rural poor in Bangladesh. BRAC works in a participatory way, where BRAC staff learn directly from the communities they aim to serve. By engaging vulnerable individuals in every phase – from identifying their needs to co-developing solutions – BRAC fosters a collaborative learning environment that adapts the intervention to local realities. This mutual learning process not only empowers beneficiaries but also continuously refines the programme to achieve sustainable transformation and long-term economic security.

A major observation from BRAC's microfinance programme was its success with certain segments of the poor – namely, the economically active poor – but not with others. Many among the poorest, with low, irregular incomes, were either considered too risky for microfinance loans or themselves considered their situation too dire, so that they were reluctant to add to their vulnerability through taking on debt. Their vulnerabilities were multidimensional, and easing off only the credit constraint was insufficient to break the cycle of extreme poverty they were in. This led BRAC to develop the graduation strategy of multiple layered interventions for those among the poorest who could potentially be prepared for taking on sustainable livelihoods.

BRAC's theory of change for the segment of the poorest who could potentially start and sustain economic activities was based on locating its new model at the intersection of safety nets, financial inclusion, and livelihoods promotion, with a strong coaching and confidence building element (Figure 1.1). It rested on the following critical learning:

- *Careful targeting.* A rigorous selection process is essential to identify those who are most vulnerable yet capable of benefiting from economic opportunities. Community-based assessments and means testing help capture individuals living on the margins who might otherwise be overlooked. Avoiding exclusion errors in graduation programmes is absolutely critical because the ultra-poor – the intended beneficiaries – often reside on the margins of society and face profound social exclusion. These individuals are not only economically disadvantaged but are frequently too impoverished to participate in community activities, attend ceremonies, or engage with peers in ways that could open up opportunities for growth and empowerment. When such vulnerable households are left out, the programme fails to reach those most in need, thereby perpetuating cycles of deprivation and isolation. Ensuring that the most marginalized are included is essential not only to maximize the programme's transformative potential but also to uphold the social justice imperative of supporting every community member, regardless of their current level of participation. On the other hand, inclusion errors are less concerning in very poor geographies since even those mistakenly included are very poor and stand to benefit substantially from the intervention. This means that while precision in targeting remains vital to reach the truly needy, the overall impact of the programme remains robust because its beneficiaries are uniformly people in severe poverty.

- *Time-bound limited consumption support or stipend (a safety net) to provide the breathing space to engage in new economic activities without having to worry about the next meal.* A temporary, carefully calibrated stipend provides critical relief, enabling participants to devote time and energy to developing new livelihoods without immediate financial pressure. This time-bound support acts as a safety net that addresses urgent household needs while creating the mental space for learning and growth. It helps alleviate the constant worry over basic sustenance, thereby fostering an environment for sustainable change.
- *Careful market assessments to determine the feasibility of new economic activities (new livelihoods pathways) and to avoid market oversaturation or constrained demand.* Comprehensive market assessments are conducted to evaluate local or regional market opportunities, ensuring that new livelihoods can be sustained over time. These assessments help to avoid issues such as market oversaturation while ensuring that the supply of goods or services aligns with local demand. This informs the design of interventions, ensuring that each livelihood pathway is contextualized and sustainable.
- *Simple, short training on running and managing specific economic activities (managing livelihoods).* Concise, hands-on training sessions equip participants with the practical skills required to manage and sustain specific economic activities effectively. The training emphasizes real-world applications and is designed to be immediately actionable, making it accessible even for those with limited formal education. By focusing on clear, targeted instruction, these sessions empower beneficiaries to quickly translate knowledge into productive outcomes.
- *A small grant, rather than a loan, to kick-start new economic activities because of the inability of the poorest to take on debt (seed capital).* Providing a small grant instead of a loan eliminates the risk of indebtedness for individuals who lack the financial capacity to shoulder even a very small loan. This form of seed funding offers an immediate boost,

allowing participants to invest in income-generating activities without a long-term financial burden. Such grants serve as a catalyst for entrepreneurship, unlocking new opportunities and paving the way towards financial sustainability.

- *Savings services and basic financial education to start participants on a course of better financial management (financial inclusion).* The introduction of savings services paired with basic financial education lays a critical foundation for sound financial management. These initiatives promote regular savings habits and enhance financial literacy, empowering participants to better manage their resources. This early exposure to formal financial services helps build long-term economic resilience and supports gradual upward mobility.

- *Close monitoring, consistent hand-holding and planning, and peer group interactions to build hope, confidence, and support that would enable participants to start and stay on course with their economic activities (coaching).* Close monitoring combined with coaching sessions provide continuous guidance and ensure that participants are able to navigate challenges as they arise. Peer group interactions create supportive environments, where shared experiences and collaborative problem-solving reinforce individual confidence. This comprehensive coaching model is vital in maintaining momentum and fostering sustained progress towards self-reliance.

- *Utmost attention to balance the support being provided with the risk of external dependence of participants through the creation of village community groups (social inclusion).* Striking a careful balance between providing necessary support and fostering self-reliance is critical for long-term success. The establishment of village community groups encourages internal capacity building and mutual support among participants, reducing reliance on support from the programme. These groups serve as the foundation for cultivating sustained social capital and are essential for integrating economic gains into the broader community fabric, even after the programme intervention is over.

- *Where possible, linking participants, after the end of the programme, to community organizations to allow for continued peer group social capital development.* Where feasible, connecting participants with existing community organizations ensures that the social networks and support systems built during the intervention continue to thrive. This linkage promotes ongoing mentorship, shared learning, and resource exchange long after the programme concludes. Continued association with established groups helps reinforce the gains made during the intervention and supports long-term economic and social development.

These conditions as well as the model for TUP programming were derived and developed based on an organic learning between the rural poor and BRAC staff. But the experimentation and the learning has continued throughout the

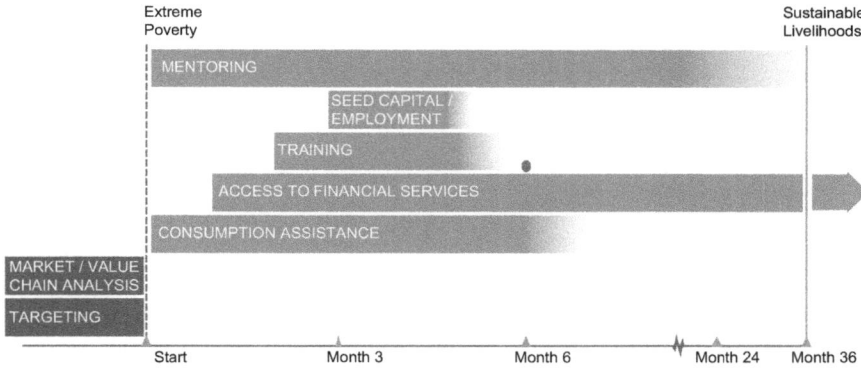

Figure 1.1 The graduation model
Source: Hashemi and de Montesquiou, 2016

last 20 years of the programme. Changes and adaptations were made based on changing contexts and new realities.

Globalizing the graduation approach

While BRAC's TUP programme represented a breakthrough, innovative model of livelihoods pathways that would 'graduate' many of the poorest out of extreme poverty and sustain them on a pathway of continued economic improvements, protracted efforts and strong partnerships with the North were required to globalize this knowledge. The key champion in this effort was CGAP.

CGAP is a global partnership housed at the World Bank. It consists of major philanthropic, bilateral, and multilateral donors focusing on expanding financial services to the poor. While central to CGAP's mission is meeting the financial needs of the poor, creating a sustainable financial sector for the unbanked requires a strong commercialization focus. CGAP recognized that extending credit to the poorest could potentially worsen their situation. Therefore, CGAP looked for models combining access to finance with various non-financial services. Inspired by BRAC's innovative approaches, CGAP advocated for BRAC's model as a pathway for the poorest to escape extreme poverty. CGAP conducted meetings and workshops with major donors and NGOs to demonstrate the graduation model's efficacy, addressing concerns about its success in different contexts (Hashemi, 2001).

In 2006, CGAP and the Ford Foundation collaborated to test and adapt BRAC's approach in diverse countries. The initiative involved ten pilot projects in eight countries, engaging various partners and extensive research. Randomized controlled trials, or RCTs, were conducted at seven pilot sites, with qualitative research in nine sites, including Fonkoze's pilot in Haiti (Huda and Simanowitz, 2010b). The programme aimed to prove the model's generalizability and effectiveness in building sustainable livelihoods for the poorest.

The **CGAP-Ford Foundation Program** included ten pilot programs in eight countries with deliberate regional, economic, cultural, and ecological diversity. The pilots were implemented through partnerships among financial service providers, nongovernmental organizations (NGOs), and government safety net programs when possible. The pilots were as follows:

- **Haiti:** Conducted by Fondasyon Fonkoze, a microfinance institution dedicated to reaching destitute clients. Research methods included mixed methods by BRAC Development Institute (BDI).
- **Pakistan:** Managed by the Pakistan Poverty Alleviation Fund (PPAF) through various NGOs. RCT impact assessment by Innovations for Poverty Action (IPA) and qualitative research by BDI.
- **Honduras:** Implemented by Organizacion de Desarrollo Empresarial Feminino (ODEF) and Plan International Honduras, focusing on women and children. RCT impact assessment and qualitative research by IPA.
- **Peru:** Carried out by Asociación Arariwa and Plan International Peru, targeting children. RCT impact assessment and qualitative research by IPA.
- **Ethiopia:** Partnered with the Relief Society of Tigray (REST) and DECSI, a microfinance institution. RCT impact assessment by IPA and qualitative research by BDI.
- **Yemen:** Implemented through the Social Welfare Fund and the Social Fund for Development, supported by the World Bank. RCT impact assessment by IPA and qualitative research by BDI.
- **Ghana:** Conducted by Presbyterian Agricultural Services, with RCT impact assessment research by IPA.
- **India:** Three pilots with Bandhan Konnagar, Trickle Up, and Swayam Krishi Sangam (SKS) in various regions. RCT impact assessment by JPAL (Bandhan) and NYU (SKS) and qualitative research by BDI (Trickle Up and SKS).

Although BRAC's TUP programme was the 'model', CGAP expanded and adapted it for changing contexts while remaining true to the vision of multi-dimensionality, big push, time-bound assistance, and close monitoring with an emphasis on empowerment and agency. In fact, CGAP started using the concept of 'graduation pathway', rather than graduation model, to suggest the necessity of adaptations. In addition, it was recognized that virtually no NGO could replicate what BRAC was doing in terms of massive national scaling up. Furthermore, most national governments were intent on initiating and expanding safety net programmes for the poor to ensure basic food security. It was felt that for graduation programming to be successfully scaled up, linkages with existing or planned government safety net or livelihood programmes would be essential.

As the pilots matured, the CGAP-Ford Foundation programme evolved. CGAP, leveraging its unique position as a convener of bi- and multilateral donors within the World Bank, started playing a lead role in building a community of practice, seeding a future global movement around graduation approaches. Starting in 2010, CGAP led deliberate efforts to cultivate a network of 'champions' within donor organizations, conducting regular donor tours in Europe, Asia, and North America to garner interest and create in-house alliances within the World Bank, the Asian Development Bank, the International Fund for Agricultural Development, the World Food

Programme, the UNHCR, and several bilateral donor agencies, in particular the United Kingdom's Department for International Development, and Germany's Gesellschaft für Internationale Zusammenarbeit. Starting in 2009, CGAP also started to organize regular 'Global Learning Events' for reaching out beyond the 'first circle' of implementers and researchers to also include two or three key staff in donor agencies – a small group that could champion graduation and move the needle within multilateral and bilateral aid agencies. In addition, key, receptive national policymakers were also invited.

From 2009 to 2015, CGAP convened Global Learning Events in Bangladesh (2009), Paris (2011, 2012, 2014) and Washington, DC (2015). These three-day invitation-only meetings were designed with multiple spaces for interaction and socializing. Their frequency meant that a group bond was created in an atmosphere of trust and shared excitement from the feeling of being at the cusp of innovation for sustainable poverty reduction. Fonkoze was always well represented with Anne Hastings, Carine Roenen, Gauthier Dieudonne, and Steven Werlin taking turns to join and present.

Research was a particularly anticipated topic, especially since the RCT impact assessment movement was starting to gain visibility, and six of the pilots were using independently conducted RCTs. The Global Learning Events brought together future Nobel winners and internationally recognized scholars such as Abhijit Banerjee and Esther Duflo, as well as Oriana Bandeira, Robin Burgess, Naila Kabeer, Dean Karlan, and more. Since early evidence was showing strong impact of the programmes, CGAP pushed for research results to be shared in the form of preliminary findings at these events, in order to create a 'drumbeat' and ready the donors and policymakers so they would be interested and likely to implement the programmes when the research became public. When the RCTs were published, they showed increased incomes and household consumption at all but one graduation site (Banerjee et al., 2015).

While the CGAP-Ford Foundation Graduation Programme started with dialogues and discussions with donors to convince them of integrating graduation programming as an integral element of their social protection commitment, efforts were also on to have these discussions with national policymakers in their own countries. CGAP and Innovations for Poverty Action, an important research institution, also produced a simple costing analysis comparing the cost-effectiveness of livelihood programmes, one-off cash transfers, and graduation (Sulaiman et al., 2016). The cost-effectiveness of graduation programmes was shown to be high, with annual household income gains as a percentage of total programme costs ranging from about 7 per cent to 25 per cent in the five sites where the programme had positive impact, suggesting that among programmes that targeted the extreme poor and with long-term impact evidence, the graduation approach had the greatest impact per dollar of cost, with positive impact on economic indicators persisting over time (Sulaiman et al., 2016).

The relationships that were developed through these meetings, the descriptions of and evidence from the pilots, and finally the publication of the results of the impact assessment in 2015 in *Science* ('A Multifaceted Program Causes Lasting Progress for the Very Poor: Evidence from Six Countries'; Banerjee et al., 2015), helped influence the global perceptions of feasibility, suggesting graduation-type programmes could be implemented at scale despite fiscal and capacity constraints to administer and manage multidimensional and cross-sectoral interventions (Banerjee et al., 2015; *The Economist*, 2015; Hashemi and de Montesquiou, 2016; Sulaiman et al., 2016) .

The uptake was slow, and rightly so, since national governments have to be extremely careful about their programme commitments and their budgetary implications. However, graduation ultimately took off. Currently, there are over 250 graduation and graduation-type economic inclusion programmes in 75 countries, reaching an estimated 92 million people. Governments started deliberately integrating economic inclusion pilots as part of national strategies and frameworks for poverty reduction as an important complement to their existing anti-poverty efforts. For example, as some countries were expanding the coverage and financing of safety nets, they started to integrate graduation-type programmes on top in the form of 'safety nets plus' or 'cash plus' strategies. In Haiti, Fonkoze's advocacy contributed to the government eventually deciding to integrate the graduation approach into its official social promotion/protection policy.

A turning point was reached in December 2015 when at a large cohort of World Bank Task Team Leaders, mostly from the Social Protection and Jobs Global Practice, joined the CGAP-Ford Foundation Global Learning Event in Washington, DC and maintained that graduation-type economic inclusion programmes were no longer perceived as unrealistic to implement, but one pragmatic option to respond to government demand for strategies that create jobs for very poor people in largely informal economies.

Of relevance to the increasingly fragile context in Haiti, World Bank 2021 data showed that economic inclusion programmes were more likely to target displacement-affected populations, particularly internally displaced populations, in contexts of fragility, conflict, and violence – referred to in the language of the World Bank as FCVs – than in non-FCV contexts (34 per cent versus 8 per cent) and focus more on increasing resilience (43 per cent versus 28 per cent), social inclusion (38 per cent versus 25 per cent), and food security (32 per cent versus 23 per cent) (Andrews, 2021). Economic inclusion in these contexts can help build resilience and develop economic opportunities that may enable people to better cope with the economic and social stress while building income and assets (de Montesquiou et al., 2017). But a lack of government systems and structures, and the presence of corruption and insecurity, make it challenging to link these efforts to government or other programmes for ongoing support. Programmes in FCV contexts are less likely than programmes in non-FCV settings to be government-led (41 per cent versus 52 per cent) or funded by government (16 per cent versus 36 per cent).

They are also less likely than programmes in non-FCV settings to be integrated with government programmes (43 per cent versus 67 per cent) and delivered by linking existing programmes (7 per cent versus 26 per cent) (Andrews, 2021).

In 2017, CGAP recognized that the pathway to scaling graduation was through policymaking and integrating graduation-type programmes with social protection systems. As CGAP was essentially about financial services, and the World Bank was the central advocate, designer, and implementor of social protection systems around the world, it was decided that graduation efforts would be far better placed within the World Bank. In July 2017, the Partnership for Economic Inclusion (PEI) was created with a mission to accelerate the adoption, innovation, and scaling of the economic inclusion programmes particularly through integrating with government social protection systems or other large anti-poverty programmes.

From the start, PEI had three core areas of focus: country engagement, innovation and learning, and knowledge management guidance and capacity building. Efforts were made to move from the 'graduation' terminology into the crafting of a joint definition around economic inclusion programmes, focused less on the operational details and more on the development objectives of the programme.

'Economic Inclusion Programmes' were defined as multidimensional sets of bundled interventions that support households and communities to develop sustainable livelihoods and increase their incomes and assets. At the onset of the global COVID-19 pandemic, economic inclusion programmes gained more popularity as a means to complement social assistance measures with additional inputs and linkages to help mitigate the impacts of the pandemic (Archibald, 2020).

The globalizing of the graduation programming is a great story of making visible Southern efforts to come up with home-grown solutions to developmental challenges. It is an example of a North–South intellectual cooperation based on deep respect for the South. The tendency to showcase Southern efforts as boutique, ethnic models, to be explained and narrated, conceptually and analytically by the North, was completely rejected in the two-decade long interactions with BRAC and other developing country partners like Fonkoze. Therein, hopefully, lies the basis of future North–South cooperation that can be learned and practised.

CHAPTER 1
To eliminate poverty

Lucienne lives along Ravin Gwomòn. Her home sits on the raised bank of the river that runs south and west of downtown Gwomòn, a broad commune in northern Haiti. With every heavy rain, waters stream down from the surrounding hills, rushing through and flooding the channel and more or less of the land on either side of it. The plots scattered along the banks can be fertile, but farming them can be risky, too, depending on how much rain falls, how quickly, and when.

Only a few years ago, Lucienne had nothing. She would occasionally look after a goat or a pig for one of her neighbours, hoping she would someday acquire livestock of her own. In rural Haiti, folks who take care of a neighbour's female livestock are normally paid in kind, from the young of any female animals they care for. If they are caring for a male, they get a cut of the sale price. But the system depends on livestock owners' willingness to be fair. People like Lucienne, who do this work, have little leverage over the owners, and the owners who used Lucienne kept taking advantage of her. They would take back the animals from her before she could profit from the work.

She and her four children lived in a small two-room house. The children's father had passed away. Lucienne couldn't afford to pay rent, but the owner of the home just let them stay in a corner of one of the rooms.

She struggled to provide for her children and herself. She would buy small quantities of produce on credit from nearby farmers who knew her. She'd then divide what she purchased into smaller quantities for sale in downtown Gwomòn. She could break down a sack or a half-sack of sweet potatoes, for example, and sell it in piles of four to six potatoes each, enough for a single meal. She might earn enough from a day of sales to make her family a meal, but she wouldn't earn more than that. She could not send her children to school.

Lucienne joined a programme designed for families in especially deep poverty, and she asked the programme to help her raise goats and invest in small commerce. She received a grant of three small female goats and some merchandise she could sell.

The commerce she chose was the same one she was accustomed to. Sometimes Haitians call it *kase lote*, which means to break up and parcel out. A merchant buys wholesale and sells retail, though 'wholesale' here means much less than one might normally take it to mean: a sack or less of something like sweet potatoes, sour oranges, or okra. Having joined the programme, Lucienne could buy her merchandise with cash, which gave her more freedom to choose what to buy and how much. Her goats prospered. In less than a year and a half, they had more than doubled their value.

Even after she completed her time in the 18-month programme, Lucienne continued to make further progress raising livestock. She began to buy additional animals with proceeds from her small commerce and from the farming she had started to do. She eventually bought six sheep to add to her goats. But she never was especially attached to any of the animals, or even to the notion of keeping livestock at all. She had learned from the programme's staff to view them simply as investments.

When she saw a chance to buy a plot of land that had already been planted with sugarcane, she jumped. She sold all the animals she had accumulated to assemble the cash she needed for the purchase. She sold her first cane harvest and bought more land with the proceeds, which she and her new partner quickly planted. She planned to use the harvest from the new land to start buying livestock again.

She was determined to keep moving forward. 'I was so poor. The programme helped me pull myself out. I have no right to go back. The humiliation that I used to feel keeps me from slipping back.'

And she developed a larger vision for herself as well. She wanted to be able to help others. 'If somebody comes to me with a problem, I have to be able to tell them that half of their problem belongs to me.'

***

In 2000, the United Nations approved a set of eight Millennium Development Goals. The first of those goals was to eradicate extreme poverty and hunger. The UN also established two criteria for evaluating progress towards that goal: halving, between 1990 and 2015, both the proportion of people in the world living on less than US$1.25 per day and the proportion of people suffering from hunger. In the *Millennium Development Goals Report* that it released in 2013, the United Nations had announced that the first of these targets had been met five years early and that the other was 'within reach' (UNDESA, 2013).

Certainly, that was very good news, but it also begs a question. What about the other half?

In the light of such rapid success, it might be tempting to assume that we should continue to do whatever we've been doing. Economic growth in some populous nations that were home to lots of poverty drove the improvement, so maybe a continued focus on economic growth will take the world the rest of the way.

The anti-poverty effects that the world has seen from economic growth, especially in southern and eastern Asia, are surely worth celebrating. More economic activity probably means more opportunity, even for those whose poverty is deepest.

But if all poverty is not the same, there is little reason to imagine that all can be addressed the same way. Economic growth could be helpful to some, maybe even many, but it might not by itself be the solution for all.

The work that this book describes starts from the assumption that the families who live in the worst poverty deserve, that they have a right to, the tools they need to improve their lives. And that the right is theirs now, not whenever increases in their countries' GDPs might trickle down to them.

This is Haitian work, done by Haitians in Haiti, and that country's recent history suggests that overall economic progress – when there is progress to talk about at all – does not reach the most vulnerable part of the population. Although the percentage of Haitians living in extreme poverty decreased through the first decade of the 21st century, any positive impact from that growth stayed in the nation's urban areas. The percentage of rural Haitians living in extreme poverty did not change, remaining at 38 per cent from 2000 to 2012 (World Bank and Observatoire National de la Pauvreté et de l'Exclusion Sociale (ONPES), 2014.) Insofar as things in Haiti improved, the improvement passed by rural Haitians living in poverty. And degradation of the economy since then has only made the figures more alarming. In 2023, the UN reported that nearly 5 million Haitians were experiencing acute food insecurity. That's almost half the nation (UN, 2023).

In addition to the belief that overall economic growth will not reach the poorest Haitians any time soon, the work depends on a related proposition. We know from both experience and research that well-designed programming can help people living in especially severe poverty build a first measure of the well-being they are entitled to. This has been well established through various studies, for example in the work of Nobel Prize winning economists Abhijit Banerjee and Esther Duflo (Banerjee, et al., 2015).

Since 2007, a Haitian non-profit called Fonkoze has worked with more than 10,000 of the poorest families in Haiti, providing them with the tools and the accompaniment they need to improve their lives. Fonkoze's programme is called Chemen Lavi Miyò, the Path to a Better Life. Since it was first tested, the programme has proven successful for over 95 per cent of its participants. It's one of dozens of similar programmes in countries around the world that are usually called 'graduation' programmes. Families join Chemen Lavi Miyò with little or nothing. They have no way to generate even a minimal income consistently. When they enter the programme, many are frequently going more than a day at a time without a meal. Their income depends on intermittent day-labour, which is paid atrociously when they can get it at all, or on occasional and unreliable charity. They have children they cannot send to school. They live in homes that, as Haitians say, 'can fool the sun but not the rain', which is to say that they might provide shade, but no protection from tropical downpours.

After 18 months of their own hard work, all that has changed. The families have developed ways to earn the income they need to begin to manage their lives. They have plans for the future and the confidence to know that they can continue to succeed. And a large majority do continue to succeed.

A short description of Fonkoze's programme can sound like a fundraising appeal or an infomercial, because its results are reliable and dramatic and the level of poverty it addresses is striking. But there is a lot to learn from a more detailed account. Seeing the path that one institution took to build a programme for families living in the harshest poverty can teach us what an all-encompassing commitment to alleviating poverty could look like. Studying the nuts and bolts of a comprehensive approach to poverty alleviation can teach us what such an effort might involve. Reading about the paths that individual women navigate as they move through the programme can teach us something about what it means to live in the most extreme of extreme poverty and what it takes to overcome it.

In 2016 my first book about this programme, *To Fool the Rain* (Werlin, 2016), came out. I was feeling a sense of wonder and of privilege because of my place on a team of Haitians addressing extreme poverty in Haiti. The people I was meeting through the programme – both the women whom we sought to serve and my coworkers – inspired me with awe: their strength in the face of impossible-seeming circumstances, but also their generosity. And it was a privilege to be part of it. I imagined that few people like me – people who came from where I came from geographically, economically, culturally, ethnically – had the opportunity to live among the folks who populated the world I was moving within. I felt obligated to share something of their stories.

It's been nine years since that book came out and longer than that since I did most of the writing it involved. A lot has changed since then, and in Haiti much of what's changed has been for the worse.

The economic environment has become more difficult. The cost of food and other essentials has steadily increased, with a range of factors contributing. According to Haiti's central bank, the annual increase in consumer prices has not been less than 20 per cent since 2021 (Banque de la Republique d'Haiti, 2025). The increasing irregularity of rainfall has made farming less reliable, as crops are lost to drought or to excessive, untimely rain. One of the country's most important staples, millet, was lost almost entirely for two years to crop disease, creating an annual gap in the domestic food supply during what used to be millet season. For these and other reasons, the country's dependence on food imports has grown while its currency lost value against the dollar.

Transportation costs have increased as well. The country's regime of heavily subsidized fuel finally burst when the government could no longer fund the subsidy, and the price of getting around using the privately owned motorcycles, cars, trucks, and buses that provide the closest thing to public transport rose correspondingly.

And that is when transportation has been possible at all. The deterioration of the security situation accelerated after the murder of Haiti's president, Jovenel Moïse, in the summer of 2021. Gangs took control of stretches of important roads, greatly complicating the movement of people and goods. Though violence has affected Haiti's capital, Pòtoprens, more directly than it has most areas of rural Haiti, the loss of access to Pòtoprens as a market for their produce and as a source of imported consumer goods has affected rural Haitians as well, as has the steady displacement of residents of the capital into safer, rural areas.

But as much as has changed, two things have remained the same. First, everywhere our staff looks, we encounter the same awful poverty: families with children they cannot send to school or even adequately feed. And second, almost all of the women we serve prove that they can change their lives for the better given the tools they need to do so.

In what follows, I weave together distinct but interrelated threads. I'll introduce the institution that decided to work with women who live in especially deep poverty and explain how it came to that decision, I'll describe the programme it established to work with these women, and I'll share the stories of some of the women who've participated in the programme. I hope that the beginning of an understanding both of the extremes of extreme poverty and of the demonstrably effective path out of it can add impetus to the United Nations' millennial commitment to eradicate extreme poverty in its various forms. We have been at this work for over 15 years, but the problem is large, even just in Haiti. Solving it will require a broader commitment than there has been to date.

CHAPTER 2
Defining poverty

The population of Gwomòn is about 160,000, of which three-quarters live in its rural areas. Lawa is a hilly part of Moulen, one of the commune's eight communal sections.

But 'hilly' doesn't really capture the feel of the place. The hills are not high, but they are steep and closely packed around rock-lined ravines. More like mountains in miniature, not at all gentle or rolling. Small, mostly straw-roofed homes dot both the tops of the hills and any flat little areas cut into the slopes. The few dirt roads that cross Moulen keep their distance from Lawa. Motorcycles can get part of the way by using one of the flatter ravines as a road. At least during dryer times. But the closest approach for a motorcycle still leaves a hike.

Clotude lives with her two young girls in Ravin Volè, or Thieves' Ravine, one of Lawa's small sub-neighbourhoods. 'I'm not sure who the thieves were', she explains with a laugh. She arrived from another part of Gwomòn, just beyond the hills across the ravine, when she moved in with her late husband about 20 years ago. 'I'm not from here, but I don't think I'll be leaving now.'

She's 42, and had 10 children, though just 6 of them survived. Her husband's death left her a widow in 2017. Two of her children moved away as soon as their father died. 'I had family members who asked me for them.'

Such informal adoptions are common in Haiti. Sometimes, it's just a matter of kind people who want to help out an unfortunate child. Sometimes, a family with some means brings a child from a poorer family into their household to help with chores. Some such families do so with a commitment to taking good care of the children; some just to exploit them. Clotude thinks that her children are treated well where they are.

Two more of the children eventually left Clotude's house as well to try to make their own ways in the world, so she now lives with just her two youngest. She cannot afford to send the older of the two to school. The younger one isn't ready yet.

Clotude does what she can for herself and the two girls by farming. She plants corn and pigeon peas on the small plot of land that slopes steeply down from her home towards the bottom of the ravine. She even has a space where she plants beans as a cash crop. But her income opportunities are otherwise limited because she is not willing to leave her young children alone to trade in a regional market, and she doesn't see business opportunities in Lawa itself. She says that there's no way to 'do commerce' there.

In Haiti, '*komès*' is used to describe a wide range of trading activities. Most involve merchants' inserting themselves into a distribution network that depends on multiple small actors at various levels rather than on a small number of larger actors, like Amazon, Walmart, and UPS. *Ti machann*, or traders, buy a quantity of something somewhere, and they change either the quantity, the location, or both. They might break a single large pile of something down into smaller ones. Someone could buy a sack of sweet potatoes and divide it for sale into small portions, maybe just enough for a single meal. Or they might take smaller piles and make them into one large one. They could, for example, buy measures of dried beans from farmers and sell them by the sack to wholesalers at a regional market. There are many variations of these general schemes. Add to this the possibilities opened by differences in prices from market to market and the work of those who simply know how to buy low and sell dear. A sack of beans, for example, might sell for less in a mountain market close to the farmers who grow the beans than at a downtown market closer to a concentration of consumers. Someone might know how to talk down the price of a goat they are buying and sell it later in the day in the same place, for more. The variations are, practically, endless.

When Clotude says she '*pa ka fè komès*', she can't do small commerce, in Lawa, she means that to build an income through retail sales of basic groceries or hygiene products or snack food or any common consumer good would be impossible there. There just isn't enough money in the neighbourhood for people to buy much of anything they aren't already buying from someone else, and she does not want to be seen as stealing someone else's customers.

So, Clotude depends on farming. When she needs cash to buy food, she looks for a day's work in her neighbours' fields. Back when I first met Clotude, such work paid 50–100 Haitian gourds. At the time, there were over 90 gourds to the US dollar so that on the days she earned a cash income she earned less than $1.10.

That level of poverty can be hard to imagine. Clotude's day of hard field labour pays her less than Americans pay for a soft drink from a vending machine.

That might not be a meaningful measure, though. Clotude would have a hard time finding a vending machine in Lawa, or a Coke, even if she looked. Much less a cold one. However, income, like the $1.10 Clotude can occasionally earn, is one standard way to measure and classify relative poverty and wealth. The World Bank Group's *World Development Report 1990* said at the time that over 1 billion people lived in 'absolute poverty' (World Bank, 1990). By this, its authors meant people living on less than $370 per year, or about $1 per day. That $1-per-day cut-off for absolute poverty has since been revised upward. It was $1.90 when I met Clotude, or over 170 gourds, much more than Clotude could hope to make in a day of field work. And her income had to feed a family of three.

Clotude's neighbour, Jeanna, has a much larger family to feed. She lives in a shack that sits on the edge of a cluster of similar homes on top of one of Lawa's small peaks. Her mother and sister live in two of the others. She's 29, and she and her husband Nelso have six children. They would have seven, but they lost one of their twins.

She did not grow up with her parents in Lawa. She's the fourth of their 12 children, and early in her life she was sent to Gonayiv, a large city just south of Gwomòn, where she lived with one of her father's cousins. The family there began to send her to school, but when she turned 14, she asked to return home. She was unhappy in Gonayiv. 'I didn't feel at home there. They hit me too much, and the boys were starting to bother me.' So, the cousin brought her back to Lawa, and she joined her parents' crowded, struggling household. When Nelso offered her a home of her own, it seemed like a good idea. She had known him since they were young children, even before she was sent away to Gonayiv.

Jeanna describes Nelso as a hard-working farmer on unproductive land that doesn't belong to them. They are sharecroppers, so they always owe the landowner half of their harvest, however insufficient that harvest might be for a family of eight.

But unlike Clotude, Jeanna avoids depending entirely on farming. In fact, she turned herself into her household's main earner. She goes to Senmak, a port city on the highway that connects Gonayiv and Pòtoprens. She sometimes spends a month or more there, staying with her younger sister. With only 75 gourds of business capital, she can buy a small sack of single-serving bags of water, already iced. She carries the sack on her head around hot, dusty, busy streets until she sells out. Then she buys another sack. She might sell as many as four or five sacks on an especially hot, crowded day, making 25 gourds on each sack. Late in the day, she takes the water money and buys kerosene, which sells well in the early evening to people who need it for cooking fuel or lamps. That can earn her another 75–100 gourds. Once a week, she buys provisions for her family and loads them onto a direct truck from Senmak to Moulen. Nelso meets the truck and carries the provisions home to Lawa.

But frequent pregnancies have meant that months often pass without Jeanna bringing in any income at all. She stays at home for the end of each pregnancy and for each baby's first six months or so. During those periods, the family really struggles. Unless her pregnancy happens to coincide with a harvest, the family is especially badly off. Then they must depend on Nelso's day labour, the same 100-gourd-per-day work that Clotude uses. But there are eight in her home.

She has two children attending school right now. They are only in the second grade, though, because they often lose time. Sometimes the school sends them home because Jeanna and Nelso owe too much money. Like most schools in Haiti, it is private. Jeanna says that the school's director likes to show patience and understanding to parents who struggle to pay, but he can only do so much because he's responsible for paying the teachers, and he cannot pay them without the fees that parents are supposed to pay him. Sometimes Jeanna just keeps the older children home to take care of the younger kids.

***

By any reasonable standard, both Clotude's family and Jeanna's are terribly, terribly poor, but there are several different ways to measure poverty. Considering how very little money Clotude or Jeanna and her husband earn, it is worth trying to understand how the UN came to define extreme poverty as $1 per person per day. Neither family earns nearly that much money.

When the *World Development Report 1990* notes how many people live in 'absolute poverty', it also explains the calculation. But perhaps we should call it an 'approximation' instead. It is a rough average of the poverty lines of a handful of poor countries (World Bank, 1990: 27). In other words, it does not itself define 'poverty', it rather averages a number of other calculations that attempt to do so. Each country's line, it explains, is a separate calculation:

> A consumption-based poverty line can be thought of as comprised of two elements: the expenditure necessary to buy a minimum standard of nutrition and other basic necessities and a further amount that varies from country to country, reflecting the cost of participating in the everyday life of society. (World Bank, 1990: 26)

Haiti's own poverty lines were detailed in 2014 in a report published by the World Bank. The poverty line for the country was fixed at $2.41 per person per day, and the extreme poverty line at $1.23 (World Bank and ONPES, 2014). These lines were determined by a group of Haitian government offices that collect and treat economic data, especially data relating to poverty. They imagined a basket of 26 different goods that would collectively cover 85 per cent of a person's food consumption, and they calculated its cost. The report distinguishes between poverty, which refers to an inability to afford 'essential needs', and extreme poverty, which refers to an inability to meet 'nutritional needs'.

And though $1.23 per day is very little, it is much more than Jeanna and Nelso can depend on. Sometimes Jeanna's pregnancies fall during the season between harvests, and the family needs cash income to get by. If all they have comes from Nelso's day labour, the 100 gourds that he brings in works out to about 13 cents per person.

These calculations are very rough, mixing data from different years, years with different costs of living and different dollar/gourd exchange rates. But by any measure, the cash Jeanna's family has available to them classes them well below Haiti's extreme poverty line, particularly when Jeanna is at home.

To distinguish the very poorest families among those living in extreme poverty, some people and organizations began speaking of 'ultra-poverty'. A report released in November 2017 by two organizations, Uplift and the RESULTS Educational Fund, explains the term (Reed et al., 2017). Rather than simply setting ultra-poor apart from extreme-poor with a still-lower income or consumption threshold, the report takes a different approach. Its authors use a tool developed by the Oxford Poverty and Human Development Initiative, the Multidimensional Poverty Index (MPI), which, as the Oxford initiative explains, 'complements traditional income-based poverty measures by capturing the deprivations that each person faces' (Oxford Poverty and Human Development Initiative, 2024).

The index considers three 'dimensions of poverty': health, education, and living standards. Each dimension determines one-third of a person's score, and each comes with indicators that specify what it means to be deprived. Deprivations with respect to health and education are measured by two indicators each, and living standards are measured by six. Applying the indicators might be complicated, but we can gain a rough sense of it, and how it applies to the women of Lawa, by considering the case of a third woman, Itana.

Itana has seven children, but only four live with her. She keeps up with the other three kids, always asking for news of them. They are in school, but she doesn't support them. They depend on the families they live with. She doesn't like the fact that they aren't with her. 'If I had the means to support them, I'd call them back. They are growing up, and there's a lot I'd like to give them.' The children who live with her no longer go to school. 'I can't pay for school. I can't buy shoes. I can't buy books.'

Her husband used to contribute a lot to the household through his farming, but he's been sick and unable to work very much for years. 'Every morning, I have to figure out what I can feed him. Every afternoon, I have to figure it out again. If someone gives me 50 gourds, I can go out and look for medicine to buy for him.'

At least she can when she isn't struggling just to buy food. She often buys on credit, and she owes money to many of the merchants in the area. She waits for the occasional 50-gourd gift from a friend, and she uses it to pay down what she owes.

We can look at Itana's situation, indicator by indicator.

The two indicators that the MPI uses to consider health are whether an adult under 70 years of age or a child is undernourished and whether any child under the age of 18 years has died in the five years preceding the survey. Itana's household regularly goes hungry. Three of her children had to leave because she couldn't feed them. So, they may meet the first indicator, and while she has not lost a child, both Clotude and Jeanna have, Clotude several children. The only question is whether they lost them in the last five years.

The two indicators respecting education are whether no household member aged 10 years or older has completed six years of schooling and whether any school-aged child is not attending school up to the age at which they would complete the eighth grade. Itana and her family meet both indicators. The only members of the household who are progressing in their studies are the children who had to leave home.

Itana meets all six of the indicators respecting the third dimension of poverty, living standards. She uses foraged wood as cooking fuel, she does not have improved sanitation or an outhouse at all, her family does not have access to improved drinking water, she has no electricity, the materials used to construct her home are inadequate, and she owns none of the assets that the MPI identifies as indicating a better living standard. She has neither radio, nor TV, nor telephone, nor computer, nor animal-drawn cart, nor motor vehicle.

Itana is thus deprived according to 9 of the 10 indicators. The indicators are weighted. The two indicators for health together make up one-third of the household's score. The same is true for the two indicators for education and the six indicators for living standards. Itana's family thus scores as 5/6, or just over 83 per cent, deprived. The report from Uplift and RESULTS defines ultra-poverty as deprivation of just 60 per cent, so Itana and her family comfortably exceed the standard. Clotude and Jeanna do as well.

CHAPTER 3
A little history

In May 2019, Jeanna, Clotude, and Itana joined Chemen Lavi Miyò, or CLM, a programme designed to help Haiti's poorest families. The name is Haitian Creole, and it means the path to a better life. It's important to understand the path those three women took to enter CLM, but even before that, it's worth considering the one that led to the programme's existence in the first place. Fonkoze's emergence was part of a particular turn in Haitian history, and before it could serve families like Jeanna's, Clotude's, and Itana's it had to become something slightly different from what its founders foresaw.

Haiti has had a difficult history. In 1804, Haitians became just the second people in the Western Hemisphere to win independence from a European colonial power. It is hard to overstate just how remarkable that victory was. A violent revolution, a rebellion of slaves, drove Napoleon's army from the island at the very moment when they were coming to dominate much of Europe.

In the years following that beginning, continual interference from foreigners has combined with conflicting interests within the country to undermine stability, and the early 1990s were typically tumultuous. After Jean-Bertrand Aristide was elected president of Haiti in 1990, a *coup d'état* replaced him for three years. Aristide's election might have initially seemed to mark a turning point for Haiti. The Duvalier dictatorship had held power for almost 30 years, and abuses continued in the years that immediately followed the 1986 overthrow of the second Duvalier, Jean-Claude. Aristide's landslide victory over the American-supported economist Marc Bazin seemed to promise a different future. His overthrow and the ensuing violence against the popular movement that had carried him to victory had to be been sobering.

Aristide returned to Haiti and to power in 1994, and community organizers could meet openly once again. Conversations turned into reflections as to what had gone wrong. One network of activists, led by a Spiritan priest, Father Joseph Philippe, believed that the survival of democracy would require broader participation in the economy than was possible at the time. They began the work that would establish Fonkoze.

'Fonkoze' is short for 'Fondasyon Kole Zepòl', the institution's legal name. '*Kole zepòl*' is Haitian Creole, and it means to put shoulders together. The expression is a Haitian way to speak of solidarity. The legal recognition of the founding, Fonkoze's *certificat d'inscription*, was published in the Haitian government's official journal, *le Moniteur*, on 20 November 1995. It shows how centrally grassroots organizing of the sort that had propelled Aristide to power was on the founders' minds:

> The Foundation's objectives are:

> To bring technical and financial support to cooperatives, peasant organizations, and other social associations in general for the advancement of their activities.

> To facilitate access for the [types of] organizations mentioned above to the means to realize their activities. (My translation)

The intent was to support the activities of organized Haitians, and this meant their economic activities. In the institution's first statutes, a short description of the means it would employ follows immediately after the statement of purpose (Fonkoze, 1995):

> As its ways and means, the foundation can make [the following] services available to members: Credit and Savings, provision of food and agricultural products (both tools and [farming] inputs), or any other activities that will enable it to achieve the ends it envisions. (My translation)

Early documents refer to the institution as an 'alternative bank', and credit and savings would be the key services it would offer, along with literacy programmes. But it would offer its services to 'members'. And Fonkoze's statutes make it clear that membership was designed for groups, rather than individuals. Father Joseph explained this clearly: 'Only organizations can become members of the foundation.' The document mentions *ti machann*, or small traders – the people who would eventually be the centre of almost everything the institution does – but only as part of '*Asosyasyon Ti Machann*', or associations of small traders. Such associations are one type of group cited as eligible for membership in the new organization.

In early 1996, the founders recruited a former management consultant from the United States as executive director to implement their vision. Anne Hastings was looking for more meaning than she found in her work in Washington, DC which was mainly for government agencies. As Hastings was in the process of applying for a placement with the Peace Corps, an executive there referred her to Father Joseph instead. Hastings came to Haiti as a one-year volunteer, but stayed for 17, leading Fonkoze until she moved over to take the helm of the commercial entity that it eventually created.

Serving the poorest Haitians emerged as an explicit Fonkoze goal in two steps. First, even before Hastings was hired, the institution began to shift its emphasis. It moved from a focus on providing accompaniment to existing associations and organizations to a new focus on helping rural Haitians, especially the women who make their living as small traders, to organize themselves to receive the credit and other services Fonkoze could offer.

This shift, from loans to peasant organizations to loans for groups of women in the informal economy, happened early on. As Father Joseph and Marie Plaisival, Fonkoze's first employee and now its director of HR have explained, Fonkoze's small team of founders had discovered that they could not count on organizations to repay their loans because organizations did not have reliable economic activities.

A request from a Dutch priest led the institution on a different path. The priest wanted to offer credit to the mothers of young people who were participating in programmes run by the Spiritan fathers in Nazon, the neighbourhood of Pòtoprens where the priest lived. He also wanted the women to receive some training, but he couldn't provide it himself. So, he deposited $3,000 in a Fonkoze account to fully guarantee the loans and had Fonkoze manage them. Fonkoze organized the women into groups of five, four members and a *manman*, or 'mother', and gave the groups their loans together.

This programme for market women succeeded, and as its success pushed Fonkoze to offer its services increasingly to market women, those services took off. Through the late 1990s and early 2000s, Fonkoze grew. Under Hastings' leadership, it built new branches and expanded its loan portfolio. Table 3.1, taken from the Fonkoze 2004 annual report, demonstrates that growth.

The previous year's report, however, includes an early statement of the second step in Fonkoze's march towards serving the poorest of the poor. Written nearly 10 years into the institution's existence, it mentions for the first time a split. Fonkoze had spun off the largest of its branches into a new commercial entity, Fonkoze Financial Services, or SFF, using its Creole name. Dramatic growth in services to Haiti's poor became the goal for SFF. The institution would spread into more areas of Haiti, working with and for more and more of the *ti machann* whom it had learned to serve.

That freed the non-profit side of Fonkoze to adopt a new focus. 'Reaching the poorest' became the first of the goals attached specifically to the Foundation, the part of the institution left over when SFF split away.

The section of the annual report describing Fonkoze's financial services had previously been devoted exclusively to its efforts to improve and enlarge its loan portfolio. Fonkoze's leadership had initially believed that rapidly expanding its capacity to provide loans to the poor rural Haitians who made up its membership was the best way to attack poverty in Haiti. But by 2003

Table 3.1 Fonkoze's Growth in its first years, 1996–2004

Indicator	1996	1998	2000	2002	2004
Branches	1	15	16	18	20
Clients with loans	110	2,607	4,794	10,000	28,183
Loans outstanding (US$)	23,234	426,580	938,527	1,127,285	4,992,265
Savings accounts	193	5,134	13,260	32,000	69,297
Savings (US$)	78,386	598,711	1,716,090	3,063,773	5,233,879

Hastings and the rest of Fonkoze's leadership understood that there were different levels of poverty, which required different services, and that its core microcredit programmes were not serving the poorest Haitians.

This shift towards a focus on the poorest Haitians received an initial impetus towards the end of 2001 thanks to focus groups about client satisfaction that were organized in and around Sodo, a small commune in the southwest corner of the Central Plateau. At the time, the community was being served by Fonkoze's office in Mibalè, the larger town to Sodo's east. Fonkoze undertook the focus groups together with Concern Worldwide, an international humanitarian organization from Ireland that had an office in Sodo. By then, Concern was already an important Fonkoze partner.

The groups included questions about the conditions one had to fulfil to receive Fonkoze credit. At the time, borrowers had to deposit 15 per cent of the value of their loan in a savings account before receiving a loan. The deposit served as collateral. Each one of the five members of a Fonkoze solidarity group also paid her 250-gourd share of the one-time 1,250-gourd fee that organizations paid to become members of Fonkoze.

From Fonkoze's perspective, the fee bought the borrowers a membership – really, a part-ownership – in the Foundation. It entitled them to participate in regional and general assemblies. These meetings included reports from management and opportunities to air grievances, and the general assembly would elect members to the Foundation's board.

At informal discussions in credit centres, however, members consistently showed that they viewed the fee as a meaningless charge. It stood out all the more so because Fonkoze's pricing policies at the time eschewed such charges, opting instead for the simplicity of charging borrowers nothing but interest on loans. During my time as the manager of a Fonkoze branch, questions about the 250-fee came up frequently in conversations with borrowers. When they asked about it, they regularly referred to it as lost money, in Creole the *'fon pèdi'*.

But in the client-satisfaction focus groups that Concern's staff conducted, borrowers spoke in favour of the fee and the required deposit because of the way each helped prevent even poorer women from joining the credit programme. This explanation comes from an unpublished internal report, written by Sonia Lee. Borrowers didn't want to be stuck bailing out other borrowers who could not repay their loans.

One of the principles underlying early solidarity-group credit was that members of a group would take a measure of responsibility for assisting their fellow members. It was a way for microfinance lenders like Fonkoze to diminish the risk inherent in an otherwise unsecured loan. When she joined four other borrowers to make a group of five, a woman was vouching for the other four women, both for their ability to reimburse a loan and their good faith. The arrangement enabled Fonkoze to offer the loans without asking for a well-to-do co-signer or larger collateral, things that conventional banks typically required from poorer loan applicants. If one of the women was unable to make a payment, the others would be expected to lend her what she needed. That way, they'd keep their group's repayment record intact, which was in their best interest as long as they wanted additional, larger loans. If the sum necessary was more than the four women could manage together, Fonkoze staff would ask members of the credit centre's other solidarity groups to help out. So, borrowers were reluctant to take out loans in a centre with women whom they viewed as too poor or as potential trouble, and they were pleased that Fonkoze had set up barriers to keep the poorer women away.

The focus groups confronted Fonkoze's staff with a disturbing truth. They showed that there were Haitian families it could not yet serve. Fonkoze had seen in itself a champion of economic inclusion, but excluding the poorest from membership turned out to be a hidden part of the way it went about its work. That realization pushed Fonkoze's leadership to look for an approach appropriate for those poorer families.

The journey towards a separate programme for the poorest of the poor received further impetus when Hastings invited Kathleen Cash, an alternative education expert, to develop a reproductive health module for Fonkoze's education unit. While SFF was emphasizing the provision of credit and other financial services, the Foundation continued to develop education programmes. It would offer them to Fonkoze borrowers as funding permitted. At first, these programmes included only modules teaching basic literacy and business skills, but Fonkoze's leadership felt that they could offer more. Fonkoze's credit centres met twice a month, once for loans and repayments, and once for conversation. A class on reproductive health was a way to use the organization inherent in them as a platform for providing important programming of a new sort.

Cash's module focused on prevention. As Cash explained in her 2017 book, *Sex, Shame, and Violence: A Revolutionary Practice of Public Storytelling in Poor Communities*, the programme she created was designed to help people confront feelings of shame, which can lead to dangerous behaviour. When the module was complete, Hastings suggested taking it to Paul Farmer, who was working to provide healthcare in central Haiti, to see whether he would be interested in partnering with Fonkoze in its use.

Cash doubted that Farmer would be interested. She suspected he would want to emphasize treatment, rather than prevention. At the time, he was dividing his time between Kanj, in Haiti's Central Plateau, and Boston, helping to build Partners in Health. He already had an international reputation as an expert in the treatment of both AIDS and TB, having made a name for himself in part by working to provide the best possible care, at whatever the cost, to even the poorest patients.

But Hastings insisted that they show him Cash's finished product, and she remembers the conversation with Farmer vividly. He said that Partners in Health needed a much bigger partnership with Fonkoze than one focused just on reproductive health education. He said that he was sick of taking people on the verge of death, bringing them back to life, and then having to watch them suffer because they had no way to make a living. Farmer himself explained his reasoning in the introduction he wrote for *To Fool the Rain* (Werlin 2016).

Farmer laid out a challenge. If Fonkoze could find a way to help the poor and sick of the rural Central Plateau build livelihoods, Partners in Health would build Fonkoze branches. Partners in Health would make people healthy. Fonkoze would help them develop the means to take care of themselves. Hastings and Farmer even developed a joint logo for the partnership, which was painted onto the first Fonkoze branch that Partners in Health built.

In the face of Farmer's challenge, the problem was to determine what would work for women too poor for Fonkoze's credit programmes, and Hastings led Fonkoze forward along two lines. One approach was to modify its credit programme to serve poorer women. Fonkoze introduced a product called 'Ti Kredi', or 'Little Credit', which was designed with two goals: to eliminate the main barriers that could prevent a woman from joining the standard loan programme in the first place and to provide extra accompaniment that poorer women might need, at least at first.

Eliminating the barriers meant allowing women to join Fonkoze without payment of the 250-gourd registration fee. They would save the money they would need for the fee while participating in the programme. They could then pay the fee after graduating from *Ti Kredi* if they decided to move on to standard solidarity-group credit.

It also meant starting with only a token savings requirement. Women would use their six months in the programme to save up the 15 per cent deposit – 450 gourds – that they'd need for their first standard 3,000-gourd loan.

The added accompaniment came in a number of forms. It started with special training for the credit agents, who worked with fewer women than those who served borrowers in the standard loan programme, met with them more frequently, and offered them more training and a more carefully structured training curriculum than other Fonkoze borrowers would usually receive.

The programme's design included other special features as well. The initial training period was shorter than the one for regular borrowers. Training to take out a first loan in the standard solidarity programme, at that time, took four sessions that were held over two months. In the *Ti Kredi* pilot, the training was completed in two weeks. That way, borrowers got their loans as quickly as possible. The loan terms were shorter. The first *Ti Kredi* loan was for one month, the second for two, and the third for three. Loan amounts were also smaller, starting at 1,000 gourds, at that time about $44. The first standard solidarity loan averaged three times as much. And the women received their loans and their training at credit centres that were distinct from the ones that served regular borrowers. *Ti Kredi* had its own credit centres, filled with women too poor for Fonkoze's standard programme. There was thus no need to look for better-off women willing to risk letting poorer neighbours enter their centres.

The *Ti Kredi* pilot began in 2003. By the end of January 2004, there were 100 *Ti Kredi* clients with zero defaults. A number of graduates had moved into standard solidarity lending as well.

But Hastings' conversation with Farmer led her to look in other directions as well. A donor offered to pay for her to visit a successful microcredit programme in the Philippines, and Hastings arranged to go to Bangladesh as part of the same trip. She knew about the Grameen Bank's Struggling Members Programme, initiated mainly for beggars in late 2003, and she wanted to see how it was working.

While in Bangladesh, she also went to BRAC, and there she met with Rabeya Yasmin, who spent two–three hours describing BRAC's Targeting the Ultra Poor (TUP) programme. TUP featured careful selection of participants, enterprise training, transfers of the assets necessary to establish a small business, a small cash stipend during the first months of the programme, and months of individual coaching. The programme was reporting a high graduation rate for less than $300 per family.

Hastings knew right away that it was what she wanted for Fonkoze and Haiti's poorest. Her dual challenge then became to see the approach adapted for Haiti and to find the money to implement it.

As a first step, she organized a summit about extreme poverty in November 2004. Yasmin attended, along with other experts from around the world. Fonkoze also invited them, along with partners and potential partners from within Haiti, to Tomond, in the middle of Haiti's Central Plateau, between the Lower Plateau to the south and the Upper Plateau to the north. Back then, getting to Tomond by car meant a difficult six-hour drive from Pòtoprens. Most of the summit's participants took the short flight from Pòtoprens to Ench, just north of Tomond, instead.

They spent three days in the field, visiting rural families living in poverty. They then spent three days in design workshops, sharing thoughts about what a programme in Haiti would look like. The summit convinced Yasmin that Haiti's poverty called for an approach such as the one BRAC had developed in Bangladesh. Other visitors were convinced as well. And Hastings and Fonkoze began to look for the money necessary to adapt the programme and fund a pilot.

Their timing was good. The Consultative Group to Assist the Poor (CGAP), a think tank connected to the World Bank, and the Ford Foundation were just then planning to test adaptations of the TUP programme outside of Bangladesh, and Fonkoze secured a place in that project.

The negotiations that led to Fonkoze's place in the larger pilot programme were difficult. For one thing, significant funding was slated to come from the Ford Foundation, but the Ford Foundation was not willing to support programmes in Haiti. For another, the Fonkoze team itself created further reluctance to include Haiti as part of the pilot with its unwillingness to join a random control trial of the approach's impact, which was an important part of the CGAP/Ford Foundation plan.

Fortunately, Fonkoze found a willing partner in the Haiti office of Concern Worldwide. With its commitment to alleviating poverty, especially extreme poverty, and its history in Haiti, Concern had a strong interest in trying out the BRAC approach, and its access to flexible funding from the Irish government gave it the capacity to invest significant resources. Concern was willing to support the programme, but it wanted to do more. It decided to implant a field officer within the Fonkoze team, thus ensuring it would be positioned to learn as much as possible from the experience.

The pieces for the pilot fell into place. CGAP and Concern Worldwide provided the funding. All agreed that there would be no randomized controlled trial but, rather, a detailed qualitative evaluation conducted by independent experts. Participants would be evaluated when they were nine months into the programme and then again at 24 months, six months after graduation. The joint Fonkoze/Concern team chose three sites, in the three communes that the Haitian government's poverty map identified as the poorest in the country, and while the new CLM staff spent a month in Bangladesh, learning the programme from BRAC, a second team, led by Concern, began the preliminary steps which would lead to selecting the first group of CLM members.

The team that spent a month in Bangladesh returned to Haiti with BRAC staff, who would help with the adaptation. One, a BRAC trainer, worked intensively with the new CLM staff both in a classroom and in the field to help them iron out the details of implementation. The other, a field supervisor, stayed for almost a year, working closely with the team to establish the necessary practices of supervision and support of field staff.

Launching the pilot included determining a name for the programme. Bethony Jean François, at the time Concern's project manager for the effort and later a CLM regional director for Fonkoze, proposed the name 'Chemen Lavi Miyò', Haitian Creole for 'the Path to a Better Life'. The name seemed appropriate as a way to indicate that the programme could not pretend to provide a better life to the poorest Haitians but that it could show them the path to such a life and then accompany them as they take their first steps forward.

The pilot succeeded. Of its 150 families, 144 met simple graduation criteria after 18 months. The formal, external evaluations confirmed the dramatic progress that programme members made. And a follow-up evaluation undertaken four years later by Concern Worldwide showed that much of the progress was sustained (Concern Worldwide and Fonkoze 2014).

Having established the value of the approach as a tool to combat the worst rural poverty and knowing how important such a tool could be in Haiti, Fonkoze set out after the pilot to raise funds to implement the programme at scale. But the necessary funds were hard to come by. Concern itself continued to finance the programme in a small way after the pilot, and a small American foundation, the Haitian Timoun Foundation, joined the effort as well. Yasmin returned to Haiti to work with Fonkoze on a strategy for scaling the programme and again agreed that BRAC would provide support.

The efforts supported by HTF and Concern were meaningful because keeping the work going even as a small undertaking was important in ways beyond its effect on the couple of hundred families Fonkoze could serve with the funds that the two organizations could provide. It enabled Fonkoze to keep key staff together, allowing learning to go on and ensuring the staff would be in place whenever the opportunity for a scale-up might arrive. It also meant that Fonkoze would have work going on in the field that it could show to potential funders and other interested parties.

Fonkoze's opportunity to scale up finally came in the aftermath of the earthquake that ravaged Haiti in January 2010. The MasterCard Foundation was willing to make a large investment in Fonkoze to help the institution re-establish itself in the wake of the destruction, and Fonkoze convinced it to include funding for 1,000 families to participate in the CLM programme.

Fonkoze hired four middle-managers. The programme director would no longer be able to supervise all field staff directly. Bethony Jean François and Hébert Artus had both been working as part of CLM as employees of Concern Worldwide, and they simply moved to Fonkoze for their new posts. Wilson Ozil had been a successful credit agent at Fonkoze and then had served in a number of other roles before moving to Concern and then coming back to Fonkoze to join the team. I had been working in various capacities for Fonkoze, first as a part-time helper mainly focused on the education programmes and then as manager of Fonkoze's branch in Marigo, in the Southeast. The four of us travelled to Bangladesh together for a month of training from BRAC, and we returned to Haiti with a BRAC manager, who had a mission to support documentation of the scale-up.

From the pilot's completion until 2017, the team worked almost exclusively in the Central Plateau. Thanks to Partners in Health's strong presence in the region, Fonkoze could ensure that the programme's members would have access to the healthcare they need. But in 2017, the Sisters of Mercy, a group of Roman Catholic nuns, asked Fonkoze to establish a CLM team in Gwomòn, where they had been supporting various projects for years. A first cohort of 200 families graduated from the Gwomòn programme in January 2019. That first cohort included Lucienne, whom I introduced at the very start of the book. Work on a second cohort, which would include the area around Lawa, began right after that graduation.

CHAPTER 4
Selection: making lists

The CLM programme, as it developed from the pilot forward, lasts 18 months after the initial selection of participants. It principally depends on accompanying women living in ultra-poverty closely, helping them build agency within their own lives.

It includes a lot of training. Participants learn to manage economic activities and also a range of skills and habits that can contribute to their good health. The training is offered both in group sessions and during weekly home visits from Fonkoze field staff.

But it is not just an education programme. People say that if you give someone a fish they will eat for a day, but if you teach them to fish, they will eat for a lifetime. CLM and other similar programmes exist because, as popular as the old saw might be, it is only half-true. Know-how lasts longer than a single meal, but it solves nothing by itself. Fishing depends on knowledge, but also on tools, good health, and access to opportunities. Rather than just teaching its members how to manage businesses, the programme aims to address the full range of barriers that stand in their way. So, it also includes grants that give members the tools they need to put their developing know-how to work. It is built around four elements: careful selection of participants, support for their economic and social development, health interventions that emphasize prevention and access, and evaluation and graduation.

Families do not apply for admission into the programme or ask Fonkoze to work with them. Nor are they drawn directly from a list of a region's poorest families that might already exist somewhere. CLM begins with a multiple-step selection process. That process includes social mapping, participatory wealth ranking, preliminary selection, and final verification. Its object is to find families living in ultra-poverty and distinguish them from other families who might also be very poor, but not quite poor enough to need CLM.

The concept of 'ultra-poverty', as something distinct from poverty or even extreme poverty has been important to the approach since the approach was first developed by BRAC. In its 2016 programme brief, BRAC explains how it distinguishes those living in ultra-poverty:

> People living in **extreme** poverty survive on less than $1.90 a day. People living in **ultra** poverty are the most vulnerable subgroup within them, suffering income poverty compounded by sociocultural dispossession.

> These people are forgotten. They suffer every day from food insecurity, own no land or assets, and lack basic education and

productive skills. They are mostly excluded from social services and healthcare, generally live in remote areas disconnected from markets, and are often unable to work due to prolonged illnesses or disability in the family. (BRAC 2014, emphasis in the original.)

Jeanna, Clotude, and Itana fit the definition neatly. They lack financial means, which is to say that they all suffer from income poverty. But lack of income is just the beginning of each family's deprivation. They all suffer from food insecurity compounded by hunger, as well. They have minimal access to land. The remote corner of Gwomòn where they live makes basic services, like education for their children and healthcare, difficult to access. There is little in the way of economic activity that they could latch onto to build a modicum of wealth.

Jeanna and her husband work hard. But although she invests time, energy, and imagination into a small business, and although she has shown in her activities in Senmak that she has the skills that managing a business requires, she has not been able to build a stable income because of her frequent pregnancies. She expresses interest in family planning, but she doesn't know how to access appropriate services, and thus she and Nelso have been adding children to their household every couple of years. Nelso farms, and Jeanna joins him in the fields when she is able, but since the couple doesn't own the land that they work, they cannot support themselves and their rapidly growing family through farming alone, and probably wouldn't be able to even if harvests were abundant and reliable, which they are not.

Most of their children should be in school by now, but they couldn't send the younger ones even if they had the money. The nearest school is too far for small children to walk to. They've sometimes been able to send the two oldest ones, but the kids cannot complete school years because Jeanna and Nelso can't pay the whole tuition bill. And worse than their inability to afford school is their inability to buy enough food. The family regularly goes a day or more at a time without a hot meal.

The CLM programme has used various survey tools over the years. At the time the families from Lawa joined it, we were using two different, internationally recognized tools for evaluating poverty. One is called the Poverty Probability Index, or PPI. It was developed as the Progress out of Poverty Index by the Grameen Foundation in 2006 as a quick way to assess the likelihood that households fall into a given wealth category. It was subsequently taken over by Innovations for Poverty Action.

The idea behind the Index was to establish a simple way to assess the poverty level of microfinance clients and to track the progress that programmes helped them make (Innovations for Poverty Action 2016). Experts study extensive data about poverty in a given country until they can identify 10 questions whose answers correlate strongly with different degrees of poverty. Once the questions and their answers have been identified, assessing the probability that a given household lives with a given degree of poverty is a matter of just those 10 questions, rather than a detailed survey.

Jeanna was given the Index's survey for Haiti, and she scored only seven out of one hundred. And even those seven points came to her only because the Artibonit, the department of Haiti where she lives, is not one of Haiti's poorest departments. In other words, her score did not show that she was very marginally wealthier than someone who scored zero would be. It said only that the likelihood that she would be as poor as she in fact was would have been greater if she lived in a poorer department of Haiti.

The programme also evaluates food security, and at the time we were using a survey developed by an organization called Freedom from Hunger. The tool includes questions like whether a person was worried in the last month because they didn't have enough food in the house, whether they have eaten the same thing over and over because it is all they've had, whether they or others in their family have lost weight because of a lack of food at home, and whether anyone in their household has had to go a whole day without a meal. There are nine questions in all, and a family can score from zero to nine points. Zero to three points indicates that a family is food secure, four to six that it is food insecure, and seven to nine that it is food insecure with hunger. Jeanna and her family scored nine, as badly as they possibly could have. They were, among other indications, occasionally going whole days without a meal.

Clotude scored 21, three times higher on the poverty index than Jeanna did. But all of her additional points came from the fact that her household is smaller. The larger a family is, the more likely it is to be in poverty, and so the survey awards points to smaller households. In Clotude's case, the higher score, which still gives her a very high likelihood of living in poverty, is misleading. Her household would be larger if she hadn't had children leave it because she couldn't afford to keep them fed.

On the food security survey, she scored the same nine-point maximum that Jeanna scored. But that's not the whole story, because the survey collects additional information that isn't reflected in a family's score. Each question that a woman answers affirmatively points to an experience of food insecurity. The survey then follows up affirmative responses by asking how often the respondent has had the experience. So, for example, if a woman reports that her family has gone a day without a meal, she is then asked whether she has had the experience occasionally, sometimes, or frequently. And while Jeanna responded 'occasionally' or 'sometimes' to all of the questions, Clotude answered 'frequently' to seven of the nine. She and her girls are often hungry.

Itana's score on the poverty index is the same as Jeanna's. Her larger family means that she receives the lower score. And her food security survey looks a lot like Clotude's, except that she answered 'frequently' for every question. She and hers are, apparently, even worse off than Clotude's family is. She has nothing planted in her garden that could help her. She would willingly work as a day-labourer in her neighbours' fields, but she reports that they rarely offer her the chance to do so.

And these surveys do not capture the additional deprivations that each family faces just because they live as the poorest residents of a neighbourhood like Lawa. The lack of economic activity in the area would make it difficult for anyone to establish a business. And even if any of these women could start one, they would have a hard time getting their neighbours, who are generally as poor or almost as poor as they are, to pay them for any purchases. And none have the social status in their community that helps successful merchants collect what others owe them.

The nearest school is too far for their younger children, and none of the families can afford to maintain a place in Gwomòn, Gonayiv, Senmak, or Pòtoprens, where wealthier families from distant rural areas of Gwomòn commune, like Lawa, install their children so that they can attend school. All three families would have a difficult time affording any medical care they might need. Itana must sometimes choose between buying food and buying medication for her sick husband. They would all struggle just to pay just the transportation costs of getting to the closest hospital, which is in downtown Gwomòn, let alone the hospital costs themselves.

***

The selection process that Fonkoze uses to identify families living in such deep poverty can take three months or even more. It is designed both to engage an entire community in identifying its poorest members and to ensure that those who join the programme are the ones who genuinely need it. Selecting the right families for CLM is a key part of its success.

In 2015, Fonkoze began to study its selection process. It seemed important to invite an independent expert to judge whether the CLM team was correctly identifying especially poor families. The study was produced by Martin Greeley, a research fellow with the UK's Institute of Development Studies, and it showed that those whom the programme selects are, on average, significantly poorer than the larger group that a standard Haitian poverty survey places in the poorest of the four categories of vulnerability that it uses (Greeley, 2019).

Before the selection process can even start, however, the CLM team needs to learn what it can about the lay of the land in the communities where it plans to work. We call the programme's principal field staff 'case managers'. These undertake the initial work towards selecting new families for the programme, and they do most of the work of accompanying the families they select.

Case managers go out and begin to walk around, chatting with people they meet. Other programme staff may join these exploratory visits. We want to identify how a region divides into separate communities. Haiti's rural population is not distributed between obvious villages, so we look for coherent groupings of 50–100 households. The first steps of the selection process, called 'social mapping' and 'wealth ranking', take place at a community meeting, and the community in question must be small enough for the people who attend the meeting to know its other residents well. During this initial walk-around, the team also tries to meet the community's leaders, because CLM needs to identify someone who can invite residents of the community to a meeting so that they will decide to attend it.

The selection team that found Lawa had been working in Morel, a neighbourhood that's part of the same Moulen section of Gwomòn commune, adjacent to neighbourhoods where the team had just completed 18 months of work with another group of CLM families. While in Morel, they heard rumours about Lawa. Folks talked about a corner of Moulen cut off from the rest of the section, more oriented in a sense to the neighbouring section, Savann Kare. The team's supervisor, Gissaint César, immediately sensed that he and his team would need to explore the area.

Getting there, however, proved to be difficult. Our staff first tried going directly from Morel. Their motorcycles could not get anywhere close, however, and the hike into Lawa was long and hilly. Gissaint went with two other staff members, Wilny Désius and Josette Hyacinthe. When they first approached the area along a ridge, it looked unpopulated. Only as they got close did they begin to see how many homes were hidden among its several hills. They weren't able to reach the middle of Lawa that first day, but they decided they had to return.

When the team returned to Lawa to plan, they found a cock-fighting ring. Men were hanging about, chatting, as is common at an active ring, sometimes even on the days without cockfights. Someone was selling lottery tickets, and someone else had a solar panel, charging telephone batteries for a small fee.

The team spoke with Merilès, the neighbourhood representative of the KASEK, the group of three elected officials responsible for local affairs in a communal section in Haiti. When the CLM staff members have identified a willing and capable community leader, we provide the leader with written invitations to distribute. Those invitations call residents to attend a meeting at which social mapping and wealth ranking will take place. The invitation does not mention the two activities or explain the meeting's purpose. It simply invites community members to participate in a conversation. Merilès was happy to distribute letters of invitation, so they passed some of them along even before they left the ring.

Our team came back after a few days and held the meeting. These meetings follow a standard set of steps. After we introduce ourselves, the CLM team goes directly to social mapping, an activity that defines the community and identifies the households in it.

We help participants draw a map of their neighbourhood on the ground, using whatever materials are handy. A stick will do nicely if it can scratch lines into the dirt. The participants note landmarks: large trees, churches, graveyards, water sources like springs or wells. Then they place a small card identifying each household in its proper position on the map. One member of our team copies the map while another copies the names of the head of each household onto index cards. These cards are then collected in preparation for the next step in the process.

A key aspect of social mapping is the atmosphere it creates among participants. We get as many people involved as we can, having them take the stick from one another to trace corrections or elaborations of the map. We encourage disagreements about the map's details because these disagreements, though usually harmless, can bring more people into the conversation and add to the map's precision. The disagreements and the discussions they occasion also help us evaluate the meeting's participants, which becomes important when we must choose a small group of them for the next step of the process. We create a space in which participants feel safe to disagree with one another, because getting accurate information both in the mapping and the second part of the meeting can depend on the participants' willingness to correct and be corrected.

The meeting in Lawa took place at a chapel that belongs to the Roman Catholic church, just a few yards from the cockfighting ring. It started with 15 participants, 11 men and 4 women, but observers kept joining it throughout. The participants identified 125 households.

We would not normally want to hold one meeting for so many families. The efficacy of the process depends on the intimate knowledge that close neighbours have of one another. We often split a neighbourhood into two meetings if it seems too large for a single one. But we can't always foresee how many households an assembled group will identify, and when we are working in a neighbourhood as inconvenient to reach as Lawa, we have to think twice before we add an extra meeting.

The second step, participatory wealth ranking, takes place at the very same community meeting and involves a handful of participants who have shown themselves, through the mapping process, to be knowledgeable, well-respected, and willing to speak. Case managers invite them to participate by drawing them aside while serving a snack to everyone who's been part of social mapping. In Lawa, our team picked five of the mapping participants for this step.

Wealth ranking uses the index cards that have the head of households' names written across them. A member of the staff starts with two cards and asks participants which of the two families is wealthier. It can take a lot of discussion to arrive at an answer, and here is where the environment that social mapping creates really matters. Differences of opinion during social mapping – like where to put the big mango tree or the spring – don't usually get people angry. But disagreements about various families' wealth could. If participants are already comfortable exchanging opinions, it can go more smoothly.

The two cards are then placed in separate piles, unless the group answers that the families are more or less equally wealthy. The staff member then takes a third card and asks participants to compare the third family to the first two, adding it to one of the piles or placing it in a third. We go through the whole stack of cards, aiming to get the participants to separate them into five piles, which represent five different wealth ranks.

We then ask participants to look at each pile, at all the names in it, with two tasks in mind. First, they have a chance to move any households that seem to be in the wrong pile. Are the families in each pile really more or less equally wealthy? Second, they identify the characteristics that define each pile. This conversation leads to extensive notes, which give us a sense of how the community evaluates wealth.

The characteristics that folks from Lawa identified are set out in Table 4.1. Those from Fagè, another neighbourhood in the region, are there for comparison. Participants classified 3 families in Lawa as belonging to the wealthiest category, 12 to the next wealthiest, 55 as poor, 40 as very poor, and 15 as poorest.

Table 4.1 Characteristics that define 'wealth' in two neighbourhoods of Gwomòn

Category	Lawa	Fagè
Wealthiest	Families own a home in a nearby city, where their children live to attend school.	4–5 *kawo*.
		2–5 cows.
	They own 2–3 large animals: mules, horses, or cows.	A mule or a horse.
		Own a home in a city.
	They own cane fields.	Children go to school in the city.
	They have 4–5 *kawo* of land.	Children go to university.
		They buy more farmland.
Next-to-wealthiest	A horse or a mule.	1–2 *kawo*.
	A cane field.	1–2 cows.
	A cow.	A horse or a donkey.
	They send their children to school in Gwomòn. They have 2–3 *kawo* of land.	Children in school in Gwomòn.
		Children go to university.
Poor	Goats.	Children in school in Savann Moulen.
	A bean field.	Own a donkey.
	A donkey or a horse.	Own goats and/or pigs.
	Children attend a local school.	
Very poor	Support themselves with day labour.	Children go to the local school.
	Live in a shack.	Own goats because someone let them take care of theirs and they earned offspring as payment. (They did not buy them.)
	Own some chickens.	
	Own a goat.	Own some chickens.
	Some children might attend school sometimes.	

(*Continued*)

Table 4.1 Continued

Category	Lawa	Fagè
Poorest	Support themselves with day labour.	Own some chickens.
	Live in a shack.	Live on day labour and asking for charity.
	No goats.	Children not in school.
	No chickens.	Live in a shack.
	Children aren't in school.	
	Own only a small plot of inherited land.	

Note: Author's translation

This is slightly different from the wealth ranking process that was used when the CLM team got started. Fonkoze began wealth ranking even before meeting the team from BRAC. Bethony Jean François had first learned participatory rural appraisal, the basic technique that underlies social mapping and wealth ranking, as a student at a Haitian university. Even while the original CLM team was in Bangladesh, getting their first training from BRAC, he was already leading a team of Fonkoze and Concern staff back in Haiti as it began selecting families.

That original process involved inviting everyone who participated in social mapping to participate in the wealth ranking process as well, rather than selecting a small group. The team would then start wealth ranking by asking the group to describe different levels of wealth. What characterizes the community's wealthiest members? What defines the households that belong in the next rank after that? Once the categories were defined, participants were then asked to place every household in one of the five categories.

But involving everyone led to very long meetings. On one memorable occasion in Nikola, a neighbourhood in southern Boukankare, the team was unable to complete the activity in a single, long day. It was forced to invite everyone to return the next day to finish up. So, the staff decided to shorten the meetings by reducing the number of people who would participate in wealth ranking.

At the same time, it also decided to ask participants to draw their criteria from their ranking of their neighbours, rather than working the other way around. They found that discussions of the criteria that occurred before the families were organized into ranks were needlessly long and artificial.

Since the conclusion of a pilot undertaken with Haiti's Office of the Secretary of State for the Integration of Persons with Disabilities in 2015 and 2016, we added an additional line of questioning to the social-mapping/wealth-ranking process. We now ask participants for information about any individuals with disabilities who live in the area. Such individuals are invited to join the programme if they are sufficiently poor, even if they do not meet the programme's other criteria.

Wealth ranking allows us to reduce the time needed for the third step in the process, preliminary selection. But for someone like me, it is surprising that the process works at all. A small team of strangers appears in a neighbourhood asking for a lot of information. They take down every family's name, put each home on a map. They ask detailed questions about the possessions various families might own. They ask participants to compare families' wealth with one another. It all seems so indiscreet. Where I come from, most people would refuse to answer. In the best case.

But that's not what usually happens. People are generally happy to share what they think and what they know. And it's not that they buy into Fonkoze's objectives, because we say as little as possible about those objectives before the activity. If people know we are looking for the households who most need comprehensive assistance, some are bound to try to direct the assistance where they want it to go rather than where it is most needed. And that's understandable. While most of the folks who attend these meetings do not qualify for CLM, many could use some kind of help and even more have friends or relatives who could.

But the fact that we say so little makes it seem even more surprising that we get as much cooperation as we do. Generally, folks are happy to jump into social mapping, and the handful we ask to stay and help with wealth ranking are usually happy to do so as well.

There are probably a few reasons for this. First, both groups are selected. Neither group is a random assemblage. The larger group consists mainly of folks who decided to respond to our invitation to talk. The smaller group includes only those we observed to be active and constructive in that first activity. Second, Haitians value hospitality. The Fonkoze staff involved are almost always outsiders. The participants in the event may want to make them feel welcome and successful. Third, there may be a tendency to respond to authority. A team of young professionals appears in a neighbourhood that may not be used to such visits. Doing what is asked might be the residents' first reaction. Finally, even if we say nothing about our intentions, they might be inclined to imagine that the visit is a precursor to some kind of hand-out. Various organizations have crisscrossed Haiti practising development assistance or simply charity. Participants in these meetings might join in with the vague expectation that something good will follow.

The most important products of these meetings are the lists we acquire of a neighbourhood's poorer families. Having such a list reduces the number of families we need to survey more thoroughly. Without a preliminary list, we would have to survey every family, so having one saves time.

In recent years, however, these meetings have become just one of two ways that the team acquires such lists. A growing collaboration with Haiti's Ministère des Affaires Sociales et du Travail, or Ministry of Social Affairs and

Labour, in some cases provides a second source. The Haitian government has been working to establish comprehensive registries of economically vulnerable families. It does so through detailed surveying that attempts to reach all households in an area. By applying an algorithm to the data from these surveys, they place each household in one of four different levels of vulnerability.

Creating lists for the entire country would be an enormous job. And the need to keep them up to date if they are to be useful only makes a huge job much larger. But in regions in which the Ministry has lists that are relatively recent, we can use them in place of the social mapping and wealth ranking. It saves even more time, and it puts us where we feel we ought to be. Namely, underneath the umbrella of the Haitian government's anti-poverty activities.

CHAPTER 5
Selection: with lists in hand

Case managers now return to the community with lists of the households that fall into either the two poorest wealth ranking categories or the most vulnerable families according to the Haitian government's list. They visit each one of those families and each individual with a disability. In Lawa, wealth ranking eliminated 70 of 125 homes, leaving just 55 families on our list to be visited.

This is where the team has employed the Poverty Probability Index, or PPI, and the food security survey. The PPI is actually imbedded within a broader survey, which collects a range of information about the family in question: what kind of house they have, whether they own it, what other sorts of possessions they own, what their sources of income are, whether there is a husband or partner who helps, how many children there are, whether the children are in school. This broader survey is based on one that Fonkoze has been using for years to evaluate women in its credit programmes. Each visit is time-consuming, so having eliminated the need to visit many of the community's households shortens the process.

Case managers work in pairs. One interviews the potential CLM member while the other takes notes and makes additional observations. Visitors whom residents don't know can attract attention in the countryside. The curious can want to follow what is going on, and their presence can disrupt what can be a delicate conversation. So, the note-taker will also help the interviewer by drawing interested bystanders away from the main conversation.

While filling out the forms, case managers compare their findings to a list of the programme's inclusion and exclusion criteria. Based on these surveys and on their observations, they make a recommendation: Does the family or the individual with a disability qualify for CLM? Table 5.1 shows our list of criteria when we entered Lawa.

The list is occasionally updated. Its criteria are not absolute but more of a guide. They can't cover every case the team encounters. Case managers can make recommendations that go against the criteria, but they must then add a note explaining their decision. A woman might be over 65, but she could be capable of working and have grandchildren who depend on her. A woman might manage a small commerce worth 2,000 gourds or more but depend on a neighbour who lends her the capital. She might have no investment of her own. A family might own more livestock than the programme would normally accept, but they might have 8 or 10 children as well.

Table 5.1 Basic inclusion and exclusion criteria

Inclusion	Exclusion
A woman between 15 and 65 who can work.	The woman is over 65.
A man or woman with disabilities in ultra-poverty.	
The woman has at least one child under 15 who is dependent on her.	The woman has no dependent children.
A woman living with her parents who has more than one child whose father provides no support.	A young woman who has just one child and who lives with her parents.
A mother living with her parents, who have more than four other children living with them.	
A woman who has not passed 10th grade.	A young woman with only one child who made it beyond the 10th grade.
A woman whose husband cannot help the family	A family with a man who earns a salary of more than 2,500 gourds per month.
A woman with a husband who either has no trade or who doesn't earn money with his trade	A woman with a husband who has a profession that earns money.
A family without an expensive animal, like a cow or a mule.	A family with large livestock.
A family whose livestock is worth less than 2,500 gourds.	A family with more than one animal and total livestock holdings worth more than 2,500 gourds.
A family who cannot send their children to school or whose children are sent by someone else.	A woman able to send more than half of her children to school.
	A family with irrigated land.
A family without irrigated land and with no more than a 'ka' of mountain land.	A family with an inherited mountain plot larger than a 'ka'.
A woman with children who has no regular income or is a day-labourer.	A woman who earns more than 2,000 gourds per month at a job.
A woman with dependents who has a small commerce worth less than 1,500 gourds.	A woman with commerce worth more than 1,500 gourds
A family receiving support from no other institution.	
A family with a home in poor repair or with a home they received through a project.	

Note: A *ka* is one quarter of a *kawo*. A *kawo* is 1.29 hectares.

As case managers work out their recommendations, they are careful to observe, and not merely to ask questions. Seeing whether a cooking fire has been used recently shows whether the family has food to eat. A dry, black spot, without recent ashes, in the middle of the three rocks that make up a typical rural stove, is a reliable sign of hunger. Are there many pots and pans, or does the family do its cooking in a single pot or an old can? Case managers notice the presence or absence of children's clothing of different sizes or of men's clothing in any laundry that might be lying around the yard. They assess a person's housing with their eyes. They try to understand the character of any support that individuals with disabilities receive from their families.

While they are doing this work, they are also looking for families and individuals who were not mentioned at the community meeting or are not on the government's list. They ask questions about homes they come across that do not appear on their map. Sometimes the families who live in them are so isolated that they are ignored or forgotten, even by their close neighbours. Case managers also find people who are without their own home. They live with parents, other relatives, or even strangers. Communities do not mention them, and the government's survey does not include them. Both the community meeting that Fonkoze holds and the government's list focus on households, not people. An adult woman, forced to return to her parents' home, will go unmentioned at the meeting, even if she has children of her own. Her neighbours think of her as part of her parents' household. A homeless mother, sharing the corner of a neighbour's room with a child or two, isn't a separate household either. A case manager named Christian was once walking by a water source in western Boukankare. He saw an adult woman he could not identify carry a five-gallon bucket on her head, walking with it towards a wealthy farmer's home. It turned out that she had been living in the farmer's home as an unpaid servant since she was a young girl. Case managers look for such people and are careful to visit and assess any they find. Often these are the very people who need the CLM programme most.

This process, which we call 'preliminary selection', produces a list of families and individuals with disabilities in a community whom the case managers believe to be qualified for the programme. In Lawa, all 55 families in the last two categories received preliminary selection visits, and case managers reported that 23 of these families seemed to qualify for the programme.

The case managers then return to the households on their list with a member of the CLM management team for the last step in the selection process, called 'final verification'. The manager conducts a one-on-one interview with everyone who has been recommended for the programme.

These interviews are free form. They aim to uncover how someone lives: the means they have at their disposal and how they come by those means. The manager is looking for women, or occasionally single men, who have dependent children without productive assets or economic activities to support them. They are looking for individuals with disabilities who lack the means or the structure of family support to lead their lives. The families or individuals who qualify frequently spend days without eating a hot meal. The children often are not in school. They have neither a plan for the future nor any hope that they could somehow improve their lives. Managers need, fundamentally, to ask themselves whether the person in front of them needs CLM. Do they seem stuck in poverty that is likely to continue to darken their life without Fonkoze's help?

Managers can approve or deny the programme to anyone on the list that the case managers have assembled. They cannot, however, add anyone to the list. If they come across someone who is not on the list who appears to qualify, they ask a case manager to survey them.

The manager's decision is final. Case managers are expected to think of themselves as advocates for the families they have recommended, and they can, and often do, ask managers to reconsider. And managers must be careful to let them make their argument, and to consider what they have to say. But no further appeal is possible.

Final verification interviews are challenging. Sometimes interviewees are understandably reticent. They don't know you, so they don't know why they should talk to you. They feel uncomfortable, unaccustomed to visitors. They may be ashamed of what they feel as their violation of the laws of hospitality: they have nothing to offer you and might not even be able to provide a chair. They may find their poverty so embarrassing that they decide to conceal it, or they may exaggerate their poverty, hoping that it will qualify them for some sort of benefit. One has to find a way to put an uncomfortable stranger at ease and to collect convincing information, whether through their words or through one's own observations.

One tries to learn about the family's assets – what kind of livestock and farm holdings they might have – but it is hard to know whether what they tell you is true. You may see a pig tied up in a shady corner of the yard, or a couple of turkeys wandering through it, but they might belong to a neighbour. Or the person might tell you that they belong to a neighbour even if they belong to her or that they belong to her even if they do not. A small goat may have been left in someone's hands for them to care for. They could eventually earn their own goat from that work, but they would have no guarantee. On the other hand, a yard may seem lifeless, though its owner has livestock – even larger animals – out of sight.

When I am assigned to verification, I focus on any family expenses that I can identify and then try to get the person to explain how she meets those expenses. Even a family who frequently misses meals eats some of the time, however inadequately. Where does the money for ingredients come from? If any of the family's children are in school, how much does it cost? Have they paid the fees? How much do they owe the school? Where will the money come from? How were the fees paid the previous year?

One of the original members of the programme's staff, Hébert Artus, did final verification in Lawa. He joined CLM as an employee of Concern, implanted in the CLM staff in Concern's effort to learn from the pilot. When the programme scaled up in 2010, he became a regional director, working for Fonkoze. By the time he visited Lawa, he was the programme's assistant director. In 2020, he became its director. Of the 23 families who appeared to our case managers to qualify, he and the case managers could only find 21 for him to interview when they returned. The other two had abandoned the area. Of those 21, Hébert approved 19. One of the families he rejected turned out to have livestock that was undiscovered during preliminary selection: two small pigs and three goats. Hébert's note at the bottom of their selection form reads, in part, 'Things might be hard for them, but they have a minimum'. On the form of the other rejected family, he noted that all the family's children are in school and that they eat, at least something, every day. He added, however, 'They are vulnerable because the husband has three other partners'.

Hébert described his experience of final verification in Lawa in a blog post in which he spoke of Itana, Jeanna, and Clotude:

> At 11:20, I started my work at a household with nine members, a small, one-room house covered in straw. It's home to a father and mother, with their children and grandchildren. At this hour, the kitchen still gives off an air of abandonment. Between the three rocks that would normally hold up the pot, there's nothing to suggest that the fire had been lit even the previous day. Two five-year-old boys – an uncle and his nephew – play naked in the yard, covered in white powder as though from rolling in the dust. They were trying to cut up a stalk of sugarcane that they would afterwards taste instead of a breakfast.

> I sit powerless in the face of this sad sight, forcing myself to interview Serena Nicolas, who, despite it all, maintains a constant smile.

Serena is the same woman we've referred to as Itana. We learned her true name well after Hébert's verification visit. Unlike many of the men and women who live in rural Haiti, she has a legal ID, her voting card, which lists her as 'Serana', but she explains that she had the ID made using her sister-in-law's birth certificate. Her own birth certificate had been lost. 'They used to keep important papers with elders. My parents gave my birth certificate to my grandfather for safe keeping. But it was lost in a fire.' The fact that her daughter's name is Italène, a variation of 'Itana', lends credence to her explanation.

Hébert's description continues:

> Maybe [Serena] does it to drown her hopelessness, or maybe she sees a glimmer of heaven-sent hope behind this visit. Though she and her husband have been living together for more than 25 years, they have no productive assets worth mentioning. The family earns its income through agricultural day-labour, but the prolonged drought gripping the area has eliminated such work for the first part of the year. No work. No hope of access to cash. Buying food on credit is the only alternative, but as mounting debt begins to harm the sellers, trouble sets in.

> Her neighbour would like to share and show solidarity, like many rural Haitians, but she has her own burden to manage. A mother of three children whose father died more than 20 months ago, Clotude has to depend on herself now. It's a fight that's too hard

for her. Just feeding her household is a terrible challenge. She lives every day with her children's lack of education, of healthcare, of opportunities to flourish. It has come to feel like destiny. She has just one question constantly on her mind: how to appease the hunger of the children she loves. Her 14-year-old girl has never been to school. No need to even mention the other kids. It was 1 pm, and she had given nothing more than a small stick of sugarcane to each child. She hadn't fed them anything the previous day. She didn't yet know what she would do for the rest of the day or, for that matter, for the rest of the week. As I left her home, she told me, with her generous smile, '*M pa gen anyen pou m ba w*'. That means, 'I have nothing to give you'. It struck me hard that, despite her sharp and chronic deprivation, she thought she was supposed to share.

At 1:34, my route brought me to the home of Tibolo, the one man working to feed a collection of families including the one he grew up in, his wife's family, and his own family as well. His wife Jeanna, who's been nursing their infant for ten days, hadn't eaten anything since the previous evening. She described the families' ways, how they all depend on the labour of a single man. Twenty-two people to feed with about five cups of rice per day. Telling me the story leaves me thinking of a similar story, the miraculous tale of Jesus multiplying five loaves of bread to feed 5,000 people. Tibolo seemed to have learned the secret.

Only one of [Jeanna's] children goes to school. In fact, hers is the only one of the three families to have managed such a feat. The school meets in the bowels of a Roman Catholic chapel, where the classes sit in beat-up benches and desks in rooms without anything to separate them, studying in a single, great cacophony. That is where the sons and daughters of peasants have to consume the bread of instruction, risking ridicule at the hands of those who correct the entrance exams that determine whether one can go to high school, something few such children can hope to achieve.

The day was long, and the cases I saw were similar. Circumstances that elicit indignation, shame, and frustration are everywhere in rural Haiti. And the dominant class – the state and its accomplices – seem proud of it.

And what of the women in all this?

The women stay at home, while the men wander. They wander to places where they are not directly subjected to the sound of their children's hungry whimpering. To places where luck might bring them to share a shot of local liquor, a bit of fried dough, or a little bread. But the women, despite the horrible suffering brought on by days without nourishment, suffer just as much by watching their offspring groan and cry with hunger, by watching them starve.

Final selection is hard, and not just because of the complex decisions we have to make using information that may or may not be reliable. The process forces you to encounter the most difficult parts of a family's struggles. Even the knowledge that you will be able to offer the neediest families tools that may help them change their lives cannot soften the frustration, the anger, that their situations occasion.

And one frequently encounters families who clearly need something, but probably don't quite need CLM. In the earliest years of the programme, such cases found an easy solution. CLM staff could refer families to Fonkoze's *Ti Kredi* team, which would invite them to become part of that programme. The two programmes worked almost in parallel. Fonkoze was able to offer appropriate services to anyone capable of using them.

But the two programmes slowly grew apart. Each followed its own geographic priorities, which were often determined by the donors funding them. Where they did work together, *Ti Kredi* focused on CLM graduates, rather than on their poor neighbours who did not quite qualify for CLM. Eventually, Fonkoze's commercial sister organization, SFF, assumed management of all Fonkoze credit, and it eliminated the programme, at least in its original form. Since then, CLM staff have been constantly facing a gap in the services that Fonkoze could offer.

Staff members struggle with the obligation to reject very needy people because they just aren't needy enough. But that is only part of the frustration of final verification. The mere fact that families are as poor as the ones whom one encounters during this process is enough to enrage. Hébert's account is full of his anger, and it ends on a bitter note:

> Facing this hideous situation, I can't keep myself from asking certain questions: Where in the constitution, in the list of human rights, in the various treaties and conventions are the rights of this forgotten segment of the population inscribed? Aren't they also Haitians? Should they always remain on the margins of social programmes, of access to quality education? What do the slogans – and I really mean 'slogans' – mean: universal rights, education for all, social justice?

> The women whom I met this day, despite their helplessness and hopelessness, hold onto their desire to share. Do we live, then, in a nation where the culture of sharing is the business of the underprivileged? The state, human rights organizations, feminist movements, peasant movements: When will we arrive at a real advocacy on behalf of the majority of the population? When will the misery of peasants' lives cease to nourish comedies in Haitian

theatre and films and instead find its place in the nation's plans for the future?

To those who have positioned themselves comfortably within this sad reality, I say 'Enough!' It is time to realize that on the day when the despair turns into rage, violence will be the weapon this forgotten mass takes in hand. I know that, on that day, repression will be disguised as the law, as the establishment of order, the order according to which the dominant dominate most easily. But the dominant class will be the great losers because the disinherited have nothing more to lose. (Artus, 2019)

CHAPTER 6
Joining CLM

At the end of their long day of final verification, Annel and Hébert climbed onto Annel's motorcycle and headed back to our office in a small, unmarked building in downtown Gwomòn. Annel was one of the case managers on the CLM staff in Gwomòn. He had been assigned as Hébert's guide for final verification. The two of them rode across the whitish stones that carpet the narrow ravine, through gardens of plantains and fields of sugarcane, until they got to the rocky dirt road that traverses Savann Moulen. They took that road back to the river, and forded it, slicing through the cloudy, knee-deep current. Taxi drivers were washing their motorcycles and bathing after a day of hot, dusty work. A couple of women were scrubbing the last few items of laundry, but most were collecting clothes and sheets they had left to dry on the rocks under the tropical sun. From the river, it's just a few minutes across the downtown area to the office.

They returned with nothing but a list of families who qualified for CLM. Beginning to help families involves a lot more than just choosing the ones who qualify. After the families have been selected, we still must integrate them into the programme.

Annel and the other case managers based in Gwomòn had to return to Lawa to visit each prospective member in her home once again. After preliminary selection and final verification, this would be, at least, their third visit. The process often requires even more than three trips, however, because staff members do not inform families when they will show up, so they sometimes arrive to discover that the person they need to talk with is somewhere else. Rural Haitians leave their homes for a range of activities: day-labour, farming, laundry, bathing, or shopping. And those are just the departures that fit into regular routines. Someone's uncle or sister-in-law could be sick, and require temporary, full-time care. Relatives or friends could be dealing with someone's death, planning a funeral or receiving visitors at a wake. Planting or harvesting a crop like beans might require someone to live, for a short time, away from their home to be close to a distant field. A woman may have gone to Pòtoprens or another of the country's cities or towns for a month or two to work as a maid to earn needed cash. Or someone might, like Jeanna, live away from home much of the time to make whatever living she makes.

And the team can't justify simply moving on to the next person. Families who qualify for the programme cannot afford to miss their chance.

We used to call this third visit 'enterprise selection'. In the programme's early years, it involved three steps. First, a case manager would explain the

CLM programme to the woman who had been selected. She would hear what it would offer her. Then she'd be invited to join. Second, if a woman agreed to join the programme, she would hear about the different businesses that Fonkoze could give her, and she'd be asked to choose a combination of two of them. That was her enterprise selection.

Finally, she'd be asked about the leaders of her community: Who is there in her neighbourhood she feels comfortable going to with an urgent problem? This last piece of information becomes important when the CLM team begins to establish local assistance committees. Almost all the women would agree to join the programme, and the case manager would invite them to attend an initial six-day training workshop.

The fact that some women refuse might seem surprising. They are unimaginably poor, and someone they don't know comes along with a comprehensive set of offers. They have almost nothing, and they are told that Fonkoze wants to give them lots of stuff.

But even those who accept our offer generally do so without enthusiasm. Agreeing with an unfamiliar professional must seem like the easiest thing to do. Most do not feel comfortable saying 'no' to a visitor who looks like an authority figure. They may not be accustomed to receiving visitors at all. But the programme sounds too good to be true, so families very reasonably disbelieve what they're told. They just go along with it.

Those who refuse the invitation outright tend to think that the offer is worse than untrue. They imagine that it's some kind of trap.

Some of their suspicions are easy to understand. For example, we come across men who worry that our programme will interfere with the authority they are accustomed to exercising over their partners, so they insist that their partners refuse to participate. And they're right. We hope that we'll be able to help women assert themselves more forcefully in the decision-making that affects their lives and the lives of their children. That is part of what we mean by 'empowerment'. We can talk to the men about how their children stand to benefit if we can help their wives establish their own economic activities, and sometimes we make our point. But not always.

Other suspicions are more surprising, at least to anyone unaccustomed to the ways of rural Haiti. Potential members can think that there is something diabolical about the programme. That it is, literally, Satan's work. We hear our work described as something right out of *Revelations*. We hear that it carries the mark of the beast or the number 666.

It is hard to be sure just what harm an individual who believes such things thinks they will suffer if they join our programme, but women have told us that we will keep a key to their home and that the livestock we give them will be cursed. I once heard about rumours of CLM turkeys that would hatch only snakes. One woman told us, after we had finally convinced her and her husband to join the programme, that she had heard we would make her dance '*san kilòt*', or without underwear.

When we started hearing such stories, we realized quickly what was happening. Community members, either jealous of the help that their poorest neighbours were about to receive or accustomed to benefiting from their neighbours' poverty, looked for ways to dissuade them from participating. They did this without even knowing what the programme was about. We knew that the secrecy we tried to operate with could only have been feeding distrust, but we felt we needed to undertake the selection process without telling anyone too much about our plans. If people knew from the start what we were prepared to offer, some would try to fool us into offering it to those without particular need. At the same time, that same secrecy left people with a lot to wonder about.

Our first response was to hold meetings in the neighbourhoods where we encountered resistance, even while the enterprise selection visits were going on. We'd talk to local leaders, explaining to them what we wanted to offer to their poorest neighbours. We'd ask them to help us convince those neighbours to take advantage of the opportunity.

I once held such a meeting in Mannwa, a mountaintop community in north-central Boukankare, where fully one-half of the women we invited to join the programme declined our offer. A case manager named Sammuel Eugene and I hiked up the hill to see whether we could get help changing at least some of the women's minds. We stood in a small circle with a dozen or so farmers under a mango tree. The tree and its shade dominated a small clearing in the midst of a broad ridge planted with corn and pigeon peas. Sammuel and I were surrounded by the wealthier landowners in the community, and they listened patiently and with interest. Some even with sympathetic understanding. Eventually, they were able to help us change one woman's answer, though she had to leave her children's father to do so. One of the members of the group also referred us to a woman fully as poor as anyone we had selected, whom we somehow had missed.

But not all the farmers' responses were encouraging. One man told us that he was against our programme because, if we succeeded, he would have trouble finding neighbours to work his fields. At least he was frank.

We soon decided to make these meetings part of our routine. We hold them after inviting families to join the programme, but before the initial training that follows that invitation. We ask all the people we've selected for the programme to come, along with any community leaders we can mobilize. The meetings are the team's first chance to tell a community what we intend to do. We want everyone to understand our programme and its selection process, and to see the results of that process. A representative of our management team explains the programme in detail, focusing especially on selection and the need for community support for those who will participate. The newly selected members are encouraged to attend these meetings so their neighbours can confirm that we have selected the area's poorest.

This might seem like an odd solution to the problem. Potential participants were refusing to join the programme, but the meetings that we instituted in response were held after the invitation process was complete.

Most of the folks who refused, however, did not do so initially. It's part of the fact that they find it easiest to go along with an authority figure standing in front of them. They would accept our invitation, but then they wouldn't show up for the training they'd been invited to. In Mannwa, only a few women told us outright that they wouldn't join our programme, but on the first two days of their initial training, at a school downhill from them at Kafou Jòj, we didn't see everyone we expected. The meeting that Sammuel and I held took place while the third day of training was going on. We left our responsibilities to hike up and speak with them and with the community leaders.

Once the CLM team has described the programme to prospective members and their neighbours and the new members have agreed to join the programme, they are ready to start their training. They begin their journey with us at a six-day workshop. The CLM team generally tries to organize these workshops in schools. Schools are useful because they have multiple classrooms. And we can usually find an open space that's a little out of the way but somewhere on the school's grounds, where we can establish a kitchen. If there is no school available, the team will look for a church or a small cluster of churches near one another.

The workshop for the women in Lawa was at the Ecole National de Moulin, the section's public primary school. It brought together 103 women from across Moulen, breaking them up into smaller groups, one in each of four classrooms. Moulen is a broad area, and many of the women had a long hike to get to the school. Some of the women from Lawa, for example, walked more than an hour and a half each way, every day, for six days.

The women receive two large meals a day during the workshop, and some of them begin to gain strength visibly as the week goes on. They often gobble down the first meal on the first day, and it's no wonder. Many are hungry. By the second meal, however, they are looking around for plastic bags or cloths – anything that they could wrap food in – so they can carry some of it home. The next day, some bring a small child or two.

So, food is an important part of the six days, even if it is a major investment of effort and expense. Case managers spend the days before the workshop preparing. They go to local markets, buying the groceries they'll need to feed the women, themselves, and others who might show up for six days. They can find some basic items, like rice, oil, sugar, spaghetti, and beans, in one stop at a large merchant. But they also need onions, vegetables like carrots and okra, seasonings like garlic, cloves, dried herring, and leeks, sour oranges or key limes for cleaning meat, other fruit for juice, and either meat or livestock for slaughter. Those smaller purchases can involve a lot of running around. They contract locally with folks who will haul the water and provide the necessary firewood. They recruit a chief cook and hire a kitchen staff.

Cooking in Haiti is time-consuming and labour-intensive. Everything must be done from scratch, from starting the wood fires and butchering and cleaning the fresh meat to grinding the seasonings with mortar and pestle and scraping out and cleaning the locally hand-cast aluminium pots when the cooking is finished. Often the cooks and their assistants simply sleep at the training site for the workshop's duration. It is the best way – really the only way – to ensure they can serve breakfast first thing every morning.

In addition to meals, the women receive a small daily stipend. In the programme's first years, it was 75 gourds, now much less than a dollar per day. At the time, that was worth about $2.

The stipend was originally conceived for transportation. It was a way to help women get to and from the training. It was thought that it would enable them to rent an animal or to pay for a seat on a truck or the back of a motorcycle.

But few members ever use the money for transportation, even if they live somewhere that presents options like motorcycle taxis or pick-up trucks and even though they may have to walk for an hour or more to get to the training each morning. Most use it to put a little food in their home for their kids on the days of the workshop, but some use at least some of it to buy a chicken or some other small asset, their first investment as a programme member.

Originally, women received the stipend each day for the day to follow. They received the first day's stipend at home, with their invitation to come to the training. This seemed important because the team thought members might need the money just to get to the workshop. It was also a small gesture showing that the invitation was serious and that attending might be worthwhile.

As it became clear, however, that the stipend would be used for a range of things, but not usually for transportation, the pressure to provide it in advance, or even in six daily payments, diminished. The team started handing it out at the training itself, often two or more days' worth at a time. It was much easier. Getting enough small bills to be able to hand each member 75 gourds was challenging because few members came to the trainings with change. Knowing that members were not depending on the stipend to get to and from the workshop freed the team to provide it in larger chunks.

Doing so also saves time. Distributing cash takes a lot of time. Each member has to sign or make a thumbprint on a distribution sheet, which serves as the receipt that shows that they received the money. We need to be able to show accountants, auditors, and donors that the money actually gets into our members' hands. Going through that long – and frankly tedious – process less often than every day speeds things up.

The workshops have always had a fixed agenda for all six days, but that agenda has evolved over the years. Originally, members spent three days learning about each of the two enterprises they had selected upon their invitation to enter CLM. The team organizing the training would have to figure out how to divide the members so that each received training in the two enterprises that she chose. As the number of enterprises that the team could offer increased, the task became more complex. Most, but not all, families would choose goats as one of their enterprises, but the fact that a few would choose pig-rearing to go with poultry or small commerce or, eventually, agriculture meant that it was not as easy as simply offering everyone goat-rearing for three days and then giving each her other choice.

This all changed in 2017 because, after 10 years of experience, the team decided to change the way members were choosing enterprises. CLM's management team had become suspicious of the results of enterprise selection. Some case managers would have all, or almost all, of the families they worked with choosing the same thing. It led the team to wonder whether new CLM members were being allowed to choose for themselves.

And it was easy to understand that members might find their choice being made for them. As case managers' experience grew, their tendency to believe that they knew best grew as well. They might have found a lot of success with women who chose goats and a pig, for example, so they might more-than-encourage women to make that selection. Or they might see something in the details of the evolving menu of fixed choices that offered a member a way to get slightly more than those who chose something else. In other words, they would find ways to game the system. Staff meeting after staff meeting included words encouraging case managers to let members decide, but the case managers were too anxious for the families' rapid progress to take the words seriously. Especially when the members themselves often preferred to leave the decision in their case manager's hands. When we'd ask some members what sort of assets they would like us to give them, their first response would be to ask for whatever we decide.

CLM's management decided that members should choose their enterprises after the initial training, rather than before it. Women would be likelier to make good choices if they could learn something about their choices before they had to choose. But that meant the team could no longer offer members two three-day modules because they didn't know which enterprises each member would receive.

So, the programme started offering one day of training in five different areas – goats, pigs, poultry, small commerce, and agriculture – and a one-day introduction to the programme. The curriculum for the five days of enterprise training would focus on the advantages and the challenges connected to each kind of enterprise. More detailed discussions would have to wait for members' weekly one-on-one conversations with programme staff.

The new first-day programme includes a full introduction to CLM and features visits from members of CLM's management team. Members are asked to invite their partners to come as well. Single mothers can bring a parent, an older child, or any other adult or near-adult who plays an important role in their household.

The decision to spend the first day with couples is the result of an evolution in the programme's attitude towards the men in members' lives. When Fonkoze first established CLM, it decided it would integrate only women with dependent children. Although it thought of itself as a programme for families, it would work directly only with women.

There were several reasons for the focus on women. For one thing, Fonkoze had long been a women-focused organization. Long before it launched CLM, with its focus on women with dependent children, over 95 per cent of the institution's borrowers were women. For another, the BRAC programme that Fonkoze was replicating also served only women with dependents.

But there were more particular reasons as well. The team saw two aspects of rural Haitian culture that argued for a focus on women. First, the structure of the typical rural family is such that, whoever might be responsible for a household's income, a household's principal woman would generally manage its resources to care for the whole family, especially the children. This is just a fancy way of saying that in Haiti, as in many places, basic household tasks like cooking and cleaning mainly fall to women, whether or not the women are also busy outside the home. Women buy food, prepare it, and serve it when it's ready. And that tends to be true if they are producing the food's ingredients or if they are generating the income to buy them, and it's also true if someone else – like a husband – is providing them with what they need. Working with women would help the women establish a measure of independence while providing the shortest, most direct route to improving the situation of their kids.

Second, the team was trying to identify the poorest households, but many men in rural Haiti have more than one family. The practice is so common that there is a word in Creole for a husband's other wife, '*matlòt*.' If we were to work principally with the men in families, we could find ourselves selecting a household because of clear need, then seeing resources directed towards another of the man's households, one with less need.

So, we have always felt that we should work with women principally, but in the programme's first years, the team didn't work with the women's husbands or male partners at all, at least not formally. Individual case managers, willing to try anything they thought would help the women succeed, would encourage husbands to help their wives, but the husbands were not invited to meetings, and the home visits that case managers made were one-on-one conversations with the women.

But the staff knew that families with two adults working as partners would have a better chance of succeeding than those in which the man was absent, uncooperative, or worse. More and more, they tried to encourage the men to participate. They started inviting men to a single day of separate meetings each time it gathered the women. These meetings had little structured agenda at first, but the men had a chance to talk about how the programme was affecting their families. Often, they would want to vent. Some would complain that their wives were starting to assert themselves. We'd hear men say that CLM was teaching their wives to be pushy, that it was teaching them disrespect. The expression they'd use, '*mal leve*', literally means 'badly raised', and is usually used to describe naughty children. The meetings also gave the CLM team a chance to talk to the men about the progress of the work, how it was designed to benefit their children especially, and how they could contribute to the effort.

But few of the men would attend these meetings. Part of this was connected to how little time rural men in Haiti spend at home. The hardest-working men leave early every morning and don't come home until the evening. And they stay active all this time. They are taking care of livestock, farming, or doing other odd jobs they find. Their families' very poverty would make it hard for serious men to sacrifice a day's work to attend a meeting. And maybe because this is the pattern for hardworking men, it is often imitated by those who work less hard, whether or not idleness is their own choice. They may have nothing useful to do, but they disappear early morning and stay out until late in the day.

But additional factors complicated the task of getting the men to participate. Long before they had received the invitation, they had convinced themselves that CLM was for their wives, not really for them. Case managers would work harder and harder during home visits to contact and encourage women's partners, but the programme's initial focus on women – both during the selection process and the initial training – left case managers with too much to overcome. Inviting the men to join the very first day of the initial training workshop and using that day to explain how the programme could work for their family, not just for their wives, seemed a possible step towards integrating the men more fully.

After the comprehensive introduction to the programme, we spend the rest of the first day teaching a module on savings. Few of the new members are saving when we begin working with them. They live hand to mouth, focused each day on feeding their family. Developing the habit of saving, however, can open doors – even for families who have little that they could save. It can give them resources to draw on in response to the setbacks that they will surely encounter. Starting to save can create investment opportunities down the line and it can insure a household against the kind of total loss that a hurricane-prone place like Haiti can bring. So, we discuss both the importance of saving and various ways that a family or an individual could choose to save.

And these workshops involve more than just food and training, too. They are six busy days. The CLM team has a lot to accomplish in a short period. It photographs each new member for a CLM ID card, making an effort to verify the spelling of their name using any ID they might have. In addition to serving as a temporary substitute for the government picture ID for members who lack them, the CLM ID links them to free medical care for themselves and members of their household.

Getting the names right can be difficult. For one thing, the women themselves are unlikely to know how to spell their own names. Of the 200 women who joined the programme with the group from Lawa, for example, only 63 could write their names, and this proportion is probably relatively high. They may never have attended school. Many lack government IDs, and some lack even birth certificates. When they joined the programme, only 87 of the 200 women had voting cards, the standard official ID in Haiti, and only 115 had birth certificates. The CLM ID may initially be the closest thing to an official document that programme members have.

And then there are more complicated stories to sort out. Itana's is just one example. She does have an ID with her photo, but it has her sister-in-law's name and date of birth. Some women give us a false name when they first meet us. They don't know us, and they don't trust us. Why would they?

Sometime during the six days, the women also sign a contract with Fonkoze. Because many cannot write their names, their signature is usually just a thumbprint. They agree to abide by the programme's rules and to do their best to manage the assets they will receive. Each member agrees to five stipulations:

- Not to liquidate anything that CLM gives her, nor to give it away to anyone else, nor to sell it, nor to mistreat it, nor destroy it.
- To take good care of everything that CLM gives her and to use it all to change her situation, earning an income both for her and her family.
- To work hard to solve her problems while she is in the programme and to make the CLM team aware of them.
- Not to look at what Fonkoze gives her as a gift, but as a means, something that she owns for the purpose of earning the money she needs to support her family.
- To follow the rules set out by Fonkoze to help her escape her situation and find a better future and to work closely with Fonkoze.

Shortly after the initial workshop, we hold a launch ceremony. It's a major event. The new programme members are encouraged to invite members of their family to attend, and we invite guests, especially any leaders of the community we can mobilize. That includes local elected officials or their representatives, along with pastors or other religious leaders. Or even just some of the wealthier folks who live in the area. We also bring as many members of our staff as are available. We want the new members to feel as though they have joined something large.

Most of the ceremony consists of short speeches. The women hear advice from CLM staff, from community leaders, sometimes even from women who have previously graduated from the programme. There are two longer speeches as well: one explaining the programme in detail and a second one, usually delivered by the most senior staff member present, ideally the director, welcoming new members into the programme and offering them more advice. In addition to the words of welcome, the second speech aims to make two main points: that the women should no longer think that they are alone and that they should recognize that the programme will expect them to work hard for all the progress they will make.

The director lets women know that they can call on programme staff to help them in an emergency. He tells them that he and his staff will have their backs. He will mobilize his team at any sign that one of the members is suffering from discrimination or abuse. But he also wants them to know that having a team to back them cannot be their excuse to mistreat their neighbours.

Each woman receives an envelope. The director calls one name after another, and they stand in place in what is usually a hot, crowded space. The CLM team organizes itself into a network of chains to pass the envelopes hand to hand to each member. These envelopes contain their picture ID; their contract, which has now been signed by community leaders as witnesses; and a book that they will keep at home, which will eventually contain a record of the member's work with her case manager.

The launch for the women from Lawa took place on Thursday 9 May 2019. Initially, the team in Gwomòn intended to organize two separate ceremonies in the two different communities because they couldn't find a central place where all 200 members could gather. The few sites that they found in the city of Gwomòn were too small, and they lacked space to prepare food.

After talking with the parish priest in downtown Gwomòn, however, the team received permission to use the church. It was badly damaged by an earthquake in the fall of 2018, but a large space in the churchyard had been covered with a high tin roof as a temporary house of worship, and the team held the ceremony within it. The priest also made a space on the church's grounds available for cooking and plating the food.

Gissaint César, CLM's regional supervisor for Gwomòn, demonstrated the use of the water filter, and each member received one to take home. At the end of the ceremony, we shared a meal.

***

At this point, at the end of the launch ceremony, we have done very little for CLM families. Other than an almost-trivial stipend for attending their initial workshop and a water filter – if we can get the filters we need in time – we have given them nothing. The individual coaching that our programme is built around has not yet begun. But if their six days of training and their launch ceremony have gone well, some members might have started to hope. It is our job to see to it that their hopes are not disappointed.

CHAPTER 7
Getting started

The CLM team is busy leading up to the launch. Selection and initial training both involve a lot of hard work, and the fundraising and project planning that must happen even before any of that starts also require time and effort. But the real work – the 18 months of close, personalized accompaniment at the programme's heart – begins after the launch. The CLM team assigns a case manager to each new member, and that case manager will visit the member in her home once each week. Eventually, these visits will have a regular agenda, but there are a couple of things that need to happen first.

These case managers are the programme's centrepiece. In Creole, we would say they are the '*poto mitan*', the central support post for a construction. More than anyone or anything involved in CLM, they are the key to its consistent success. Everything that we try to do for participating families depends on them. They are social workers, helping families consider and plan for the issues that affect their lives. They used to purchase the assets that members use to establish economic activities, whether merchandise for commerce, livestock, or farming inputs. As we have transitioned to providing cash for investment instead of assets, case managers hand members the cash and coach them through the process of acquiring assets. They are business consultants, coaching families to recognize and take advantage of whatever income opportunities they might encounter. They are financial advisors, helping members accumulate and make good use of savings. They are veterinary technicians, helping with questions about livestock, and agricultural extension agents, providing advice about farming. They are health and wellness advisors, transmitting messages that can help families stay healthy, but they are also patient advocates, facilitating members' access to healthcare, encouraging them to seek attention when necessary and linking them to whatever care is available.

The women from Lawa were part of a cohort of 200 families that were CLM members in Gwomòn. The CLM team in Gwomòn included four case managers, and each was assigned to work with 50 of the families. In assigning the families, the supervisor for Gwomòn had a number of things to consider. He was looking at 200 families, distributed very unevenly over a wide area, an area that includes obstacles like rivers and hills. The area has few roads, almost all of them bad. He would need to divide the two hundred into four manageable assignments. You can't just draw straws or use the alphabet. And his challenge involved more than just creating assignments that can work in principle. You have to make sure each assignment can work for the particular case manager you give it to. Not all staff members are equally capable of getting to all members. Some areas require strong motorcycle skills. Others require extensive hiking. Still others, like Lawa, require both.

And Gissaint needed to consider how best to serve each neighbourhood. Some are best given to a single case manager. Doing so can favour strong relations with the community, since all of its residents can identify the programme with a single face. It can also mean that the case manager is in the same neighbourhood more than one day each week, which can help us ensure members get quick help when they need it. In remoter areas like Lawa, however, we sometimes prefer to have multiple case managers working on the same day. That way, a case manager who runs into a problem can be sure of having a coworker close by. It can also help ensure that more than one case manager knows each household, which can be helpful at various stages in the process. The supervisor combined Lawa with the area the team would cross to get there, Savann Moulen, and the two neighbourhoods together were home to enough CLM families to provide a full day of work for all four case managers, so the initial plan had the four working in both areas.

Supervisors assign each case manager a list of 50. But the case managers cannot know where to go first. They may remember the homes at which they did selection, but the 50 families they have been assigned may not have many of those homes among them. And the families can't know when they should expect their case manager's visit each week. Each case manager needs to turn the list of 50 names into a clear weekly schedule. The first week after the launch ceremony, the members from each neighbourhood meet with their case managers in small groups somewhere in the neighbourhood.

At the close of the launch ceremony in Gwomòn, Gissaint had announced when and where each of these group meetings would be. The meeting for the women in Lawa took place on a bald, flat space of packed, brown dirt somewhat elevated over the main path into the area. Two buildings sit on that shelf of land, a church and a *gagè*, or cockfighting ring.

The church, which is also the local school, is a medium-sized cinder-block structure with an old tin roof. Looking at it, one is bound to contemplate the labour and expense involved in bringing all the cement and roofing tin that went into its construction all the way to Lawa. Trip after trip by mules and men, carrying a sack or two of cement or a few sheets of roofing. The *gagè* is a smaller and simpler structure: covered but not enclosed by anything more than the spectators' benches, planks nailed to wooden posts driven into the earth. The benches form a rectangle around the space where the fights take place.

Fonkoze's four case managers used both buildings to organize their groups, each finding a small, separate space where they could meet with the women assigned to them. Two groups met in each building.

These meetings can be awkward. Though the members have already attended six days of training, they can still be wary of the programme. They can be reticent and passive, all of which makes the work more difficult for the case manager responsible for leading the conversation. They let members know which of them will work with each family, they advise them that they will soon be asked to choose the assets the CLM programme will provide, and they work with the members in their group to determine the order of the home visits for the following weeks.

They need to agree on a day for these visits, and though the team would prefer to give each member her choice, it really can't. The kinds of regular community events, like market days, that determine which days would work best for a community are generally large enough to affect broad regions. In Gwomòn, the principal market is the one held downtown, and it happens several times a week. So, case managers must see families on market days, even if it inconveniences the families. And they have to be able to look at all 50 families they will work with and come up with something that works more or less for everyone. In Lawa, everyone was lucky. They were generally satisfied that Tuesday was to be their day.

A weekly home visit takes approximately 30 minutes to complete, and the case managers work with the members to establish a schedule that respects both those 30 minutes and the distance between their homes. The day's first visit in a distant area like Lawa might be scheduled for 8 or 8:30. It is hard to schedule anything earlier because it takes time just to get to a place like Lawa. If it will take 10 minutes for the case manager to get to the next home, they cannot slot the next visit until 8:40 or 9:10.

The week following the group meetings, case managers begin seeing members individually, in their homes. At this point, the supervisor was faced with a challenge. Staffing for the CLM programme is generally stable. The scarcity of jobs in Haiti means that those who have jobs are inclined to keep them. Though Fonkoze loses CLM staff because the grants that allow us to employ them run out, and though we have had to fire a few for other reasons over the years, relatively few have chosen to leave their post.

But one of the case managers on the team in Gwomòn left immediately after these small group meetings, so when the team was ready to start visiting CLM members individually in their homes, one of the case managers was new at her job. The case manager assigned to Itana, Jeanna, and Clotude was Molène, the new member of staff. She had received her training, but she had no experience whatsoever in what she would have to do. So, the initial visits for these women were led by Gissaint instead.

This first home visit was the members' chance to choose which enterprises the programme would plan to transfer to them, and the supervisor took them through the process. He went through the same procedure with each one, starting by asking them to review the advantages of each of the various enterprises Fonkoze routinely provides and the challenges each presents.

Jeanna spoke at length about both poultry and small commerce. The former gives you small assets that you can sell off quickly whenever you have a small, urgent expense to manage. If a child is sick, for example, you are sure to find a neighbour willing to buy a chicken, and that will generally give you the

Table 7.1 Change in the price of goats, 2014–2025

	Exchange rate (HTG* per US$)	Young female goat (HTG)	Young female goat (US$)
January 2014	43.89	1,500	34.17
November 2021	98.81	5,000	50.60
January 2025	130.28	7,500	57.57

* HTG, Haitian gourd

money you need initially to get the child to a doctor. And because Jeanna has many children, medical needs are a strong consideration. She then explained that commerce, by ensuring a stream of cash, enables you to 'pay into a *sòl*' – a Haitian savings club – 'or buy a little bit of food' when you need to.

But she chose goats and a pig: the goats because they are easy to care for and require no special food and the pig because pigs can accumulate value quickly. She specified that she'd rather raise a boar than a sow. 'Piglets get into people's gardens, so they throw rocks at them and kill them'. It can lead to serious conflict with neighbours.

The supervisor asked her to identify her goals for the enterprises. Jeanna explained that she wanted to be able to sell offspring from her goats to buy a larger animal. 'I want a horse so I can get into commerce again.' A horse, or another pack animal, like a mule or a donkey, would be transformative for her since it would increase the amount of merchandise she can bring to market, from the very limited amount she can balance on her head to that much plus all that her animal's strength permits. And even though the price of horses has increased significantly in Haiti over the last few years because the demand for horse meat has increased, using goats to purchase one should still be possible. Goats are, after all, getting more expensive as well. Table 7.1 explains the change in the price of goats in the markets in Central Haiti from January 2014 to January 2025.

Jeanna has been managing a business on and off for years. At least any time she is not in the last stages of pregnancy or nursing a baby. The business takes her to Senmak, where she sells drinking water and kerosene. Her husband stays in Lawa with the kids while she's away. But when asked about her hoped-for horse, she makes it clear that she does not imagine returning to that life. 'If I had a horse, I'd do my business from home. I wouldn't have to leave my children anymore.'

Clotude sees her options as limited. Whereas Jeanna refers several times to the role that her husband will play with her in managing their new activities, Clotude comes back repeatedly to the fact that she has no such support. Her husband is dead, and her older children live away from home. She's alone in the house with three daughters, ages 12, 7, and 2. 'I can't leave.' At the same time, she feels a strong need to get something started. 'I have to have something in my hands.'

She'd like to raise a pig. If you take good care of one and get a little lucky, your wealth can increase quickly. Boars gain value rapidly as they grow, and sows produce saleable offspring more quickly than goats do and tend to produce a lot more of them, too.

But pigs are also demanding. 'To manage a pig, you have to have means in hand,' Clotude explains. They need to eat well. Unless you can afford to buy a lot of feed, you have to take on the labour-intensive work of foraging for them, and even with that you can still have to buy pig feed regularly as well.

So Clotude chooses goats instead. They don't require much care beyond moving them around. You just have to keep them tied up out of the sun and within reach of food. Though many Haitians let their goats wander, finding their own food, our team strongly discourages programme members from doing so. Clotude says her 12-year-old daughter Claudine can help her with that.

She also chooses small commerce. She'll sell groceries along the main path. It is her only option until she can find a way to leave her girls for longer periods and thus set up her business further from home. But a grocery business close to home involves a lot of risk. Neighbours often want to buy on credit, and it can be hard to say 'no'. If they don't pay on time, you can run out of merchandise without a way to restock.

Clotude is nevertheless anxious to try. And when the supervisor asks her to explain her goals, she shows that she has the beginnings of a plan. 'Once it gets going, I can start buying a chicken or two now and then. Eventually, I'd like to buy farmland so I can plant sugarcane.'

Itana remembers much of what she learned at the six-day training. She has little trouble going through the advantages and disadvantages of each business. Goats are easy to take care of. Chickens are easy to sell quickly in a pinch. Small commerce is the one way to a steady cash income, and a pig makes money quickly.

Her initial reaction is to thank the supervisor for whatever he might decide to give her. 'You have to take whatever falls your way,' she explains. But the supervisor is in no hurry. He is happy to take the time he needs to make her understand that the choice is hers, that he will not make it for her. Eventually, she relaxes enough to let him know what she thinks.

She sees problems everywhere. Pig feed has been expensive lately. Small commerce can disappear if customers buy on credit. And poultry is subject to disease and theft. So Itana asked to receive goats, and nothing else.

At one time, this would have been a problem for the programme. CLM used to insist that all members choose two different kinds of assets as a way to lessen their risk. They would be presented with a menu of two-asset packages – goats or a pig with commerce, goats and a pig, goats or a pig with poultry – and choose their package.

In recent years, however, the approach has become more flexible, emphasizing a more detailed conversation with each member about how she would like to invest a certain amount of money – an 'envelope' – that is available to purchase assets for her. In practice, rural members still tend to choose goats, usually with a second asset as well. But we thought that the longer, freer conversation there would be if the choice was less constrained would be a useful way to review key lessons from the training while helping us ensure that the decisions women make are their own. Case managers, anxious for members' quick success, are too inclined to want to make decisions for them.

Itana knows what she wants, and the supervisor is willing to give it to her. Her plan is to use the first offspring from her goats to buy a pig. By then she hopes to have the means to take good care of one.

The supervisor held these same conversations with all of Molène's members, just as the experienced case managers held them with the other families. He had, after all, spent years as a case manager before receiving his promotion. After a week of visits, the team knew what assets it would need to purchase, and it began to make its plan.

The week following that first visit, the case managers held individual home visits again, but they still weren't ready to start the work of accompaniment that will help families change their lives. Instead, they undertook a survey, called the 'evaluation of assets', which is designed to verify exactly what productive assets each family owns.

This isn't really new information for the team. Or it shouldn't be. The selection process includes extensive surveys, and identifying the assets that a family owns is one of its central goals. But checking it all once again has two big advantages.

First, the information that we get at this point is more reliable. Before families are part of the programme, they are more likely to lie to us. We have done nothing to earn their trust. They don't owe us the truth. They do not know why we are asking so many questions, so they can decide to conceal the truth in various ways and for various reasons. Having been through initial training, the launch, and a couple of weeks of conversations with their case manager, new members are more at ease. In addition, a couple of extra weeks walking around the neighbourhood, talking to folks both within the programme and outside it, makes case managers more knowledgeable questioners.

So sometimes case managers learn, at this point, about assets that disqualify members for the programme entirely. Maybe the pigs that the member said belong to a neighbour are actually hers. Maybe they've heard about a cow that's kept grazing away from the home. A few weeks into the 18 months, the team can decide to remove someone and replace them.

But replacing a CLM member at this point is uncommon. The more important role of these surveys is to enable the member and her case manager to start the 18-month coaching process with a detailed, shared understanding of where the member stands. The extensive coaching that the programme depends on requires that the case manager know the resources that each member has available. Simply assuming that none start with anything would leave too many possibilities unexplored.

And identifying the resources available to a member can be complex, both for us and even for her. This is especially true of any household assets that a woman identifies as belonging to her partner. He might own livestock that could, in principle, disqualify the household, but the new member might not really have access to it if her partner thinks of it as being for another spouse. The more a case manager knows about anything that is or could be available to the household, the better.

The narrow survey of members' assets goes along with a broader survey of various important aspects of their family's life. This broader survey serves as a baseline that we return to later in the process, at 12 months and at its end, to see the changes – the progress, we hope – in that life.

CHAPTER 8
Home visits

Dieunel St. Fleury is a quiet man from Boukankare, a broad rural commune north-west of Mibalè. He's neither especially big nor tall, but he has an athletic build. His light brown face flashes a ready smile behind his moustache and the short, dark beard, which runs the outline of his jaw. He's been a case manager for the CLM programme for over two years. This morning, his schedule was taking him to Kapab, a small community along the Artibonit River, in Laskawobas.

Getting to Kapab is quite a haul. There's no road. It's served by canoe ferries that crisscross the lake formed by the hydroelectric dam in Pelig, the Artibonit River, and the many small inlets that lead up to the dam. But for someone as athletic as Dieunel, it is simpler and more sensible to get to Kapab on foot, especially since he cannot swim. Dieunel hikes there.

In Lonsi, a wide path winds upward from the long, rocky, rain-gashed road that connects the Pelig dam with downtown Laskawobas. Dieunel can take his motorcycle part-way up that path. But he must leave it behind below the final rise to the hill's main ridge. The path gets too steep, too crooked, and too rocky to drive, so he walks the rest of the way. Then he continues on foot down the winding path into the valley. The descent makes for a long, but comfortable morning stroll, but promises a much harder trip back up the same hill when he returns to his motorcycle at the end of the day, when the late-afternoon tropical sun is hot.

He visits 50 CLM families in their homes every week, spending about half an hour with each. Thirteen of those families live in Kapab, and he needs to see them in one day, because the trip to Kapab and back is too long to make twice a week. That means 6½ hours of work, not including the hikes to and from Kapab and the time it takes him to get from one home to another. By any reckoning, it's a long day.

He sees his first two families just after he crosses over the ridge, before he descends the main part of the slope, but the other 11 families are all down towards the river. Mariciane lives nearly all the way down. Her home sits on its own small rise, bald and covered with packed, light-brown dirt. As low as her yard is, the slight rise and the bareness of the space opens a wide view of the small plots of farmland that sit along both sides of the water, towards the east. Dieunel slips through the small garden between her house and the main path. The garden grows mostly half-dead weeds this time of year, with the dry season starting to take hold. As he approaches the back of her house, he calls out:

'*Onè!*' Literally, that means, 'honour'. It's a customary way to announce one's arrival at a rural Haitian home. Dieunel doesn't hear the traditional response, '*respè*', or 'respect', so he keeps calling as he enters the *lakou*, or yard.

'Hey! Isn't anyone home?'

Dieunel turns, crossing in front of Mariciane's narrow, tin-roofed house. Mariciane calls from where she's sitting, behind the house and to its right, under an old, thick, twisted tree. A couple of kids sit around her on the tree's exposed roots.

'Here we are. Here we are'.

'Mariciane?'

'Yes.'

Mariciane is a tall, slender woman who's almost 50. She has seven children, the youngest six of them with her current partner. She keeps her steel-grey hair pulled back close to her head. She has lively eyes above a subtle but ready smile. As soon as Dieunel can see her, he begins to ask her how things are.

'How are you? How are you?'

'We're fine, and you?'

'Ah, well. I'm struggling along. How's the family?'

'*Yo pa pi mal, non.*' This means, 'They are no worse.' It's a typical Haitian way to answer the question.

Mariciane rises and asks Dieunel to sit in the chair she's been using. It is important to her that her visitor have the best chair she can produce. She sends a child to bring another for herself, but none are available. So, she takes a bright yellow five-gallon water jug. It has a flat top, and she lays a pillow across the top and settles down on it.

Dieunel turns to Mariciane's approaching husband. 'Zando?' The man's name is Frankel, but his friends and neighbours use a nickname, Zando, and so does Dieunel. Like Mariciane, Frankel is slender. He's somewhat older looking than his wife, and a little bit shorter than she is. He has the slight but sinuous body of an active farmer and a short, greying goatee.

'How are you, *konpè*?' Zando answers. Literally speaking, my '*konpè*', or my '*monkonpè*', is my godson's father or my child's godfather. As a more general form of address, it conveys familiarity, comfort, and respect among equals. And this is how Frankel addresses Dieunel.

***

No part of the CLM programme is more important than the time that case managers like Dieunel spend with programme members at the members' homes. Their weekly visits drive everything we try to accomplish. The visits target improving members' economic situation, protecting their health, and changing their social status. They aim towards building members' capacity for future-planning and their self-confidence, two things that good decision-making depends on.

The first few visits can be awkward, however. New members can be unaccustomed to visitors, but they can nevertheless have a strong sense of what it means, in rural Haiti, to receive someone. They want to provide at least a comfortable chair in a shady spot in their yard.

They may, however, own no chairs, and they may not have enough authority over the space where they live to decide either where they will sit down or where they will seat someone else. Curious neighbours or other people from the member's household sometimes want to follow the proceedings, which can only make everyone involved even more uncomfortable. Members may even want to offer some kind of refreshment, but they rarely have anything they can give. They themselves probably have too little to eat. But as little as they have, their parting words are often apologetic: 'I didn't give you anything'.

At first, members might want to remain standing in front of their case manager, who seems like an important authority figure they need to respect. They tend to look away, either to the side or down at the ground, an echo of the way that Haitian children are taught not to look adults in the eye. Case managers are taught, on the other hand, to speak with members face-to-face, whether seated in a chair, on the ground, or in the shady roots of a mango tree. They might find a discarded cinder block, a bucket, or a relatively smooth rock. Some simply carry their motorcycle helmets with them, using them as stools in the homes that don't yet have anything better to sit on. They make a point of showing that they feel relaxed and at home.

The case managers' attitude is part of helping members see themselves in a new way, but it initially causes some stress. Members rush to find a chair wherever they can, sending a child to beg the loan of one from a neighbour if necessary, and they will gasp in distress when their case manager sits down without one. '*Ou chita atè!*' 'You're sitting on the ground!' The young husband of a member once saw me sit down on a large, smooth stone in his yard, leaving two chairs for him and his absent wife's case manager. '*Sa w ap fè m, granparan?*' he shouted. 'What are you doing to me, grandfather?' As though I had somehow injured him. He insisted I take one of the chairs, and he lifted and carried the large, heavy rock over to where we sat so that his wife could sit on it. Case managers have to balance the strain they cause by violating important behavioural norms against the opportunity the violations create for easy, face-to-face conversations down the road.

There is a lot to accomplish in a visit, but because case managers have to see 50 families every week, the visits must be short, scheduled for just 30 minutes. There's a fixed agenda, and it's tight. It takes discipline to get everything done. The programme provides a checklist to guide the process, and we neither expect nor even encourage case managers to memorize it. They carry it with them. The list has changed some in the years since we started in 2007, but not very much.

Visits start with a greeting, like the one that Dieunel offered on his arrival at Mariciane's home. They could hardly start any other way. Greetings are important in Haiti, where it's sometimes said that your '*Bonjou*' is your passport. And greeting, for CLM, means more than just saying 'hello'. Though there is time reserved in the visit to talk in detail about the member's health and the health of the rest of her family, these initial greetings inevitably include a few words asking how everyone is. The greeting is also the time to make sure that a member is ready for her visit. The greeting between Dieunel, Mariciane, and Frankel continued:

> 'Mariciane, where are the animals? You know I have to see them while I'm here'.
> Frankel: 'They're not far'.
> 'Okay. Bring them here for me, konpè. Do it quickly. You know I have other families to see. Let's sit down, Mariciane. How was your week?'
> 'It wasn't bad.'
> 'Are the kids well?'
> 'They're no worse.'

After completing this initial chat, a case manager can move to the second item on the checklist: verifying the state of the member's business assets. Case managers are trained in basic livestock care, and they go over each of a member's animals. They give particular attention to simple health issues, like various internal and external parasites that can lead to serious problems, but they also look for signs that members are taking good care of the animals. Does a goat appear well-fed? Does the area around a pig look clean? Are the ropes used to tie them in good shape?

If a member is managing small commerce, they go over the week's purchasing and sales and discuss any problems that might have arisen. Are clients buying on credit and not paying? Has rain damaged any merchandise? Did a day spent at a local market fail to go as planned? Has the member suffered any unusual losses?

But Dieunel had a problem. Mariciane had goats and turkeys, but she and Frankel had neglected to keep the goats near their home for the visit. He had to wait while Frankel went to get them. So Dieunel moved to the next item on the list, checking the hygiene around the home.

Case managers look at household hygiene for two reasons. Most importantly, cleanliness helps families stay healthy. Good hygiene can do a lot to prevent water-borne diseases especially. And taking good care of one's home, one's yard, and oneself also helps improve a family's social status. It is part of helping families come to be seen and to see themselves as full members of the communities they live in.

And improved hygiene around the house is something like the low-hanging fruit of life changes. Case managers can help members take on easy-to-address problems. Before they join the programme, families can be careless about simple things, like sweeping and cleaning. We come across families with holes in the walls of their houses that they could easily repair, with trash strewn in their yard that they could easily remove, with dirty laundry lying around that they could easily clean. They ignore all that because persistent hunger is a much more urgent problem. Sweeping the yard in front of their home is no step towards getting a meal every day. But it takes very little time or effort, and it can serve as a helpful first step on the way towards social inclusion, even while a family is still working on solving the problem of daily meals. So, case managers not only preach good hygiene, but they look to see whether their sermons are having an effect.

> 'Let's get up and have a look around the house. Come along, Mariciane. Let's go. What are you looking for?'
> 'I'm bringing in my laundry.'
> 'My visit isn't the time for that, is it? Which door is open? Let's have a look at your water filter.'

Mariciane laughs.

> 'Last night a bunch of *mizango* passed through and they took away our laundry.'

A '*mizango*' is a kind of low-level evil spirit, but the word can also be used for a low-level thief. Someone, apparently, had passed the home during the night, seen laundry still drying outside, and taken some.

> 'I don't know anything about that, but let's look at your filter.'

All CLM families receive water filters. It's important for them to drink treated water. Water-borne diseases, from simple diarrhea to cholera, can be enfeebling or even deadly. Though chemical treatment products are readily available in Haiti, even in more rural markets, it is easier to get families to commit themselves to treat water if they can initially do so free of charge. A water filter helps, and many families perceive the difference in their health that clean water makes.

But families don't always see the importance of the filter right away. Case managers have to keep after them, checking the filter to see whether it's being used. If you merely ask a member whether she has been filtering her family's drinking water, she's likely to say that she has been. But inspecting the filter makes it easy enough to tell. And knowing that their case manager will check the filter, and not just ask questions about it, can encourage a member to use it. It can seem easier than getting an earful.

> 'You haven't been treating water, have you, Mariciane?'
> 'No. I wasn't here.'
> 'You weren't here? Where have you been?'
> 'I've been making charcoal. I just don't have time. I haven't had time for anything at all.'
> 'No time to treat water? What water do you drink?'
> 'We put a couple of grains of stuff into it.'
> 'What stuff?'

'Either Aquatab' [a water treatment product widely available in rural Haiti] 'or a few grains of bleach.'

> 'And when you're out making charcoal, you find treated water to drink?'
>
> 'What? Are you kidding? I leave the kids here, and they treat a jug of it. I don't have time for anything. For anything. Last night, I didn't get back from the charcoal 'til after dark. Now I need to collect my laundry to go out to wash. Then, when I'm done, to come back here and ... I just don't have any time.'
>
> 'Okay. Come here. Come here. Let's sit back down together. I'm glad to see the area around the house is ... Mariciane, Mariciane, pay attention. You're with me right now. The area is not too bad. But you really have to keep at it, inside and outside, to keep your family from getting sick, especially from cholera.'
>
> 'I know. I know. I don't really treat myself too badly.'

Frankel arrived with the family's goats. The CLM programme had given them two young nannies and three turkeys as productive assets. And though Dieunel is not a veterinarian, he has been trained, like all case managers, in basic livestock health.

> 'Here they are', Frankel announces.
>
> 'Yeah. I see. Looks like that one's had some diarrhea. We'll be treating them for parasites, internal and external, soon. We'll look at the medication we can give them. In the meantime, they get sick sometimes. Animals are no different from people that way. But there are some natural remedies I can show you. You can feed them guava leaves. It looks like the diarrhea is passing.'
>
> 'That one's Darline's', Mariciane answers. 'But mine has diarrhea, too.'

Darline is one of Mariciane's daughters. A mother of two young children herself, she is also a CLM member, and Dieunel will have to work with her after he finishes with Mariciane. But, for now, he wants to focus on Mariciane's issues.

> 'Okay. I see it's not too bad right now. Feed it guava leaves, and we'll see.'

After looking over Mariciane's livestock, Dieunel is ready to help her learn to write her name. Members who cannot sign their name – and that's the majority – learn to do so by copying it in a notebook they purchase. Some are able to copy their name easily the first time they see it. With just a little practice, they've mastered the skill. For others, the challenge is greater. For older women, vision problems can make things difficult. Others show signs of what might be dyslexia. They have serious difficulties trying to copy even simple shapes.

A case manager must guess what a member is going to be able to do and then push her to her limit. Dieunel decides to focus on just the first letter of Mariciane's name, the M, but he does more than simply give her a model for her to copy. He provides a description of the process he follows as he draws a simplified M. Mariciane thus has more she can depend on than her ability to see the model. She can work from a simple description of the way the letter takes shape, too.

'Where's your little notebook, Mariciane? Bring it over so we can have a look. Where is it? Don't you remember that I said you should keep the envelope with all your stuff in one place, and make sure your notebook is always inside it? And where's your pencil? Mariciane doesn't have a pencil!'

'Here it is. I found it. I found it.'

'Does it have a point? You can't write with a pencil that's not sharp. Sit close so you can see! Come closer, closer! Today, you'll learn how to make a letter called 'M'. What do we call this letter?'

'M.'

'Look at what I do. If I want to make an M, I make a first little stick standing upright, then a second. Then I connect their heads, and I draw a third standing up in the middle. Do you think you can make one? I'm sure you can. Give it a try.

'Let me make another one for you. Here's the first little stick, and here's the second. I connect their two heads, and then I draw a third stick down from the middle. That's an M. See how easy it is? It's the first letter in your name.

'Now you should make one. No. No. Start there, like I did. Go ahead. The first stick, the second stick farther along, then the one across the top, and then the one down the middle. That's a good start. You can make another. That's right. The first stick, the second Connect the tops and drop the third down from the middle. Okay. Isn't that easy? Great job! You're really good.'

'I'm a good student,' Mariciane chuckles.

'Now, fill up the page with M's before I come back next week. And don't let Darline or the other children do it. It has to be Mariciane. If the kids do it, or someone else does it, I'll know. Next week, when I come by, we'll make another letter.'

After they've worked on name-writing, Dieunel and Mariciane are ready to review last week's 'lesson' or 'issue'.

Much of the CLM programme depends on teaching of different kinds. Transmitting new business techniques, for example, starts off through training in a classroom and continues in one-on-one conversations. Ongoing coaching supports improved planning and decision-making.

The lessons are another kind of teaching we do. They are short health-related messages designed to help families make simple changes that can dramatically improve their lives, and they are learned through a structured drill. When the programme was first piloted in 2007, the original implementing team worked with its advisors from BRAC to choose 10 such messages.

Simple things, like the importance of vitamin A and how to find it, the danger presented by worms and how to avoid them, the importance of clean drinking water, and the value of hygiene. There were also several messages relating to family planning and reproductive health. In 2011, the team added a lesson about cholera prevention, and in 2016 one about how talking to babies is critical for their development. In 2020, it temporarily introduced a lesson about COVID-19.

Case managers present one lesson each week in every home. They also offer a short review of the lesson from the previous week. At the end of 12 weeks, the programme starts over with the first one once again. The same messages rotate through the programme's 18 months.

> 'Mariciane, do you remember a subject we talked about last week? Remember …? Are you sure you're concentrating?
> 'I don't remember. I have too many things in my head.'
> 'Really?'
> 'There's just so much I have to take care of. I don't have time to sit and think.'
> 'Okay. What we talked about is why it's not good for a woman to be pregnant too early. But that was a couple of weeks ago. Last week, I was off buying livestock. Let's move on to this week's lesson. It's cleanliness, hygiene, and latrines.'

All the lessons follow the same three-part structure: a statement of a danger, a description of the solution, and a commitment to adopt the solution. Dieunel begins by talking with Mariciane about the dangers that poor hygiene presents.

> 'Mariciane, what's cleanliness?'
> 'Cleanliness is really important. Like this morning, you showed up and I haven't done anything yet. I'm embarrassed.' She laughs. 'I haven't swept. I haven't arranged anything. It's embarrassing. Cleanliness is really important.'
> 'But why's it important?'
> 'Cleanliness keeps you healthy.'
> 'What do you mean? What diseases can you catch when you don't keep things clean?'
> 'You can get hives or rashes. It can give you all sorts of things. You can pick up a cough. It can make you sick inside.'
> 'That's right. But do you remember another disease that spread around a few years ago, one that had folks carrying sick people away, one after another?'
> 'Yes. Yes. Cholera.'
> 'Yes. If you don't follow simple good-hygiene rules, you can get really sick. You can get cholera, you can get diarrhea, you can get typhoid. And these are all diseases that can kill you. No one wants to die, right?'
> 'No.'

They have arrived at the danger, sickness that can lead to death. Now Dieunel needs to talk with Mariciane about what she can do to avoid the danger.

'That's why your whole yard, the place you live, inside the house and outside of it, needs to be in good condition. When we say "in good condition" we mean that, even if you don't have money, or you don't have much money, the place you live always needs to be clean. Your house, your clothes, everything you use, all need to be clean. Your bed, your dishes, pots, and pans. Everything that you use. The yard, too. You need to sweep, get rid of all the nasty trash, and clear out the weeds, so you don't have bugs collecting in them that could make you sick. When you wash everything in and around your house, you'll be healthier. Don't forget, if you let things get filthy, and that makes you sick, you'll have to spend lots of money to get healthy again. You can even end up dying.

'And it's not just your house. You have to take care of yourself, too. That means bathe often, brush your teeth, keep your fingernails short. Remember to wash your hands with soap and water, especially when you've used the latrine or are going to eat. When you're hungry, even if it's just a mango or an avocado. It might look pretty, but nothing says it doesn't have germs that could make you sick. Because you can't see germs with your eyes. You need to be careful with it. Wash it before you eat it.

'And use the latrine. Don't do what you have to do just anywhere. When you don't use the latrine, you can contaminate the water you use, and that can bring other diseases. Cover the latrine's seat so that you don't have flies from the latrine getting near your food.'

The third and final step in the messaging process is to ask the member to commit herself to the behaviours that she and the case manager have discussed. Dieunel will ask Mariciane whether she agrees to implement the steps they've talked about.

'Do all that, and it will help you stay healthy. Do you think you'll remember?'
'I'll remember.'
'Really? Next time I'm here, you won't ask, "What was that you were saying again?"'
'I'll remember. I'll remember. Even if I sometimes seem out of it.'

After working on the week's message, Dieunel turns to the seventh step of the visit checklist. At her initial six-day training, Mariciane received a lot of information about managing the assets she would eventually choose. Now that she's at home, Dieunel will review something about asset management with her each week. As they work together through 18 months, Dieunel will get to know her better and better, and he'll be able to evaluate each week what she might need to work on. But early in the process, her needs can be pretty unclear, so he lets her guide what they will discuss.

'Next, do you remember what you learned at the training about taking care of your animals?'

'The animals? The goats? Well. You make sure they have food. You tie them where they have food to eat. You move them when you need to. You give them water twice a day. But my goats don't want to drink water. Neither of them do. I bring them water, but they don't drink. And it's bad because one has diarrhea.'

'I see. I think we should just keep an eye on it for now. We don't know what it was like where it lived before we got it. It might be used to eating different things. It might just be getting used to things here.'

'So, you give them water and a shed for them to sleep in. As far as the turkeys: You have to give them food, so they don't wander off. Every day. You get up and feed them, so they don't leave.'

'Yes. Good.'

'And for the goats, you said that when we build our goat shed, we should take a little hollowed-out gourd, put some salt in it, and hang it in the shed on a piece of string. The goats will lick the gourd, so they'll get the salt and that will give them an appetite for the food they find.'

'Okay. I hear what you're saying. But do you do the things you say you should do?'

'I haven't made the shed yet, but I remember what you told us ...'

'Why haven't you made the shed yet?'

'We set it up. We just haven't walled it in yet.'

'Why haven't you walled it in?'

'I haven't found the time.'

'It's been a while now, and you never have found the time. Do you think that there's hope you'll find the time eventually?'

'I'll find the time eventually, if I don't die. As long as I don't die, I'll manage to find the time. We will. Right now, it's stuff about our house that's taking up our time. Running around, collecting the lumber that we'll need. Having it cut up. That's what's taking up our time.'

'Okay. But even though it hasn't rained in a while, we know that we'll get rain again sometime, right. And when it rains again ...'

'Yes, yes. The rain will come, but the goats won't get wet. The hut is covered. It just doesn't have walls yet.'

'You mentioned salt, giving your goats salt in their hut. What's salt good for?'

'It gives the goat an appetite. It makes it drink more water so it will eat more, too. I don't remember if that was it.'

'Yes. Yes. Everything you say is true. But remember there's more. Not only does salt make your goat feel at home, but it also provides calcium that's good for its bones. I hope that when I come by next week, I'll find the goat shed walled-in. It's your responsibility. If you don't want to have trouble with me, you have to finish your goat shed. We should have been finished with this already.'

After reviewing asset management, Dieunel is ready to broaden his conversation with Mariciane. The next item on the checklist is talking with Mariciane about her plans.

One of the key changes that CLM aims at for its members is to help them think more about the future, to help them make plans. Many of the families who join the programme are so focused on the struggle to get by each day that they don't think about the medium or the longer term. They develop tunnel vision. This is a phenomenon that has been described widely (see, for example, Mullainathan and Shafir, 2013).

The CLM team has always been convinced, however, that developing members' ability to plan for the future should be an important part of the programme. From the time of the pilot, having a plan was a graduation criterion. In the first years, the question about planning on evaluation surveys focused on plans concerning the member's business investment. The evaluator would ask whether the member had a plan for her business, and most members would say something like they wanted to buy a cow or a piece of farmland, and the evaluator would give them the point that the question was worth.

But the team's experience talking with graduates led it to change the question in two steps. First, it worked to define what would count as 'having a plan'. Buying a cow might be a very good idea for a rural Haitian woman, but it isn't a plan until she can say how she is going to go about doing so and when. Where will the money come from? Will she sell other livestock she already has? Will she sell a harvest of a crop she's planted? When will the livestock or the produce she's counting on be ready? The programme came to define 'having a plan' as including an objective, a strategy, and a timeline.

We took the second step as further experience pushed the team to think about planning more broadly. Interviews with graduates made it clear that some members were unable to move forward or even lost the progress they had made for reasons that had little directly to do with their business plan. They might struggle to stay healthy because they weren't sure how to continue treating their drinking water once their filter was no longer usable or because they did not know what to do once their latrine pit was full.

In 2017, I spoke with a group of recent CLM graduates in Bakè, a community on the road that leads to the major rural market of Mache Kana, in Central Mibalè. None had had any trouble meeting the programme's graduation criteria after 18 months, but several had built their CLM-assisted homes on land they had leased but did not own. Though each had graduated with a reasonable plan for continuing to manage her business, none had planned what they would do if or when they lost access to the land their homes were built on. When the time came, they had to sell their productive assets to rent rooms where they could live with their children. They risked returning to the extreme poverty they had known before they joined the programme.

So, Fonkoze added a small worksheet to the evaluation with questions about seven key areas of a family's future: how they will ensure the children's education, how they will treat their drinking water once the filter breaks, what they will do when their latrine is no longer usable, how they will ensure they always have a secure and dry house, how they'll continue to keep their home clean, how they will grow their business, and how they'll ensure their family has enough to eat every day.

And it isn't just a matter that comes up when they use the evaluation survey. Case managers work with members about their plans every week. As they gain experience with individual members, they can guide this part of the conversation more and more where they think it needs to go. But early in the process, the case manager will try to learn what is on the member's mind, and this is what we see Dieunel trying to do.

'So, next. Let's talk about what you've been doing since I saw you last.'

'You mean about my goats?'

'Oh, I don't know. Whatever you've been working on … .'

'Whatever I've been working on? Nothing, really. Mostly stuff for my house problem.'

'What kind of stuff?'

'I've been having lumber prepared.'

'Wow. That's great news.'

'I bought palm trees and had them cut down, but we haven't been able have them cut into planks yet, because I don't have the money. But the trees I will need are on the ground. And all my support posts are ready. Now preparing the palm trees is all that's holding me back.'

'So, that's for your home. That's great.'

'Yes.'

'Okay, Mariciane. What goals do you have for the future? For you and your kids? What would you like to do?'

'What would I like to do? Well, I don't know whether I'll die first, but I'll tell you what's in my head. I'd like to fight to send all my kids to school so that, if they can stay in school, I'll have something I can draw on in the future. Because some day I won't be able to stand on my own. I'll need my kids to provide for me, to help me. And when the children start to have means of their own, it won't just be me who thinks of it, but they'll think of the family, too. Because if I worked for you, you should think of me and your family when I can't anymore.'

'Okay. So, your idea is to send the children to school so they can graduate and then help themselves and their family. That's good. But what do you plan to do for that?'

'I farm. That's all I do. I don't have a business anymore. I used to do business, but I don't anymore. I just farm to send them to school.'

'Why don't you try business?'

'No, no. What kind of business could I do? I can't. I can't carry heavy loads anymore. There's no business.'

'So, you used to carry heavy loads? What sort of business did you used to do?'

'I used to get up at 3 a.m. and go down to the water and take a canoe to buy fish from the fishermen. Then I would take it to market. I'd return home with 500 gourds or even 750. I would feed the family with 300 or 400 gourds and try to save the rest.'

'Are all your kids in school this year?'

'All of them.'

'All of them? Bravo! That's a lot of work. But what you're saying is really important, too. You know that if I hadn't gotten an education, I wouldn't be in a position to even know you. School is really important. But it isn't about just one year. It takes time for a child to get all the way through school. So, you can't fall asleep on this plan. You have to stick with it. Always save some of whatever you have. Save in your savings and loan association. Save through a *sòl*. When you go to the market with 500 gourds, buy food for 300, 400, and save 100. Anytime you have 1,000 gourds, buy a chicken to raise. When you sell a sack of charcoal, don't buy food with everything. Put something away. When your chickens lay eggs, you can eat some. But let some hatch so you'll have more chickens. You can keep farming. Your husband can keep farming. All that will help you so that you'll always be able to send the kids to school. But you need to do more than just send them. You need to make sure they're studying so that they'll succeed.'

'There's just one of my girls who doesn't like to go to school, but when she says she doesn't want to go I keep after her. I keep after her to make her go.'

'What's her problem? Why doesn't she want to go to school?'

'She just doesn't want to. She'd rather stay home. If I want her to go to school, every day it's a battle. I have to hit her. You can say what you want to her. Preaching doesn't do any good.'

'What does she say to explain it?'

'She doesn't want to go. She wants to go to the Dominican Republic.'

'Has she been there before?'

'No. But she has a sister there. Because of her sister, the child says she wants to go too. She says she doesn't want to go to school. It's not what she wants.'

'Has her sister asked her to come? Has she been giving her advice?'

'Her sister? Even if the girl saw her sister, she wouldn't know her. Her sister left back when the girl was little. It's been six years, almost seven years, that she's been away. She hasn't visited. This month makes it a year since I've even heard from her. So, would she even know that person? But she doesn't want to go to school. Sunday, I really had to whack her to get her to go to school this week.'

'I understand. A real problem. You need to encourage her. Do you ever just sit her down to talk with her?'

'You can talk with her all you want. She doesn't listen. She's just a bad seed.'

'So, you hit her to get her to go?'

'Yes.'

'She went today?'

'Ever since Sunday, when I really gave it to her, she's been going.'

'Where does she go to school?'

'In Laskawobas.'

'Laskawobas? You need to find a way to make the kid understand that school is really important for her, that it will help her.'

'That's what I tell her. That's what I tell her. I tell her I have nothing I can leave her when I'm gone. It's all I can tell her. You say you have nothing you can leave her when you're gone. You're going to die someday. There's nothing else you can do for her but work every day, spend what you have on her, so that she'll be able to learn something she can use to help herself. With a pen in her hand, she can help herself, help her family. She can get whatever she'll need with her pen with a little luck. But if you know that you're going to die someday, if you know you won't be around to do anything, and you leave something for your child, you leave the pen that you put in her hand that can give the child a way of life, she's the one who it'll be good for. But she doesn't want to listen to that. She doesn't see that.'

'Okay. I think I should talk to her. Maybe if I see her sometime when I come by, I can talk to her. Maybe she'll understand. Then you wouldn't have to hit her to get her to go to school.'

'You can see her when she's on vacation.'

'Yes. I hope so. Next, what did you do with the money from your *sòl*?'

Dieunel spends most of the time he will devote to Mariciane's plans making sure he understands what she wants to achieve, and Mariciane is perfectly clear about that. She is devoted to her children's education, and she and Dieunel talk about what she can do and about the biggest problem she faces. He gives her some advice, but there is nothing they can do right away, so he moves on.

Mariciane recently received the first pay-out from her *sòl*. That's a kind of savings club common in Haiti. Members of a *sòl* make regular contributions, and each time they do, one member gets the whole pot. CLM case managers help CLM members organize *sòl* while the members are receiving their weekly cash stipend. That way, though they still receive some of the stipend in a very small weekly payment, they are also using it to accumulate larger sums. And these larger sum become something that case managers and members can discuss to help members learn to plan how they'll spend their money.

'The money from my *sòl*? I guess I can say it passed right through my hands. I took 300 gourds to buy food. Then my boy came home. He said he felt sick, that he didn't feel good, and he asked me to give him money to go to the hospital, so I did. I spent it all. That's the way it always goes. All the money I have just goes to waste. My money doesn't do anything for me. The first 600 gourds I got, we used 100 gourds for coffee and I spent the other 500 on palm trees for the house. Then I got 1,000 gourds. I put it away. I said I was going to buy something with it. But then my boy … I saw he had a fever. So, I took the money and took him to the hospital.'

'But that's okay, because, look, a sick child has to go to the hospital.'

'I haven't done anything with the money.'

'No. Look at what you've done.'

'I haven't done anything yet. The next 1,000 gourds. I had men cutting up the lumber for my new house. I realized I had nothing to feed them. So, I took the 1,000 gourds to buy stuff to make food for the guys who were cutting it up. And the rest of the money was spent too. Whenever I have 1,000 gourds, someone comes along and takes it.'

'But it's all solving problems for your family. It's solving your housing problem. It's solving your problem with sick children. That's good. The kids depend on you. Do you think you could have means at hand and decide to let your kids suffer? You can't let your child die while you have means in your hands. Remember, we're all struggling for our family's well-being. If your family has a problem … If one of the kids has a problem, the whole family has a problem. So, I don't see that you can say you haven't done anything. You haven't done what you wanted to do.'

'I wasn't able to buy even a chicken.'

'Yes. What you're saying in that sense is really important. Buying some chickens is important. But taking your child to the hospital is really important, too. The kids' school is important, too. So, if you haven't bought chickens yet, that's not really a big problem. Could you lend me your book?'

Each programme member receives what's called an 'information book' or, more commonly, just 'the book'.' It's kept at her home, but she is not the one who uses it. The case manager uses it to record what happens during these weekly visits. Members who can read are, of course, encouraged to look at what their case manager has written. Case managers write as legibly as they can for such members.

The book had two sections at the time when Dieunel was meeting with Mariciane, though we have since added a third. In the first, the case manager records all transfers made to the programme member. That includes the regular cash stipend, but it also includes the water filter; the productive assets – whether livestock, merchandise for trading, or agricultural inputs; and materials for constructing a latrine and a home. Those are all typical transfers. All members receive them.

But any odd transfer that emerges as part of a case manager's individualized work with a particular member needs to be recorded as well. Some members receive crutches or wheelchairs through the programme's partnerships with the Haitian government's Office of the Secretary of State for the Integration of Persons with Disabilities and other providers. These must be listed in the book's front section. Some members receive cash from the programme's emergency fund, perhaps to defray the cost of a funeral or to finance a necessary medical procedure. These transfers need to be recorded as well. And the programme has occasionally received donations of clothing or shoes for members and their children. These too are to be recorded.

The second part of the book is the record of visits to the home. Each two-page spread is divided into separate columns for the date, the topic of the week, the various things that the case manager and members discussed, and any decisions they made that involve follow-up. This section is important, because any member of the CLM staff who passes by the home can look at this section and immediately talk with the member about anything that she and her case manager agreed that she would do. If she agreed on a Tuesday visit to take her child to the hospital on Wednesday, a supervisor passing on Friday knows to ask whether the child saw a doctor.

Visiting CLM members without case managers is an important part of the supervisors' role, and they are not the only ones. The team includes specialists in human health and livestock health, in agriculture, social development, and savings clubs. They act primarily as internal consultants, advising members and their case managers concerning their areas of expertise. But all of them also conduct home visits, and their access to a member's book means that their visits can fit usefully into the work that a member and her case manager are already doing.

The book's newer, third section is designed as a planning matrix. Case managers record objectives that members have set for themselves, and then list the progress members have made, the difficulties they've encountered, how they've addressed those difficulties, the member's own assessment of their progress, the lessons they think they've learned, and their expected next steps. This section helps members and their case managers see the structure that underlies the efforts they are making.

The books have another, less obvious, function as well beyond the record they provide of the work between a member and the CLM staff. Though members all have CLM ID cards, the book serves as an additional sign of belonging to CLM, and members often keep their books carefully stored years after they've completed the programme – even though few members could read what is written in their book even if they wanted to. We come across them at visits made 3, 6, even 10 years or more after graduation. Like souvenirs.

'So, I hope that when I get here next week, we won't have any arguments. I'll find that you've completed work on the shed for the goats. That's the first task I'm assigning to you. The second is to treat your goats.

Even though we'll be giving them medications for parasites soon, you can already give them natural remedies. You know sour guava? Not the sweet kind.'

'Which guava?'

'There's a sour guava and there's a sweet one. You need to find sour guava.'

'I don't know about sweet and sour guava.'

'There's just one sour guava tree I've seen around here. It's just up the hill, above the *bokò*'s [professional vodoun practitioner] house. You take the leaves and boil them. Then you pound them and give the goats some of the paste. There's another leaf you can use, called '*seretou*', or you can use tetracycline. If you give it to your goat, I think that'll take care of the diarrhea. When I come back next time, we'll see how it's going. I hope the diarrhea will be cured. And we'll be doing the anti-parasite treatment very soon. Okay?'

'Okay. Yes.'

'I hope you don't forget the things we talked about. Will you remember?'

'I'll remember.'

Once Dieunel and Mariciane have finished talking about their plans, Dieunel would normally check the health of each family member and the hygiene around the house. But since he was able to do all that at the beginning of the visit, while he was waiting for Frankel to get Mariciane's goats, he can pass to the visit's final step. He'll thank Mariciane and say 'goodbye'.

'Okay. I'm going to go. But when I come back next week, I need to find the things we talked about done. Make sure the goat shed is finished. Don't forget to treat your goats' diarrhea. I'm really happy about the progress you're making on your house.'

'All the support posts are ready now. They're over there.'

'Over there? Great.'

'The only problem I still have is the palm-wood. The trees are cut, but they're not cut into planks.'

'I think that you'll find a way to prepare them one way or another. After all, until recently, you didn't have any cut down and ready, either. But now they're cut down. So, I'm sure you'll find a way. You wouldn't have thought you'd have gotten this far, but you've been so smart. You've already come a long way. Thanks a lot, Mariciane. I'll see you next week.'

CHAPTER 9
The stipend

Something important was missing from Dieunel's visit to Mariciane.

For the first 24 weeks that a family spends in the CLM programme, we provide a small cash stipend. The one Mariciane was receiving in 2021 was 350 gourds, or just under $5 at the time of this visit. She was supposed to receive it in cash directly from her case manager each week. She could use it to contribute to her *sòl* and in other ways as well. Handing over the stipend is one of the items on the visit checklist, though circumstances can affect the ways in which case managers provide it. Mariciane's visit with Dieunel was early in her 18-month cycle, so she should have received the money, but it did not happen, and it's worth explaining why.

We call a group of CLM members who start the programme at the same time a 'cohort'. A single cohort can involve several hundred families, or even 1,000. Mariciane's group included 150. Case managers are responsible for handing the cash stipend to each member each week, and they have to have a way to get the cash they need.

The programme is constantly moving money for a variety of reasons. Cash stipends are one. Staff members who use motorcycles need to buy gasoline. Organizing training sessions and events like launch ceremonies means purchasing food to make meals. Case managers have assets to buy for members, like livestock or merchandise for small trading, and such purchases require cash as well.

So, CLM needs a reliable way both to move money around and to keep track of its movements. For this, Fonkoze depends entirely on its sister organization, Fonkoze Financial Services, usually known as 'SFF', an abbreviation of its Creole name.

SFF is a licensed microfinance institution – the first, in fact, to be licensed in Haiti. In many ways, it functions the way that banks do. It has branches across Haiti, and it offers passbook savings accounts, loans, and other financial services. It operates under the supervision of Haiti's central bank.

The CLM programme has a central account at SFF, controlled by a financial team based at its headquarters. It also has individual accounts for the programme's field supervisors. Supervisors work with 4–8 case managers, or 200–400 families, and each supervisor requests an advance of the funds their team will need each quarter. If the request is approved, the finance team transfers the amount requested from the central account into the field account. A case manager fills out a withdrawal slip, which is signed by both the supervisor and a second member of the management team. Providing that second signature is one of the less interesting parts of my job. The case manager then can withdraw the cash from the closest SFF office. Different sorts of expenses involve different sorts of reporting, but all expenses require some sort of justifying paperwork.

Dieunel couldn't give Mariciane the money she should have received during his visit because he hadn't had the chance to withdraw the necessary funds. The visit was taking place immediately following the New Year's holiday. At the end of the year, all the programme's field teams are required to return any unspent funds to the central account. They then have to be re-requested. It is a nuisance for the field staff, but it is part of what goes into Fonkoze's financial control. Dieunel had rushed into the field after his days off for New Year' without seeing his supervisor, who hadn't had time to get to the CLM office in Mibalè from his home in Pòtoprens. Dieunel couldn't have waited for him without losing too much time. He had thus not had the withdrawal slip signed, so he couldn't make the withdrawal. Mariciane would end up getting a double payment the following week. It's not ideal, but things happen.

***

A cash stipend was part of CLM from the very beginning, adopted from the original version of the graduation programme that Fonkoze learned from BRAC. The BRAC team thought that families struggling with hunger would feel pressure to sell off any business assets they might receive and buy food with the money, rather than using their new assets to start generating income. So, in the BRAC programme, families got a small weekly stipend from the moment they received the transfer of their first asset. That stipend would continue for an amount of time that depended on BRAC's calculation of how long it would take a given type of asset to start earning income. A family that received cows, for example, would receive the stipend for longer than one that received poultry would, because cows take more time than poultry to start producing.

But the stipend's simple purpose was to help a family take the edge off its persistent hunger. At times, stipends were even provided in-kind, rather than as cash, with BRAC staff delivering rice and lentils. BRAC staff would even mix the rice and lentils before handing them over to make them difficult to sell. That would help ensure that the stipend remained a nutrition support.

At first, the stipend played a similar role within Fonkoze's programme. It was conceived with a narrow focus on nutrition. The team called it 'ti tchotcho lamanjay', a name chosen by the founding director, Gauthier Dieudonne. A 'ti tchotcho' is a small gift of cash. 'Lamanjay' means that the little bit of cash is for food. The CLM stipend when the programme started was 280 Haitian gourds per week, or about $1 per day at the time. Two hundred and eighty might seem like an odd amount, but the choice of 40 gourds per day reflects the way the team understood the stipend: at the time, 40 gourds bought a kilo of rice. The stipend was pegged so that members would be able to purchase a kilo of rice per day for their families.

During the pilot, members began to receive their *ti tchotcho lamanjay* and their assets at the same time, just as the families in BRAC's programme did. This was simple to arrange because the assets were purchased before the programme's launch and then transferred to the participating families at the launch ceremony. There was no need to provide the stipend for different lengths of time to different members because asset packages did not differ greatly. Everyone received goats, along with either small commerce or poultry.

When cohorts grew larger, the team was no longer able to purchase and store assets for everyone before the launch. A single launch ceremony might involve hundreds of people and, therefore, hundreds of goats, not to mention other assets. Members began receiving their business assets immediately as they were purchased. But purchasing was done piecemeal, as early in the 18 months of the programme as possible. Members continued to receive their stipend, however, from their first weeks in the programme, even before they received their assets. Since the types of assets CLM offered still did not vary very much – only a few options have been added over the years – the team never saw the need to tailor the stipend to each type of asset.

The CLM programme's thinking about stipends began to change with an innovation that started during the pilots, in one of its three regions.

Lagonav is the large island across the bay from Pòtoprens. Lower Lagonav is on the island's western side and at the time of the pilot was among the most poverty-stricken parts of Haiti. It was one of the pilot's three sites.

The programme there faced a number of particular challenges. The residents of Lower Lagonav had only limited access to markets, healthcare, and water. The SFF branch office where they had opened savings accounts was much too far away to be useful. Farming in the region was particularly risky. Rains there had been especially unreliable, and water sources were few. The presence of anthrax among livestock in the area was a strong threat to their goats, which were the major CLM-funded investment for the families.

Hébert Artus, who eventually became the CLM programme's director, was one of the two case managers working in Lower Lagonav. The other one was Freda Cathéus. Hébert and Freda had distributed almost three months of stipends when they began to foresee a problem. The rainy season would end soon, which would mean that the families they were working with would find little to eat in their gardens. These families had been using their stipend to buy additional food, but the stipend would run out in three more months, early in the dry season, and families were sure to suffer as the dry season progressed.

The two were an interesting pair. Freda was from nearby Ti Palmis. She was a longtime community activist, a leader in her church, and a mother of four. Hébert was a young university graduate who had been born and raised in Pikmi, on the far eastern end of the island. Freda had years of experience organizing activities in her community, so it was easy for her to organize CLM events, like group trainings. As a mother from nearby, she could relate well to the concerns of the women they were working with and could communicate with them well. Hébert's student years helped him learn quickly to make short work of reports and other paperwork. His training in social work gave him a strong academic background in the kind of case management CLM depends upon.

Most importantly, however, the two enjoyed working together, sharing their challenges and their ideas. They spent weekdays away from their families, in a residence near the members' homes, so they had plenty of time to talk. Reflecting on the threat that the upcoming dry season held for the CLM families, they came up with a plan. They would organize *sòl*.

Sòl are very common in Haiti. Participating in one would seem natural to CLM members. Just being part of one would feel to them like a mark of progress.

Freda and Hébert divided the women they were working with into groups of 12 or 13. For each of the remaining weeks, members would contribute 100 gourds of their stipend to a pot. They would spend the other 180 gourds however they needed to. But one of the members would get the whole pot each week. They would take turns, and as each woman's turn came, she and her case manager would agree on an investment she could make that would help her create a source of income, at least a small one.

One woman bought *kleren*, local rum, by the gallon to sell it by the shot. Another started a business selling small bottles of kerosene for lamps. A third bought a tree that her husband turned into charcoal, which the couple then sold. In every case, the stipend retained its focus on feeding the family. But instead of simply buying food with the money, as the programme's creators had originally imagined, members would also use it as investment capital that would help them eat better and more regularly for the long term.

The plan worked well. And as the case managers watched it unfold, they noticed that it was helping in another manner. The conversations they had with members as each considered what she would do with her *sòl* pay-out provided wonderful occasions to work with the women on making and executing plans. Through the use of the *sòl*, the weekly stipend became more than a means to provide families with means. It became a key tool for teaching financial management and planning.

Freda and Hébert had been trying to work with members on planning, but as long as the women they were speaking with had very little in the way of resources, there was not much they could plan. Their *sòl* payout was a lump sum, even just a small one at 1,200 gourds, and it changed the situation.

***

Families now use the stipend in a variety of ways. Mariciane spoke with Dieunel about buying food, but also about buying structural lumber and palm-wood planking for the walls of her new home and about how she used the funds to send her child to a clinic. She expressed frustration over the fact that she had not yet used any of the money to add to her assets. She said she hadn't even bought a chicken. But that just underscored her sense that she should use some of the money that way, too.

Members use their stipend to make deposits into savings accounts, whether at SFF or at local savings and loan associations. They contribute to a *sòl*. They make small investments. And they buy food for the household. Talking together about the use of the stipend has become an important part of their weekly conversations with their case managers.

***

Although they did not receive all of their stipend in the small, weekly payments through which it is typically disbursed, Jeanna, Clotude, and Itana made use of the money in ways that were more or less typical. All three used some of the money to buy food for their families. All three accumulated some of the money as savings until they had lump sums big enough to handle larger expenses.

Jeanna bought a new mattress for her bed, and she added some of the money to the small commerce she was starting to build. But she also used some to pay for birth certificates for her children.

Children in Haiti are supposed to receive certificates at birth, but many do not. And a parent can find it hard to send a child to school without one. Principals will sometimes refuse to register them, and children without them will not be able to go far even if they do get into school because registering for state examinations requires one. As the children grow into adulthood, they will not be eligible for government IDs.

Clotude used much of the money to complete construction of her new home. Eventually, she bought a pig as well, even though the pig did not survive for very long. Itana, too, invested in building a home and in birth certificates for her kids.

But the stipend has another role, one that is unrelated to the particular choices that CLM members make about its use, unrelated too to the conversations it makes possible. A CLM case manager who begins to work with a CLM member is a stranger. They have entered the member's life to bring support, but the member has no very good reason to believe that. She's been through six days of training, and those days were perhaps fun. She also ate well and was treated nicely. She even received a very small amount of cash.

But then the case manager comes to her home, loaded with advice, advice that they very much hope, sometimes even expect, the member to follow. This can be awkward, as was confirmed in a recent post-graduation dialogue with case managers who worked in a group for which the stipend was slightly delayed. Their team was based in Jeremi, in south-western Haiti. At the time their members' stipends were to begin, political upheaval in Pòtoprens prevented the organization's accountants from going through all the steps that are necessary to get money into the accounts that field staff use. Case managers had to make home visits for the first month or so without being able to offer anything but advice. 'You have nothing to offer', one of the case managers explained. 'They wonder why they should listen to anything that you say.' Handing out cash at each visit, even if it is not much, gives the case managers standing with the new members under their care. It purchases a member's attention. It makes a member more inclined to stay and wait for her case manager's visit before she comes to value the visit for other reasons. It helps to build trust, and to show that it might be worthwhile to pay attention, to listen.

CHAPTER 10
Building wealth

I spoke of Lucienne in the first pages of Chapter 1. In the 18 months she spent in the CLM programme and the couple of years that followed, her life changed a lot. The changes involved various things, but a change in her finances – the means she used to support her family and to invest in their future – was at its core. She joined the programme as a woman treading water, one problem away from a real disaster. Hardly even treading if you consider the hunger that she and her children sometimes experienced. She became an investor, if a small-scale one. She learned to increase her possessions and to deploy those possessions to increase their value and better ensure her family's future, and she prepared herself to take on others' problems as her own.

To most of us, it might feel strange to speak of a few goats or chickens, or of a business worth less than $100, as 'wealth'. But for families who live in ultra-poverty, acquiring a few small assets makes a big difference. A collection of even a few female goats, if managed well, can enable a family to send their children to school and to build additional assets that eventually lead to the purchase of more valuable livestock or even land. Raising even a small number of chickens can mean that parents have the means to take a sick child to see a doctor. They need not choose between begging a neighbour for help and waiting a sickness out, hoping for the best. A small trading activity that reliably brings in no more than a few dollars of profit every day can mean that a family need not go a day without a meal.

The CLM programme has never been merely a way for poor people to accumulate their modicum of wealth. Even so, helping people establish the wherewithal to earn a living has always been at its core. A lack of financial means may not be the only thing that distinguishes families living in the direst poverty from their neighbours, but it is a big part of what sets certain families apart, and addressing that lack is also one key to the solution for those in the greatest need. If someone lacks the tools that fishing requires and conditions that are at least minimally favourable to fishing, merely knowing how to fish gets them nowhere.

Giving women the assets that they need to establish two income-generating activities was an original part of the CLM programme. There could be no building livelihoods without means. The CLM team took asset transfers as an element of the programme directly from the Bangladeshis who created it.

No part of the transfer has ever been a loan. It is a grant. The contract that members sign when they join the programme may say that they agree not to view the assets they receive as a gift, but a gift it is. It is entirely theirs.

Acquiring and distributing business assets for members is challenging for a number of reasons, the most important of which is the quantity of assets required in a short period. In rural Haiti, almost all programme members choose goat-rearing as one of their activities, so Fonkoze provides each with two or three young, fertile nannies. Even a group of just 50 families will likely thus require over a hundred goats, and groups of 50 are less common than groups of 150–500. One has to acquire and distribute a lot of goats quickly, and since almost all members choose at least two different types of assets, acquiring the goats is only part of the challenge.

Not only that. The staff that buys the assets is the same staff that's responsible for home visits, and you have to be able to buy them without sacrificing too many of the weekly home visits that the programme's success depends on. When Fonkoze was piloting the programme in 2007 and 2008 for the first 150 families, the team bought all the livestock that members required before the end of the initial six-day training and distributed them when the training was over. The goats were acquired at local markets, and the chickens from a large Haitian supplier of hybrid birds. Case managers provided some preventive medications and kept the animals secure and fed until they could be distributed. In the course of the month that followed the launch, members who chose small commerce – in Boukankare that was most of them, though there were many fewer at the other two sites – were invited to the market with their case managers, who purchased their first supply of merchandise with them.

Buying the goats at local markets even for the small number of families in that first group took several trips. Only so many goats of the right age would be available on any one day. If goats are too young, their first litter will come too slowly, and the programme's 18 months will be too few to enable a family to take off. If the goats are already in their prime, they will be more expensive, so members will get fewer animals for the same money. If they are past their prime, they can still be expensive if they are large, but their long-term value to someone who wants to raise goats is limited.

But buying them before the end of training was ideal in one important respect: members received their livestock quickly, even before their weekly home visits began. This meant they lost no visits because case managers were off buying assets for them and their fellow members. It also meant that they had as much time as possible – 18 full months – to use their case manager's coaching to develop the assets they received. They would have 18 months to try and to fail and to come back from their failure, all before their case manager's time with them was done.

Immediately after the pilot, however, Fonkoze made an important change in the programme that affected many of its procedures, and also the amount of time it took to acquire the assets. During the pilot, each case manager worked with just 25 families, visiting every family twice a week. Conversations held at the end of the pilot between programme staff and its Bangladeshi advisors concluded that just one visit was necessary. Finding funding to expand the work was proving challenging, and the opportunity to reduce the cost by serving more families with a smaller staff seemed important. So, as soon as the pilot was over, the number of families each case manager worked with increased to 50.

Among the implications of this change was that staff members had more assets to deal with. More members, more assets. For the first groups of members after the pilot, case managers still acquired as many of the assets as they could before or during the six-day training, but they resigned themselves to completing the transfer of assets as quickly as they could after they had started the programme.

In 2010, however, the programme experienced its first moment of significant growth. In the wake of the 12 January earthquake that levelled Haiti's capital and much of the area south and east of it, Fonkoze received the funding to work with 1,000 families at once. The programme was suddenly too large to arrange acquisition and transfer of assets in the original way, the ideal way. The team abandoned its expectation that it would buy all or most of the assets before the launch. It would have to acquire them gradually, and staff simply committed itself to getting assets into members' hands within the first 3 of the programme's 18 months.

As the programme grew and Fonkoze's team gained experience, the variety of assets offered to members grew as well. Initially, all families received goats, with either chickens or small commerce as a second asset. The team had considered offering pigs as well. Raising them is popular among rural Haitians. But two considerations argued against that plan. First, pigs are fragile. Disease often kills them. Raising them is risky. More importantly, they are demanding. The team felt it made little sense for families who could not feed their kids to take on an animal that they would need to feed frequently as well.

But the team discovered that, as soon as many members had a little extra cash, a small pig was one of the first investments they would choose to make. Some members were showing both that they were happy to take the risk involved in pig-rearing and that they thought they could manage the expenses that pig-rearing entails.

After the pilot, the programme's leadership therefore decided that they would offer members small pigs as a fourth type of business asset, after goats, chickens, and small commerce. Initially, they offered sows. Pig-rearing as a business would follow the model that Fonkoze was already promoting for goats: raising females for the young they produce. The programme would transfer each sow with a small sack of pig feed to reduce the expense that raising a pig would otherwise represent.

Members would choose two of the four different types of assets. Just as they had during the pilot, they would protect themselves from losses by establishing businesses of two different sorts. But they would not just choose two of the types of assets the programme could offer. They would choose from a menu of two-asset options.

During the pilot, all but one of the members chose goats with either small commerce or chickens. A member's goats would build lumps of value that could help with larger expenses or turn into larger investments. Her small commerce or her chickens could help her establish a trickle of steady income quickly.

Adding a pig as an option changed things somewhat, even if the change went largely unarticulated. Though some members chose a pig and either small commerce or chickens, merely replacing one type of larger asset with another, most of the women who wanted a pig wanted it with goats. Two goats and a sow became the most popular asset package by far, even though it could not promise immediate income at all. Pigs can develop more quickly than goats, but they do not provide a constant income stream. Members were choosing to continue to struggle along with day-to-day expenses almost as they had before they joined the programme, waiting as their livestock developed. Or they were coming up with plans for income that did not depend on Fonkoze's transfer of productive assets to them, usually starting some sort of small commerce. Often, they would use the pay-out from their *sòl* as their initial investment, just like the members whom Hébert and Freda had worked with on Lagonav.

But we began to see a fundamental problem. The percentage of women choosing the package of goats and a pig kept growing, even as we added more options.

There's nothing wrong with that in principle. Choosing goats and a sow was perfectly sensible, and women could very reasonably have been choosing it.

But when we started seeing instances in which all 50 of a case manager's families, or almost all of them, were making the same choice, we had to wonder. At staff meetings, case managers would agree that they had to let members make their own choices. But it was becoming increasingly apparent that some experienced case managers were so sure that they knew better than the members that they were not really letting the members decide. It was easy for case managers to do so, since many members wanted their case manager to make the choice for them anyway.

The matter was complicated. The entire team recognized that a case manager's advice about their enterprise would sometimes have to be forceful. One common instance of this was when women chose small commerce as one of their assets even though they had trouble distinguishing the different denominations of Haitian money or were unable to do addition and subtraction reliably enough to make change. Letting such a woman choose small commerce was inviting her to fail. A woman might want goats but have no place to let them graze, or she might want a sow although her home was surrounded by gardens that piglets would surely enter and damage.

Thus, case managers would explain their understanding of the best choice a new programme member could make, and these explanations were sometimes quite specific. Members who chose two goats and a pig would start with assets they could build on, then they could use savings from their cash stipend to start a small business or to invest in their farming by initially risking very little. Some case managers even found ways to play the system. They noticed that if a member chose goats and poultry, she could use the money assigned for poultry to buy a small pig and still have money left to buy a single large bird, like a young turkey, though in this case she would be getting the pig without a sack of feed.

Still, the team felt strongly that women should generally be free to choose what they wanted. So, we postponed the choice of assets until after the initial enterprise training.

Holding the training before members chose meant redesigning the curriculum so that it included a single day on each of five different types of assets. This gives members more time and more of a basis to develop their thoughts. At the same time, supervisors started flagging case managers for whom an especially high percentage of members made the same choice. The supervisor or another staff member then talks with a handful of the members assigned to any case manager who was flagged. They try to ascertain whether the members had felt free to choose. These spot-checks sometimes lead to members changing their minds, making new choices. This did not necessarily mean that their initial choice had not been free, but it leaves the team feeling more confident that members are getting what they want.

We then eliminated fixed asset packages entirely. Rather than offering a small number of pre-established combinations – like goats and a pig, goats and small commerce, or a pig and hot-pepper-farming – case managers talk with each member about the amount of money CLM can spend on assets for them, and together they make an investment plan. The conversations between members and their case managers thus became more complex, and their complexity made them longer. It encouraged more talk, and more talk seemed likely to encourage members to say more.

These longer conversations better serve to launch the coaching that the programme relies on than an invitation to order from a fixed menu of options. Families' long-term success requires them to gain skill and self-assurance as decision makers and to begin seeing possibilities they may never have previously considered. They must learn to deploy whatever resources they have to take care of themselves, continuing to progress if possible, but, in any case, at least holding their own. Lucienne's sober decision, which we described in the book's opening pages, to sell off all of the livestock she had painstakingly accumulated and then buy farmland planted with sugarcane exemplifies vision and confidence, and she herself credits the way her case manager kept after her for the success she's achieved.

In the last few years, we have taken yet a further step. Rather than buying and transferring assets to families, we now more often provide cash. Members and their case managers discuss the amount of money that will be available to the member, then they make an estimated budget for asset purchase and a purchase plan. Case managers give members the cash, usually in more than one payment, and the member goes to market to make her purchase. Often

Table 10.1 In-kind transfers vs. cash transfers in southern Laskawobas

	Total transfer value (HTG)*	Goats	Pigs	Poultry	Small commerce	Farming inputs	Horse	Cow	Donkey
In-kind transfer	26,000	339	67	77	28	37	0	1	0
Cash transfer	23,000	312	160	861	30	n/a	10	1	1

* HTG, Haitian gourd

the case manager will go to the market on the day of the planned purchase to be available for advice, and they always go over the results of the purchase during their next visit to the member's home.

The new system has advantages for members and advantages for us, too. It gives members the broadest possible field for their own action. They figure out, with their case manager's advice, both what they want and how they will go about getting it, and then they go through the process of choosing, negotiating for, and transporting the assets they buy, all with their case manager available to assist them. More than an in-kind asset transfer, a closely coached cash transfer prepares them for the way they will have to do things after they graduate.

For the team, transferring cash is simply easier. Handing over cash takes less time than buying and transferring assets does. And it is easier to make sure we are providing members with resources at the moment they are ready for them. A member should probably have a space prepared before she buys a pig, for example. She probably shouldn't have money for small commerce lying around until she is ready with a plan. Whereas much of the asset transfer schedule had to be guided by the number of animals we could acquire in local markets each time our staff went out for purchase, we can now give each member her resources as soon as, but not before, she has a clear plan.

We do not yet have much experience with this new version of the process, but early indications have been positive. Table 10.1 compares the assets acquired by two different groups of 150 CLM families.

We were struck by two things: the purchase of 12 larger animals and the number of poultry members bought. The larger animals would all have cost more than the total transfer. So, those 12 families must have added their own resources to make the larger purchase. That was never really an option while we were making the purchases for them.

The quantity of poultry is even more striking. According to the case managers, members would have change left over after buying their goats or their pig, whatever their principal purchase was. Rather than returning home with the change, which they thought would just pass in their household expenses, they would buy a chicken or another inexpensive fowl, even if they had to add a little bit of other money to do so.

***

Cenel is a CLM graduate who learned to manage his small businesses aggressively and profitably. He's a single man who lives in Tomond, along the national road that runs north to Ench and beyond. As a young boy, he used to help his mother bring mangos for sale to Pòtoprens in a large truck. Back then, the road was unpaved, and the last hill separating the Central Plateau from the metropolitan area around Pòtoprens, Mòn Kabrit, was notoriously dangerous. One day the truck they were in lost its brakes heading down the final slope. His mother was killed in the resulting accident, together with the boy's uncle. Cenel was badly hurt. He spent seven months in a hospital bed, and he lost his foot. He's been moving around on his single foot and two crutches ever since.

Losing his mother changed Cenel's life. She was the one who cared for him. Though he had been a poor student, she always made sure he went to school. He dropped out after her death. He would farm a small plot of land, but he struggled to get around in the soil during planting and harvest seasons. His crutches would get caught in the deep, dark Tomond mud. Friends would occasionally think of him, giving him small amounts of cash, but often he would go hungry. 'Sometimes I would just go off into my field to cry.'

He joined the CLM programme in early 2020. The team had been going through its selection process in his neighbourhood. He had not initially appeared on the team's lists because those are made up of households, and Cenel was not a household. He was living in his father's home, and his father did not qualify for the programme. But the team's supervisor came across Cenel and struck up a conversation. As he came to understand how difficult Cenel's life was, he assigned a staff member to do an initial evaluation. Then he verified the evaluation and invited him to join the programme.

Cenel was excited. 'I would just sit by myself by the side of the road, waiting for what might come. When they asked me whether I wanted to join the programme, I thought it was a gift from heaven.'

He chose goats and a pig as enterprises, and his results were mixed. His first pig was stolen, and when Fonkoze helped him replace it, the second pig died.

His goats fared much better. The programme gave him two, and he increased that investment by managing them carefully. By graduation he had seven, and he was planning to sell some of them to buy a cow. He explained that cows involve less risk because you can let them graze further from home, whereas goats get into peoples' gardens, which leads to conflict. He was already struggling to care for the seven goats he had, and he started to assign some to older children in the neighbourhood. Each child takes responsibility for one goat and then gets some of the goat's offspring as payment. It takes some of the pressure off Cenel, and it helps young people get started in life. This latter point also helps Cenel manage some of the jealousy neighbours might otherwise feel at his success.

That success had much more to do with his management of the resources he accumulated than with the growth of his collection of goats. When he and his case manager began to talk about home repair, he insisted he didn't really want a house. He wanted to build a small, one-room building at the side of the road that he could use as a little convenience store. He would put a bed inside and sleep there, too, but he would mainly use it to sell basic groceries.

Because the construction he planned was so small, Cenel was able to finish it quickly. He took out a loan for 10,000 gourds from the savings and loan association that we set up for him and the other CLM members who live near him, and he bought his first merchandise. He used half the money to buy food basics, like rice, oil, and sugar, and the other half to buy hygiene products, like soap and shampoo. He made the effort to travel to Ench, the Central Plateau's largest city, to purchase what he needed. The prices there are slightly lower than in Tomond because there's more wholesale business going on.

His store took off. He would return to Ench once each week, buying more and more products each time. He settled on a small number of wholesalers, so they would see him often. They quickly came to trust him, and soon they were allowing him to buy for more than the cash he had on hand. He would owe them a running balance, and that enabled him to expand his business even more.

The money he made allowed him to continue to save in his savings and loans association, but he did more than that, too. He joined a *sòl*, and when he decided that the association and the *sòl* combined still offered too little opportunity for savings, he established another device for himself and 13 of his neighbours. It is called a *sabotay*. The 14 participants each contribute 250 gourds every day, and each day someone takes the pot.

And Cenel found uses for each type of savings.

He repaid his loan from the association, and he took out another, larger one. The second was for 15,000 gourds, and he combined that money with money from his *sòl* to buy a freezer for his shop. He now sells cold drinks alongside his groceries. 'I keep the money from the groceries and the money from the drinks in two separate buckets, so I know what I am getting from each.'

When his association completed its first one-year cycle, he used the money to buy an additional goat. 'The goats are important for my business. If I have a loss, I can sell a goat and the business will keep going.' The next time his turn comes around in his *sòl*, he plans to use the money to buy a cow, selling as many goats as he needs to add to the money. He used the money from his *sabotay* to buy cinder blocks. He tore down the wooden walls of his house and replaced them with solid walls of blocks and cement.

What is most striking about Cenel's success is that all of the thinking behind it came from him. Since joining the programme, he has shown unusual creativity and initiative. Each new idea was his own. He would suggest it to his case manager to hear her advice, but he is happy to tell you that the ideas were his.

Despite the ability he quickly demonstrated, he had never started anything before joining the programme, and he can explain why. His answer involves three main elements. First, he explains that before he joined CLM he lacked vision. Even as he entered the programme, he wasn't able to imagine himself running a business. That's why he chose two forms of livestock as his initial enterprises even though the programme could have provided merchandise for small commerce in place of the pig. He didn't really think of running a business until he attended training sessions and listened to his fellow members. 'You attend the workshops, and you hear what other people are doing. It makes you think.'

He also talks about how he learned to manage money. He was always getting 50 or 100 gourds at a time from friends or neighbours who felt bad for him, but he would spend all of it on food right away. 'You learn that even if you only have 100 gourds, you should eat only 75 and save 25. Little-by-little you can build up what you need.'

Third, though his success has come from managing his shop, he talks about the importance of livestock as well. Before CLM he had none, and he was afraid to start a business because any loss would be irreparable. The goats we gave him provided insurance against losses, and that helped him feel the confidence he needed to start investing.

Cases like those of Lucienne and Cenel show how acquiring business assets works together with an improved approach to help families change their lives. They both used assets that Fonkoze purchased for them to build their income, but both needed more help than that alone. Lucienne pointed to the strong encouragement she received directly from CLM staff. Cenel cited the examples of success he heard about from his fellow CLM members. Lucienne learned to manage what she had, and Cenel to imagine what he could have.

***

Neither Itana, nor Jeanna, nor Clotude made the kind of progress that Lucienne and Cenel made. All chose to receive livestock from the programme, and Fonkoze gave each a couple of goats and a sheep, but none was able to make very much out of the animals. They were largely unable to keep them healthy.

However, managing the animals, making decisions about purchase and sale, figuring out how to respond in the face of losses, and doing all this while in regular conversation with a friendly, well-trained guide has helped them to feel differently about their lives and also to manage those lives differently. Their guide helped them to draw lessons from both successes and failures and to remain hopeful about what they can do.

All the things that CLM members do, and the new attitudes they take on, depend in part on the help of the case manager who accompanies them. But their success also depends on the fact that they now have some modicum of wealth to work with. These members need the assets that Fonkoze gives them as tools to remake their lives.

CHAPTER 11
Saving

From the time of the CLM pilot in 2007 and through the programme's early years, all members had savings accounts at the Fonkoze branch office nearest them. For one thing, there was an underlying assumption that, upon graduating from the programme, members would join Fonkoze's credit programmes to continue their march forward out of extreme poverty. Fonkoze viewed its CLM programme as the first step in what it called its 'Staircase out of Poverty', an attempt to provide services to Haitian families living at different levels of poverty. That staircase had four steps, each representing a different level of need and a different product or service. Women could move from CLM to *Ti Kredi* to standard solidarity-group credit to individual loans, or they could start part of the way up the ladder if that's what they needed. Fonkoze would meet them where they were and help them take the next step and then the next.

More importantly, the CLM programme's leadership felt that CLM members needed to accumulate some savings as insurance against the various problems they might confront. Rural Haitian families living in ultra-poverty are not the only folks in the world who can face sudden, unanticipated expenses, but they may be more vulnerable than most. A business setback, a heavy rain, a fire, a sickness or a death in the family, even a pack of hungry dogs: any of these can threaten destruction of a family's livelihood. Holding some cash savings in a small account promised a safe way to hedge against sudden losses.

And from the time of the pilot, training sessions included a focus on the importance of saving. The programme's founding director, Gauthier, used a slogan that reflects his characteristic bluntness: *'Ou pa ka fouye tout sa w gen nan bouch ou.'* Or, 'You can't just stuff everything you have into your mouth'. He told members that they needed to put something away. As Haitians say, *'si gen yon ka'*, or in case something comes up. The CLM team emphasized Fonkoze savings accounts as a method of saving both for the way they'd help the transition to other Fonkoze programmes and for the security they'd provide compared to livestock, which can die or be stolen.

And there was a third reason as well. CLM members would typically have had very little experience in formal, institutional settings. Staff members at Fonkoze offices were used to welcoming customers unaccustomed to such places, so visits could build members' social skills, helping them learn to deal with formality.

Normally, saving in rural Haiti doesn't involve a bank account. Haitians in the countryside save in several ways, but perhaps the most important is by buying livestock: poultry, goats, pigs, or larger animals. This is so much the case that an important theme of the programme's livelihoods training is to encourage members to think of livestock more as business assets and less as piggy banks. Rural Haitians can tend to want to simply hold onto the livestock they own rather than managing it to generate maximum income.

And members' commitment to their savings accounts during the pilot varied a lot by region, in terms of both the number of deposits they made and the amount they saved. The pilot involved three regions – Lagonav, Boukankare, and Twoudinò – and although the differences that emerged were unplanned, the savings habits that tended to develop were unique in each one, for a range of reasons (Huda and Simanowitz, 2008).

The differences depended in part on the way the pilot began one region at a time. Boukankare was first, and the two case managers there had the least-defined savings strategy. Thus, there was greater variation in savings habits among the members they worked with than there was among members in the other two regions, where the lessons being learned in Boukankare could be applied on the fly.

Differences in savings habits also depended in part on differences among the three regions. For example, the Fonkoze office was far less convenient for the members on Lagonav than for those in the other two areas. Bank accounts were, therefore, less useful, which contributed to the early use of *sòl*.

The differences depended as well on the assets that members in each region initially chose. More members in Boukankare chose small commerce than did those in the other two regions. In Twoudinò, 40 of the 50 women chose poultry to go along with their goats, and on Lagonav 49 of the 50 did. Since assembling the means to establish a small commerce as an additional activity was one of the goals that drove savings early on, the need for savings may have seemed less urgent where members received small commerce as part of their initial transfer.

Finally, they probably depended on the differences between case managers. The case managers in Twoudinò and Lagonav pushed savings forcefully from the start, and so the savings habit developed strongly in both places – at least as long as the weekly stipends continued – even though the amount of money that members saved was very different. On Lagonav, deposits were typically very small, but very consistent. In Twoudinò, they were less regular, but much larger.

The case managers in Boukankare, however, were especially concerned with immediate food insecurity. When members received their stipends, their case managers encouraged them to spend as much as they needed to buy food for their families. They did not emphasize savings, although they eventually took a lead from the team on Lagonav and organized *sòl* for members who had extra cash.

And encouraging members to use all or almost all of their stipend to buy food worked, at least in the short term. The nine-month evaluation of the pilot reports that families there were able to eliminate severe child malnutrition early on, though it returned in some families as soon as the stipends were over.

In all three regions, case managers facilitated deposits. They took money that members wanted to put into their savings accounts during the home visits. Fonkoze's branch offices were happy to supply CLM case managers with deposit slips. The members themselves would not need to travel to the branch. This was important because many lived far enough to make getting to the branch inconvenient.

But the smaller deposits on Lagonav presented a problem. The minimum deposit at a Fonkoze branch was supposed to be 50 gourds, and the management of the Lagonav branch insisted on it. Members there, however, rarely wanted to deposit that much at one time. Case managers would have to accept and hold onto multiple deposits, which could be as small as 10 gourds, before they could take the money to the bank. They would record the transaction in the information book at the member's home, but also in a notebook that they carried with them. When the funds a case manager was holding for a member reached 50 gourds, then the case manager could fill out the deposit slip and bring the money to the branch.

Fonkoze's practice reflected the importance it attached to savings in several ways. At monthly staff meetings in Pòtoprens, case managers from all three regions would turn in detailed reports about members' savings using a form that had been adopted directly from BRAC. The evaluations undertaken at 12 and 17 months included questions about savings. Members earned a half-point on those evaluations if they had made three transactions, whether deposits or withdrawals, in the three months before the evaluation, and they earned another half-point if their balance was over 100 gourds, an amount so trivial as to mean little more than that the account had not been closed. The two half-points were part of a 10-point scale, so while they did not count for a lot, they counted.

But savings were not as important as other things that were evaluated. At least not if we can judge by their place in the evaluation. Together, the two questions about savings were worth just a point, as much as any of the 10 groups of questions, but the evaluation questions were divided into two types, required ones and optional ones. A member could not qualify for graduation without scoring a point on all five of the required questions. A member needed at least two sources of income and business assets worth a certain minimum value. She could not have any children suffering from untreated malnutrition, she had to be healthy enough to continue to manage her business assets, and she had to have a home with a good tin roof. But she needed only score two points on the other five questions combined, so she could have made no recent transactions and have no savings at all, and she could still have qualified for graduation.

Whatever differences in savings habits there were among the three different regions during the pilot's 18 months, nowhere did members develop a long-term commitment to savings, at least to savings accounts. A second independent evaluation held six months after graduation concluded that, 'Whilst significant savings balances were developed in some branches in the first 9 months of the program, this was not sustained. In terms of formal savings culture and cash deposits in a savings account, this was not achieved' (Huda and Simanowitz, 2010a). As it turned out, within six months of graduating from the programme, most programme members no longer met even the 100-gourd minimum savings balance requirement. This is despite the fact that 92 of the 150 women joined Fonkoze's *Ti Kredi* programme after they graduated from CLM, which required a balance of 100 gourds.

In the years after the pilot, our focus on transitioning graduates directly into *Ti Kredi* diminished, and the percentage that made that transition decreased as well. In part, this had to do with an administrative separation between the two programmes, which had initially shared the same leadership. Without close coordination between the two staffs, it became harder to ensure a smooth transition. In part, it had to do with the difficulties Fonkoze encountered when it tried to manage credit programmes in especially remote areas. The CLM programme was committed to going to all areas, no matter how hard to reach. But the separation of the two programmes eventually led to the removal of *Ti Kredi* from the non-profit foundation and its transfer to SFF, the commercial microfinance institution. Within SFF, those responsible for credit programmes increasingly wanted them to focus on easier-to-access regions, closer to branch offices, where offering credit cost less and was easier to supervise.

Some CLM members continued to find their savings accounts valuable. Fedeline is an example. She joined CLM in Fon Ibo, near downtown Gwomòn, in 2017, as one of three siblings who qualified together. A sister and a brother also qualified, the latter because of his blindness. Fedeline had four children, the older two without any support from their father. She was supporting them with a small business selling used clothing. When she first joined CLM, she had no capital of her own. She depended on a neighbour, who was also a merchant. The neighbour would sell Fedeline small piles of used clothes out of her inventory on credit. Fedeline would walk around downtown with her small pile, selling it item by item. She'd return home, pay her neighbour, and use the profit to feed her kids. It gave her a trace of a living, and it gave her neighbour a way to increase her sales.

She joined the programme, and she used the capital the programme provided to buy larger loads of clothing outright. With more to sell, she sold more, and her income increased. In addition to improving what she could do for her family, she began depositing money regularly in her Fonkoze account. She never made large deposits, but by the time she graduated, she had saved over 3,600 gourds.

After graduation, she changed the way she used the account, but she still used it. She made only three deposits between her graduation and the end of 2020, almost two years later, after having made more than a dozen in the 18 months that she was in the programme. But her post-graduation deposits were relatively large ones, ranging from 3,500 gourds to almost 10 times as much. Her account became a place to store larger sums of money while she decided what to do with them. Each time that a *sòl* she participates in pays out, she uses her account to secure the money until she wants to spend it. That might mean keeping it in the account for months, as she withdraws it little by little. That's what she did while she was buying construction materials for the new, larger home she decided to build after she graduated. It might mean storing money in the account for just a few days. She withdrew her largest deposit, over 30,000 gourds, less than two weeks after she made it, as soon as her husband was ready to use the money to help buy a motorcycle as a taxi. 'I like putting money in the bank, even just for a few days, because it's safer there.'

But as fewer members looked to Fonkoze for credit after graduation, fewer made use of the savings accounts that the CLM team opened for them when they joined the programme. Fonkoze's office is convenient for Fedeline. A motorcycle taxi costs just 50 gourds, which is worth paying for a large transaction. And because the office is in downtown Gwomòn, where she goes to manage her business in any case, going by to make a deposit or a withdrawal makes sense.

But Fedeline is part of a small minority. Most CLM members have much further to go to get to an office. Many members were waiting until shortly after graduation and then going to the Fonkoze branch closest to them to close their account. We still wanted to help members learn to save, but it began to seem that we could not count on their using accounts at Fonkoze to do so. So, we started experimenting.

Wilson Ozil, one of the more experienced regional managers, wanted to try something different. He had already managed cohorts that were far enough from a Fonkoze office as to render the utility of individual savings accounts doubtful. A first experience, with 200 families in a corner of Sodo called Montay Terib, and a second experience, with 150 families in Mòn Michèl, a hard-to-access area along the border between Mibalè and Laskawobas, had shown him how hard it was for CLM members in such places to use savings accounts. CLM case managers would always be able to make deposits for members, but they could not make withdrawals. Any time a member wanted to use some of her savings, no matter how little, she would have to get herself to the Fonkoze office. This could involve a long hike, an expensive ride by motorcycle or truck, or both a hike and a ride.

Wilson was assigned another group of 150 families in Lawoy, a communal section of Tomond. Haiti is divided into 10 departments, and each department is divided into communes, which are like US counties. Every commune is run from a mayor's office. The communes are divided, in turn, into communal sections, each with an elected committee of three at its head. Lawoy is east of Tomond and across the Artibonit River to the north of downtown Laskawobas, along the Dominican border, centred on a major rural market in Kas. The closest Fonkoze office is in Tomond, and taking a motorcycle from Kas to Tomond could cost 125 to 200 gourds in the late 2010s. The trip might be worthwhile if it meant spending a day at the Tomond market or visiting the Partners in Health hospital there, but not just to make a small cash withdrawal from a savings account.

The 150 families in Lawoy would be served by three case managers, and Wilson had each of them open a single savings account for 50 families. Every week, the case managers would collect deposits. When a member wanted to make a withdrawal, she would just let her case manager know. If the case manager had the cash on hand, they could give it to the member immediately and reimburse themselves from the group account. If not, they could make a withdrawal and give the member the money she wanted the following week. For each member, there were two copies of a control sheet. One remained at her home, and the other stayed with the case manager. The sheets functioned like savings account passbooks. Case managers recorded every deposit and every withdrawal on both copies of the sheets.

The plan had several advantages. First, case managers and members would be able to talk about savings and plan how to use them for all 18 months. Second, though record keeping would be complicated, it would also be easy to verify. Withdrawals would require two signatures: the case manager's and Wilson's as well. The total balance for each case manager's account would be available through any Fonkoze office, and Wilson could compare this amount with the registers that the case managers kept with them, which could be compared, in turn, to the registers left at members' homes. Though most members would be unable to read the register to verify that case managers recorded the exact deposit or withdrawal that they made, Wilson could question them when he visited their homes and compare what they said to what the registers showed. Third, at the end of 18 months, it would be easy to pay out to each member whatever she had saved. She would not even lose the small amount that Fonkoze holds onto when someone closes an account. And it would be easy as well to open an individual Fonkoze savings account with her balance if she wanted to join Fonkoze's credit programme or she just wanted her own account.

Wilson repeated the experiment for a second cohort of 200 families in Savanèt, a small commune in the south-east corner of the Central Plateau, and it worked well there, too. Though Fonkoze's office in Mibalè had a history in Savanèt, having sent credit agents to serve customers there regularly over the years, it was far enough from the new CLM members to be very inconvenient for minor transactions. But thanks to the group accounts, members were able to accumulate savings and access those savings quickly, if not immediately, any time they had a plan for spending.

During 2015, we tested another alternative to savings accounts. Through a partnership with Texas Christian University, we had the chance to work with the Haitian government's Office of the Secretary of State for the Integration of Persons with Disabilities to pilot CLM as a way to serve persons with disabilities living in ultra-poverty. The pilot would include 30 people in Laskawobas. We foresaw that mobility issues would be one type of disability it would encounter, so the partnership decided to try a way to encourage savings that would work for someone largely unable to get to a branch office.

Each of the pilot programme's participants received a small lockbox. They kept their box with them, so their money was always in their hands. But, for the duration of the pilot, their case manager kept the key, so that it was easy for participants to avoid spending money that they wanted to save. Members made deposits or withdrawals during their case manager's weekly visits. In addition, members received an illustrated four-lesson booklet about savings, and they would go over a lesson during each visit. The lessons discussed the importance of savings, and suggested strategies designed to help one decide to save.

The experiment worked to a degree. The evaluation undertaken after the initially planned 12 months of the pilot showed that all participants had saved at some time during the 12 months and that 86 per cent had saved both during the first six months, when they were receiving a weekly stipend, and during the second six months, after distribution of the stipend had ceased (Elliott and Werlin, 2016.) This was true though almost none had been saving when the pilot began.

But the programme was extended to 18 months, the same length as the standard CLM programme. A second evaluation, undertaken after the six-month extension was complete, left less room for optimism about savings habits. Only a small minority of the pilot's participants continued to save through this third six-month period. Those who did choose to save emphasized strongly the importance of savings to their changed lives, but most of the members did not bother to continue saving at all. Despite the pilot programme's focus on savings, few members acquired a savings habit (Chemen Lavi Miyò Team, 2018).

We believed that we needed to do more both to encourage members to save and to facilitate savings, but a step forward finally came in response to a different motive. The growing realization that graduates were not, for the most part, choosing to enrol in Fonkoze's credit programmes left us with a problem. We had always felt that we could better ensure that families would continue to make progress if Fonkoze could accompany those families for a long time. A transition from CLM to credit programmes seemed like a good way to do this. Members would receive the close, constant accompaniment that CLM provides for 18 months. After that, they would be part of solidarity groups and credit centres, which would meet with Fonkoze staff at least every two weeks. As members of a credit centre, they could participate in educational and health programming. And in case of a disaster, like a hurricane, Fonkoze would do its best to provide a measure of relief.

But as it became clear that Fonkoze's credit operations would not follow the CLM programme into remoter areas, we had to admit that the CLM programme itself was the only structure of accompaniment that Fonkoze was providing. Fonkoze's leadership gave the CLM team an ultimatum. Either find another way to offer long-term accompaniment or agree to operate exclusively in areas that were served or that might be served by Fonkoze's credit team.

For the CLM team, only one of these options was possible. Giving up on people whom Fonkoze's credit programmes could not reach seemed a terrible idea. The fact that Fonkoze could not offer credit somewhere at least suggested that the place might have particular need. Remoter, harder-to-access areas often were home to the families who needed the programme most. Our only option was to find another way to organize a structure capable of providing long-term accompaniment for the families.

***

Just as we did not create but discovered the CLM programme itself, so too we discovered Village Savings and Loan Associations (VSLA). The VSLA approach emerged in areas of Africa where depth of poverty and population sparsity made it hard to build effective microfinance institutions. VSLAs were designed to enable small communities to establish their own simple financial services, even without something as sophisticated as a microfinance institution, much less a bank. A thorough presentation of the VSLA approach is available at www.vsla.net.

The central elements of the approach are simple, though one finds variations. Associations usually consist of 20 to 30 members. They meet once a week, and at each meeting members buy from one to five shares in the association. The group itself determines the share price. The money the association accumulates through these purchases becomes a loan fund. Members can take out loans, which they pay back with interest at a rate that the group also determines. The group also controls both what penalties it will impose – whether for missed meetings, late arrivals, or late repayments – and the amount of a weekly contribution to a small fund that can be used to help members deal with unexpected expenses, like sickness or death.

VSLAs are designed to function with very little in the way of equipment or supplies. They use a system of record keeping that requires only minimal skills. At the end of a year, the group disburses the money that members have contributed, along with the interest it has earned on loans, with each member receiving a pay-out proportionate to the number of shares they purchased over the course of the year. The week following the pay-out, a new one-year cycle begins with share purchases.

VSLAs seemed an attractive addition to the CLM programme. CLM members would be within a community structure that encourages them to save money and gives them access to small loans when they need them. The associations could renew themselves annually, so CLM members can stay in that structure long-term, well after they graduate from CLM.

By the time the women from Lawa had joined CLM, the programme had been using VSLAs for a couple of years. So, although they opened Fonkoze savings accounts, they also were founding members of Lawa's VSLA. Itana felt, from the start, that joining the VSLA was an important opportunity for her.

'If you don't have problems, you can just push yourself to save. You don't even need to take a loan.' And though she was committed to her Fonkoze savings account, she found the VSLA useful as well.

Itana used her VSLA to help her help her daughter Guilaine. Guilaine's partner lives and works in the Dominican Republic. He supports Guilaine and their children with remittances, but those remittances are irregular, so if Guilaine had to depend on them directly, her quality of life would be irregular as well. With Itana's membership in the VSLA, however, she and her son-in-law cooperate to ensure Guilaine's income is steady. Itana borrows money from the VSLA each time she sees Guilaine's funds are low. She doesn't worry about taking out small loans because she relies on her son-in-law to pay her back. And, so far, he has. Knowing that her daughter can depend on her means a lot to Itana, perhaps all the more so because, without the means to raise Guilaine, she had sent her away as a young girl. When the VSLA's first cycle ended, Itana took some of the money she had saved and paid for birth certificates for those of her children who did not yet have them, and she used much of the rest to further help Guilaine with medical bills. She hopes, however, that the next time she reaches the end of a cycle, she'll be able to use her savings to make an investment. She wants to buy a small pig. She'll give it to a young relative to raise, and they'll split any profit, so it will help them both.

Clotude had heard of VSLAs before she joined the CLM programme. This isn't surprising. Fonkoze was not the first institution to introduce them to Haiti in general or to Gwomòn in particular. 'I had heard folks talk about them, but I didn't understand.' When the CLM team told her that they would be starting one for CLM members in her neighbourhood, she didn't want to join. 'I didn't want to because I didn't understand. I only did it because they asked me to.'

But to describe how much she likes her VSLA now that she's had some experience with it, Clotude engages in word play that requires some explanation. VSLAs are sometimes called 'AVEK' in Creole. It is a word-for-word translation of the English acronym. But they have another common name in Haiti as well. They are often called '*Ti pa*'.

'*Pa*' is the Creole word for a 'share', so '*ti pa*' means 'little share'. The name refers to the share purchases that are the centre of weekly meetings. But '*pa*' has another, more common, meaning as well. It is the usual word for a 'step', so '*ti pa*' also means 'small step'. '*Ti pa, ti pa*' is a standard way to say, 'little by little'. Clotude explained that her '*ti pa*' is not a '*ti pa*', but a '*gran pa*', a big step, not a small one. 'If my *ti pa* fell apart, I'd look for another one, even at the far end of the country.'

Like Itana, Clotude took out multiple loans from her VSLA. But two of her loans were simple favours she did for a friend who wasn't part of the group. The friend needed money, got Clotude to borrow it for her, and paid Clotude back on time. The third loan Clotude took out for herself. She borrowed money to buy the pigeon peas she needed to plant one of her fields. She used income from a small business selling basic groceries to pay back that loan.

When the VSLA's first cycle ended, Clotude knew exactly what she wanted to do with the roughly 7,000 gourds she received. Though she could think of various ways to use the money to increase her income, she felt duty called her to make an investment of a different kind.

She was raised by a single father, who refused to find a second wife when Clotude lost her mother because he didn't want a stepmother to raise his girl. When he passed away, Clotude could do very little to honour him, much less than she felt he deserved. So, when she received the pay-out from her VSLA, she decided to use all of it to build a tomb to mark where he was buried in her yard. Her plan for the end of the VSLA's second cycle is more typical. She wants to buy a pig. 'I want one that's already big. If you buy a small pig, and it dies too soon, you've lost everything.' If her pig is already starting to get big when she buys it, she can hope to get something for the meat even if the pig dies in her care.

Itana, Clotude, and Jeanna all speak of their lack of savings before they joined the programme. As Jeanna explained, 'If you have a commerce, you can join a *sòl*, but if you don't have a commerce, you can't'. Clotude added, 'If you have just 50 gourds now and again, you go to market and you buy food for your children. You don't save'.

Data collected over the years by and for the CLM programme has confirmed that, when they first join the programme, new members do not generally have cash savings. A 2021 evaluation of 200 members in Gwomòn, for example, showed that just 10 of them had had cash savings when they first joined the programme. But learning to save, finding the resources that one needs to save, and then learning ways to use savings to one's benefit can be life changing.

And if that 2021 evaluation is any indication, the CLM team has got much better at encouraging a sustainable habit of savings than it was at the time of the pilot. The authors of the evaluation of the pilot had to conclude that the programme had not helped members establish a savings habit. By 2021, however, members showed an average savings of over 3,000 gourds even nearly two years after they had graduated, and only 27 of the nearly 200 people evaluated reported no cash savings.

It is easy to imagine that the VSLAs have been a big part of the improvement. Saving at Fonkoze itself was never going to be convenient for most CLM graduates, whatever its advantages are. VSLAs are convenient, they can offer more interest on savings than Fonkoze or other formal institutions in Haiti can because they do not have operating costs that they must cover, they unlock access to small, inexpensive loans, and they set up a social context that provides individuals with encouragement from friends and neighbours that can help them stay motivated to save.

Recent evidence shows that VSLAs work. In 2020, a Fonkoze programme established 32 VSLAs for former CLM members in southern Mibalè. These members had been part of CLM before VSLAs became a part of it. We have extensive data from 29 of the 32 VSLAs for three cycles. That's nearly three years. Overall participation held steady from the second cycle to the third, and membership among former members of the CLM programme increased by almost 20 per cent (Fonkoze, 2023).

This is encouraging. One issue that has been challenging for the CLM programme in some areas has been to maintain the VSLAs' orientation towards serving CLM families. It is not unusual for the structures to thrive even as former programme members drop out and are replaced by their better-off neighbours.

As an example, we point to data from four VSLAs that were established in Laskawobas to serve a cohort of 150 CLM families. If one considers only the economic performance of these four VSLAs, there is reason to be impressed. The average end-of-cycle pay-out per member doubled from the first cycle to the second. And the total number of participants grew by nearly 20 per cent.

All that might also seem positive. But we established the associations to provide long-term structures that support CLM members' livelihoods and help them manage their finances after they have left the programme, and in this case 50 of the 150 CLM members dropped out of their VSLA when the second cycle began.

In the case of the VSLAs in southern Mibalè, the trend initially ran in the same direction. The percentage of CLM members involved dropped between the first and second cycles. But the CLM team's VSLA specialist and the cohort of community VSLA agents that he created to support the associations identified the problem and made it a focus of their work. They made it a point of emphasis in their conversations with the elected leaders of the associations, and they sought out and encouraged members who had left the VSLAs to return, eventually bringing in some who had not even joined the VSLA programme when it began.

The financial indicators for these VSLAs are uniformly positive. Even as the percentage of members drawn from the CLM programme itself grew, the level of savings measured both in total savings and savings per member grew as well. So did the amount of loans taken out, at least from the second to the third cycle. And the end-of-cycle pay-out increased as well. The pay-out per member rose by about 20 per cent, and the percentage return rose from roughly 13 per cent in the second cycle to about 17 per cent in the third one.

So, more people and, in particular, more CLM members participated in the VSLAs' third cycle. They saved more money, made greater use of the credit available to them as members, and got a better return on the money they put into their associations. And the movement that is rooted in this project is much larger than our data reflects. The community agents who were recruited and trained to follow-up with the original VSLAs established 25 additional associations.

Fonkoze has come to believe strongly in the positive role that VSLAs play within the programme. They present a way to facilitate, even encourage, savings long term, while integrating their members socially into a group of neighbours and friends. And establishing a network of agents offers a way to make sure that the associations stay strong.

CHAPTER 12
Committees

Many of the conversations among our staff involve particular cases. Case managers are not supposed to think of themselves as implementing a rigid programme. Much of what we offer families is determined in advance, but staff are taught to think of each family and its individual situation. One of the harshest criticisms that Gauthier, the programme's founding director, used to make when he thought it necessary was that staff members had established a routine. Questions about individual situations are in our conversations all the time. This is true for informal exchanges held in passing, and it's true of staff meetings as well.

> 'Carline said that someone stole her goats.'
> 'Marie can't find the lumber she needs to build her home.'
> 'Guerline's husband hit her.'
> 'Neighbourhood children have been throwing rocks at Jeanne's turkeys.'

Case managers want to talk about the most stubborn of the many problems that families face. These problems may be very serious or less so. Children should not throw rocks at turkeys, but that and domestic violence probably don't even belong on the same list.

But all are problems. And frequently the first answer a case manager receives is a question, 'Have you spoken to the committee?' Or even just 'What did committee members say?'

We organize groups of local leaders into committees in all the communities where we offer CLM. These committees, sometimes called Village Committees for the Reduction of Poverty, or KVRP for their name in Creole, are the most difficult element of the programme to write about because they are where what we manage to do differs most from what we say we will do.

***

Like almost all the core elements of the programme, the practice of organizing committees was adopted directly from BRAC. Community leaders and representatives of the programme members are organized into a group that meets every month. At least one staff member also participates in each gathering. All local programme members are supposed to come to the meetings as well. Attending meetings regularly helps them integrate themselves more fully into the communities where they live because it brings them together with neighbours, gets them accustomed to participating in discussions, and invites them to talk about shared problems. We plan for a committee for each

25 families, although the actual numbers depend on the way that members are distributed through a region.

When the original CLM staff was in Bangladesh, learning about the programme, they saw the role that BRAC's village committees were playing. They saw relatively wealthy Bangladeshis meeting together with the women in the programme. Committee members gave the women advice. They encouraged them. They also contributed their own means to solving problems. Fonkoze's team was sceptical about doing the same thing in Haiti. They doubted whether community leaders in rural Haiti would be willing or even able to offer such help.

Some of their scepticism related to the significance of the things that Bangladeshi committee members were doing. Village leaders there were taking on what seemed like big projects, involving substantial expense. One typical project was installing a community well. Bangladesh has a problem with arsenic in drinking water, and installing high-quality pump wells offers a solution. The committees BRAC was organizing seemed to have at least some members with real means. Some were, it was true, just local professionals, like schoolteachers or principals, who could offer specific kinds of support. But others were relatively wealthy village leaders. Investing in an improved water source probably didn't strain them, and doing so contributed to their prestige.

The team in Haiti struggled to imagine where they would find such support in the communities where they were preparing to work. The folks they saw who might serve on committees were much wealthier than CLM families. Of course. But they weren't especially wealthy. The team could not see them carrying out the projects that they saw in Bangladesh.

Some of their scepticism related to what was perhaps a prejudice about the community leaders they would find in Haiti. The CLM staff felt that the men and women they would find were more likely to look for what they themselves could get out of the programme than they were to consider how they might help. Without their own vision of what the committees could accomplish in Haiti, the CLM team was tempted to leave this component out of their version of the programme.

But the trainers from BRAC insisted on the importance of the committees, and Fonkoze's staff felt that their BRAC colleagues deserved their trust. So, they decided to give it a try.

They established the first committee in Boukankare as part of the training they received from BRAC during the pilot. The BRAC trainer went to Boukankare with the CLM staff, leading them step-by-step through the process he had already explained to them in the classroom. They did all the work, but the trainer coached them closely throughout. After setting up the committees in Boukankare, the team used the lessons it learned there to establish the ones for the pilot's other two regions. In Twoudinò, then on Lagonav.

Despite its scepticism, the team was determined. Hébert Artus was a case manager then, and he became the programme's director when Gauthier retired. Looking back, he said, '*Tout moun t ap viv pilòt la, [se] komsi si nou echwe nou pral dwat devan bawon an.*' That means, 'For everyone who lived through the pilot, it was as though, if we failed, we'd go straight to meet the Baron.'

The phrase requires some explanation. In Haitian tradition, when folks die, they appear before Bawon Samdi, the master of the cemetery. They need his permission to pass. To say that they would have to appear before the Baron is a very strong way of saying that the pilot's success felt like a matter of life and death.

And the almost-desperate attention that the team paid to all the details of the procedure that BRAC taught them bore fruit in all areas of the programme, including the committees. Committee members in all three pilot regions made important contributions. In Boukankare, a local elected official bent the normal rules for handling the damage untethered goats did to fields to spare the goats of CLM families. Committee members there also retrieved the roofing tin that a member's spouse had sold to cover his gambling debts. A committee in Twoudinò, in the north-east, got together to personally bathe all the members' goats with traditional remedies to remove external parasites. One committee on Lagonav teamed up to quickly build a temporary shelter for a member whose landlord kicked her out. A committee's treasurer there gave land to a member who had nowhere to build her new home. The results that Fonkoze's team saw overcame their scepticism. Establishing and managing committees became an important part of the CLM team's work.

***

The first step towards building a committee is to identify potential members. We need to know who in a neighbourhood might be willing to help out, so we ask the people who are most likely to know, the families we have selected for the programme.

When programme members are invited to join CLM, staff members ask them to name neighbours they can turn to when they have an urgent problem. Who might let them have a cup of rice so that their children don't go hungry? Who might let them use a donkey to bring a sick child to the hospital? Who might lend them a cup or so of beans that they can plant in the small patch behind their home? Who might listen sympathetically to troubles, whether or not they can do anything significant to help? Some members will say that there is nobody, but others will mention someone or even a couple of people. Fonkoze compiles lists of the names that new members cite, looking especially for the ones that come up more than once.

These lists give us a starting point, because we know at a minimum that folks on them have a history of good will towards their poorer neighbours. We study the list with two criteria in mind. We look for names mentioned by multiple people, but we also consider who would be in a position to be useful. Is there a school director or a teacher on the list? They might be able to help get a child into school. A local elected official? They might be able to intervene if a major conflict arises. A successful local businessperson? They might be able to offer good business advice. Someone who works for another development programme or for an aid organization? They might know of resources that their own institution could direct towards CLM members.

We make a new list of the folks we will seek to recruit, and we send staff members to meet with each one individually in their home. They explain the CLM programme in detail. They talk about how committees work and the role that committee members play. They are careful to say that committee members are volunteers. If someone professes a willingness to help out, we invite them to an initial organizational meeting.

It would save time and energy if we just sent out invitations to the first meeting and explained everything to everybody all at once. These individual conversations are time-consuming. But they are worth the trouble. The social situation at a group meeting can push people to say things they do not mean. People can agree to help because they do not want to refuse in front of their neighbours. An energized conversation can create a momentum that people go along with despite themselves or without thinking. But you can't count on such people because they were never really interested in the first place. And if you had asked them privately, in their home, they might have found a way to say they were too busy, or that they couldn't participate for some other reason. Or they might have agreed to participate but then just not showed up for the meeting. So individual conversations can screen out people who don't really want to participate and whom we do not, therefore, really want. And these one-on-one home visits also begin the effort to pay committee members in the only currency that we will offer them, respect.

At the initial meeting, committee members are not just identified. They are also organized into the different positions that a committee requires. A committee needs a president, a secretary, and a treasurer, and each role requires a particular sort of person. A president must be able to lead. A secretary must be literate. A treasurer must be able to handle funds and must have their neighbours' trust. By this time, our staff has interviewed potential committee members, but it has also been chatting with the programme members in the area and with other neighbours as well. It normally has a good sense of who is suitable for the different roles.

Running these first meetings can be tricky, because we have a narrow path to follow between opposing difficulties that can arise. On one side, we want to avoid leaving the roles open completely to whomever the group might choose. We do not, in other words, want to hold elections. The group could choose someone who does not want the job or who is not really appropriate for a certain role. It could choose an illiterate secretary or, what is probably more commonly a threat, a president too bossy for the group's good. On the other side, we should not leave the group feeling as though they have nothing to say. The committee belongs to its members and to the community, not to Fonkoze. Encouraging participation in the selection, even if not holding a vote, is one step towards establishing the group's ownership of the committee. The CLM members themselves are asked to choose two of their numbers to represent them on the committee.

Once the committee's leaders have been chosen, we turn the meeting over to the president, whose role includes, after all, to preside. The president normally has a few encouraging words for the CLM members in the community. Then the group determines a monthly meeting time, and it adjourns. We will eventually provide the committee with some training, focusing on more detailed discussions of the various roles the committee's members can play to help CLM members and on the nuts and bolts of running committee meetings. Committees receive a register they use to keep notes from the meetings and to record attendance. But even before that training takes place, committee members can begin to assume their roles.

And committee members serve CLM members and the CLM team in lots of ways. Some are striking, like the examples from the pilot that convinced the team that committees could work in Haiti. Others are less dramatic. They can help members communicate with Fonkoze staff. Even today, there are many members without phones, and staff members normally pass through a neighbourhood just once a week. A committee member with a telephone can provide a key link on the six other days. They offer advice that is easy to access because it is close at hand. Many committee members depend for their income on the same sorts of activities that CLM members are trying to develop – raising livestock, farming, small trading – and they have extensive and relevant experience. Committee members also provide a measure of informal supervision, checking in on members, encouraging them to take good care of their new assets. Members often receive their new assets before they really understand or believe how the programme will work for them. They can be inclined to try to sell their assets right away, suspicious that the CLM programme might try to take them back. Committee members who live along the roads and footpaths between CLM members' homes and the markets, and who are present in the markets themselves, can discourage programme members from doing so and, so, they become one key to CLM families' making progress they sustain.

Committee members can help manage the conflicts between CLM families and their neighbours, who might not be a lot wealthier than they are and who sometimes resent the opportunity that their poorer neighbours have received. Sympathetic community leaders are the best-placed people to help address these conflicts. For one thing, they were not the ones who chose programme participants. Neighbours who've been excluded from the programme might not want to listen to programme staff, but they might listen to someone they know who is not to blame for their exclusion. For another, local leaders know things that the CLM team does not. Conflicts can have more than simple jealousy behind them. They can involve months or years or decades of antecedents. Our conflict might involve my jealousy, but it might also involve what your son did to my nephew or what my uncle did to your grandmother. Local leaders who know these stories are in a better position to address conflict than the CLM team could be.

Some committee members are large landowners. They may have a small tree or two they can give to someone struggling to assemble the support posts that a new house will require. Or a palm tree that can be turned into planking for a new home's walls. They can sometimes help members access land to build a home on. That might mean that a wealthy committee member gives someone a small plot of land, like the committee treasurer from Lagonav did during the pilot and others have done over the years. It might mean that a willing local leader helps one or more members gain the right to build a home on a piece of public land.

***

In the years since the pilot, working with committees has remained an important challenge. Fonkoze has always hoped that the committees could last, serving long term as a structure within which communities would continue to support their poorer members. But the programme struggles to hold these committees together. Attendance at the meetings weakens. The meetings gradually become less regular, too. Helping committees establish a reliable, disciplined structure takes a lot of staff time.

But with all the case managers' various and detailed duties, with all the attention they must direct to each aspect of each family's situation, they can overlook or become lax about tasks that seem less urgent. The fanaticism of the pilot, where staff members worried about the prospect of facing the Baron over each detail of a programme they were just learning, gave way to a similar – though perhaps less intense – fanaticism about the programme's final results, not the details of its method. Having regular committee meetings is useful. Participating in such public meetings is good for programme members. But for a very busy staff, the meetings themselves can come to seem less important than the way that building the committees helps the team enlist men and women who are willing to be friends and champions for the community's poorest residents.

In other words, having willing and capable committee members can come to seem more important than having working committees. Building the committees can come to feel like a mere means, a way to identify helpful individuals in a community and to cultivate strong relationships with them. Over the years, some of the most reliable and helpful committee members have not been part of working committees at all. The staff tends to cultivate relationships with committee members more than it works to build strong, lasting committees, and the regular discipline of meetings falls away.

CLM's leadership has sought to fortify the committees in various ways. Though committee members are always told that they participate as volunteers, the programme regularly organizes events in their communities – training workshops for members are the most usual example – and these can involve lots of small jobs. Someone has to supply wood and water for cooking. Someone has to cook the food and clean up afterwards. Committee members and their partners can be interested in these jobs, but more often they are just happy for the chance to choose someone else they know to do a job they might feel is not worth their time.

Because basic veterinary care is unavailable in many of the areas the team works, the team tries to address the need by offering an opportunity to committee members. It recruits interested ones, gives them some basic training, and provides them with an initial kit of veterinary supplies. They can set themselves up as veterinary technicians, and they have access to a Fonkoze veterinarian for advice about difficult cases. This enables them to serve their neighbourhoods, it is good for their status, and it can even be a small source of additional income.

All these measures encourage committee members. But each encourages them as individuals, without doing anything to strengthen the committees themselves. We continued to worry that as committees themselves became weaker, members could lose the important connectedness to community leaders that committees are designed to build.

When we began organizing VSLAs for all members, we realized that these associations could help address this concern. We discovered that there were many places where no CLM member had enough education to keep VSLA records. The associations use very simple accounting, but their secretaries must be able to read and write reliably, if not necessarily comfortably, and that includes doing figures on paper as well. The obvious solution was to invite committee members to join the VSLAs as their leaders.

VSLAs turned out to be so popular, that community members, inside and outside of CLM, wanted to be part of them. Though participation was introduced to the leaders as a service they could provide to their neighbours, it came to feel like a benefit as well. VSLAs operate as associations, so they bring CLM members into meetings with their neighbours. And, so, they contribute to CLM members' sense of belonging much as the committees are designed to do.

But VSLAs have a narrow set of priorities. Their members save. They borrow money. They repay their loans. Though participants contribute to a small solidarity fund, and they talk about one another's problems when they're deciding when to make a pay-out from that fund, their real focus must be to ensure that their procedures are correct and transparent, that they collect all the funds they are supposed to collect, and that they calculate the pay-out correctly when the time comes. Participants tend to want the weekly meetings to be as short as possible. Though a lot can be added to what VSLAs do, they are not really designed to address larger problems, whether the problems of individual members or the problems of the community at large. Fonkoze's managers wanted to take another shot at creating community committees that would be lasting.

The managers reasoned that the committees' focus on CLM members might be too narrow. Even during the programme's 18 months, committees lose the discipline of regular meetings unless the Fonkoze staff that works with them keeps them on task. Few would meet at all once the 18 months are up.

The team wondered whether the committees would hold together more if they had more to do than simply supporting CLM members. This thought emerged as two staff members were invited to Senegal to participate in a training workshop offered by Tostan, an organization based there that specializes in community development. Tostan has a long, involved process through which it accompanies communities as they build their own engagement to fight injustice. They have been particularly effective in the fight against female genital mutilation. Fonkoze wondered whether it could adapt key aspects of Tostan's process to help transform committees that were designed just to support CLM members into committees with an eye to broader community development.

Fonkoze's staff created a three-day workshop based on principles they had learned from Tostan. The training works through a series of steps. First, it encourages workshop participants to start thinking critically about themselves, then about their surroundings, which is to say about the community where they live. Then, it asks them to think about their community as it is and then as they want it to be, using mapmaking in small groups to help them articulate their vision.

Having illustrated their vision for their community, Fonkoze's staff asks them to consider the changes they hope for and to distinguish between those they could undertake themselves and those that would require outside help. A group at a training in Tomond once explained that they wanted a professional school so that local young people would be able to learn a trade. A group at a training in Savanèt explained that they wanted a bridge over the Fè a Cheval River to connect them to the main road. Groups have asked for hospitals and paved roads and new schools, things that small groups of community members consisting mainly of CLM members are not going to accomplish in the short or medium term.

But there is a Haitian proverb that the CLM team asks them to consider, '*Koke makout ou kote men w ka rive*'. That means, 'Hang your bag within your reach'. It is a way of saying that one should know one's limits. Fonkoze does not ask people to limit their dreams, but to recognize that some of the improvements they envision would be easy to achieve. There is such a thing as low-hanging fruit. The team encourages committees to choose an attainable goal as their first and to construct a plan towards achieving it. They tend to choose a range of things: community plant nurseries, goat-rearing businesses, repair of local dirt roads, work on local springs, community corn mills, and the like. They build their plans, and the team lets them know that it can offer them small grants – roughly $500 – to help them. Once a committee's plan is finished to the satisfaction of the CLM supervisor responsible for work in their area, they receive the funds and can implement the project.

In some respects, these new committees have been successful. A large majority of them have planned and then carried out projects they felt their communities needed. But as useful as such small projects might be, it is worth remembering that they are not really the point of the initiative. The idea was to use them as a way to strengthen the committees, make them more lasting, so that they remain structures that former CLM members can continue to turn to after they graduate, and there is not a lot of evidence that that is what happens.

CHAPTER 13
Health and safety

Anise is a single mother of two from Niva, an area south of downtown Mibalè. Niva stretches along both the national highway that leads from Mibalè towards Pòtoprens and an important dirt road that runs off that highway, across a river, and then all the way to downtown Sodo. Anise's older child's father abandoned them both to their fate long ago. Her second child, her son, Mackenson, was born shortly after Anise joined our programme. Mackenson's father's name is Genson. He lives close by and supports Anise and their son as much as he can, even though he and Anise are no longer together.

Anise had been in the programme for some months when we brought her and Mackenson to a mobile health clinic we organized in a small church in Venis, a more remote area of rural Mibalè, further to the south. A Haitian-American doctor of nursing was volunteering his time, seeing as many CLM members as we could get to him. Men and women waited their turn to see Dr Luke. They sat on rough wooden planks nailed onto posts driven into the packed-dirt floor, the same benches that folks use at regular services.

The clinic was not close to Anise's home, but we told her she'd need to come because Mackenson had been so sick. As soon as Wilfaut, our driver, dropped Dr Luke and his team off in Venis, he drove back to Niva to collect Anise, Mackenson, and a couple of others who needed attention. We knew there was no chance she'd be able to get to the clinic by herself, just as she had been unable to get Mackenson to the hospital in Mibalè.

When Wilfaut returned with Anise and Mackenson, Dr Luke didn't take the time to examine either of them. He was passing through the waiting area, when he took a quick look at the obviously sick infant. He told us to get the boy to the emergency room immediately. Wilfaut sped off once more with Anise, her case manager Nerlande, and Mackenson.

As they were walking out the door of the church on the way to Wilfaut's truck, someone asked Anise very pointedly how she could have allowed her baby to deteriorate to such a degree, and she burst into tears. As weak as she was, she had to hold herself up by clutching the doorpost of the church as she wept. Nerlande grabbed one of her arms – Anise was carrying Mackenson on the other – and led her to the vehicle.

When Anise and Mackenson reached the emergency room, Mackenson was admitted to the hospital right away. He was sent straight to the paediatric ward. Anise sat in the ward, day and night, cradling her boy. She would explain to anyone who asked that she was happy to see that the swelling in his feet had gone down some. The hospital staff, however, was reluctant for some time to speak of progress because even after a couple of days with them, Mackenson's diarrhea continued. Eventually both Mackenson and Anise regained their health, though we had to pay one of her neighbours to sit with the boy in the hospital so that Anise could go off to get the care she needed, too. But when the pair finally left the hospital, they were healthy, and they've been healthy ever since.

***

A moment's reflection is probably enough to help most people see that money and training would not, by themselves, enable a woman like Anise to set herself on the road out of extreme poverty. Fonkoze could have taught her to manage a business and then provided all the resources she'd have needed to start one, but it probably would have been useless. She wasn't healthy enough to manage a business if she had one. And even if she had been healthy enough herself, the demands of caring for Mackenson would have made it hard to get anything started or just to maintain anything she might have had.

Poor health is a result of poverty, but it is also a cause. It fits neatly into what is a vicious circle, one that is sometimes referred to as a 'poverty trap'. Just as we come across women, like Anise, for whom poor health bars any escape from poverty, we come across many for whom poor health is the reason that they are as poor as they are in the first place.

***

When we met Larose and Frederik, a couple from northern Gwomòn, they had almost nothing. They actually owned no productive assets that their case manager could calculate when she first evaluated them. By then the couple had been married several years and had four children.

Early in the marriage, they had farmed both their own land and additional plots they rented, and Larose sold basic groceries both in the market and out of their home. They had managed well enough until their third child, a boy, was born with severe physical disabilities. He lacks the strength in his neck to support the weight of his head. He can sit if he is propped up, but his head hangs limply in front of him. He can communicate well enough with those used to listening to him. Others find him hard to understand.

The couple spent everything they had in an unsuccessful struggle to get him the care he needed. They followed an understandable assumption that he was somehow sick and could be cured. Larose burned through the capital in her small commerce, and the couple sold their farmland. They paid for several trips to see doctors in Pòtoprens and were left with a boy who continues to need their constant attention. The one rehab hospital they were able to find gave them nothing but an estimate of 160,000 gourds for the work they claimed the boy would need. At the time, that would have been more than $3,000, and it was much more money than the couple could have hoped to mobilize.

When our team came across them, the boy was spending his days sitting on the dirt in the couple's yard, his head hanging from his strengthless neck, cheerfully talking with his sisters. A family that was once managing not well, but decently, easily qualified for a programme for those who have nothing. And if Larose's case is unusual for its details, it is not at all unusual for the fact that medical or funeral expenses drove an already-poor family into the depths of ultra-poverty.

***

Helping families establish sources of income cannot address ultra-poverty by itself, not even if it comes with extensive training. Investment and training, even combined, do not account sufficiently for the fragility of the lives of families in extreme poverty. Offering just training and resources would be a matter of, as Haitians say, '*lave men, siye atè*'. That means washing your hands and wiping them off in the dirt. It is a typical Haitian way of talking about useless or self-defeating action. A woman who can't stay healthy enough to work, or whose family members are sick enough to keep her from working, is trapped. Any progress a family does make can be wiped out quickly by disease or death.

BRAC's initial design of the graduation approach made helping families stay healthy a priority, and Fonkoze adopted that priority, adapting it both to Haitian families' needs and to the circumstances in Haiti. CLM's approach has always emphasized prevention, helping members stay healthy, and has always defined the work of prevention broadly, offering measures that protect families directly, but also training members to understand how to protect themselves.

That training is built into the home visits that case managers make every week. As part of the initial guidance that the BRAC team provided, they helped the CLM staff identify 10 important health issues that the team judged to be addressable through simple messaging and then helped the team construct the messages. These were not questions requiring complex conversations, but straightforward, easy-to-master principles: eat foods rich in vitamin A, protect your children from worms, get your children vaccinated, drink clean water, keep your family and your household clean. The list of messages has changed slightly over the years. Messages have been revised, and a few have been added. In 2010, cholera arrived in Haiti, so the team added a lesson on cholera. When a COVID-19 epidemic seemed to threaten, the team added a lesson on coronavirus as well. Conversations with Tostan staff and then a day spent with an expert in early child development led the team to add a lesson on talking to infants.

But we do not believe that teaching people to earn a living without giving them the means to do so is enough to address poverty, and we are similarly convinced that it is not enough to teach people healthier habits without helping them establish the means to live healthier lives. The programme provides education, but we also make concrete investments in families' health.

The programme's investments in prevention aim at helping families make their home environment healthier. That means helping them ensure that they have clean water to drink, their own latrine, and somewhere dry and secure to sleep.

The first thing the programme typically transfers to new members is a water filter. *The World Factbook* (CIA, 2022) reported that roughly 44 per cent of Haiti's rural population was consuming unimproved drinking water even as late as 2022. That means they were drinking water that comes straight from a spring, a river, or whatever their local water source might be. Water-borne diseases, both major and minor, are commonplace, taking a serious toll, especially on poor families. Until 2022, Haiti had experienced several years with no new cases of cholera, which killed thousands of Haitians in the epidemic that followed the 2010 earthquake, but the disease returned after that. And even without cholera, diarrhea is all too common among Haitian children. Haiti has the highest infant-mortality rate in the Western Hemisphere, and according to an organization called Haiti Water, water-borne diseases accounted for over 15 per cent of those deaths, even before cholera arrived (International Action, n.d.).

Fonkoze does not aim to convince its members to drink only filtered water. It provides filters. But the team knows that filters don't last forever. Things break. And filters are hard to find in rural Haiti. So, Fonkoze aims to convince families to drink treated water. Filters are one means to that end. Programme members hear a lot from staff about the importance of treated water and about the different ways they can treat it. Most can find the means – treatment tablets or liquid chlorine – once they decide to do it. But having their own filter makes it cheap and relatively easy to drink safe water at the start. Some begin to see the difference that treated water makes. The stomach aches that have been a common part of their lives become less frequent. They see less diarrhea. And, so, they develop a willingness to make the small extra effort that safe water requires.

Not that members' transition to treated water is always either quick or straightforward. Case managers have to keep after them. A member might say that she has treated water, but she might change her story when you ask her for a drink. She might not really care about the water she drinks but may fear that untreated water could make her case manager ill. At least in that case she's come to see that untreated water could be dangerous. Or she might just worry that her case manager will have some way to tell whether the water's been treated. Members often think that they are used to the water they drink so that it cannot hurt them, even if they are also used to stomach aches and diarrhea.

When visiting a member in her home, a case manager inspects her filter to see whether she's using it. A dry, dirty filter probably isn't seeing water regularly. Sometimes filters are so little used that they start to accumulate roaches. Staff members go over and over the benefits of drinking treated water. And most families are eventually convinced. A broad survey of CLM families showed that over two-thirds were still treating their drinking water even five to six years after they left the programme (Shoaf and Simanowitz, 2019).

But improving sanitation involves more than clean drinking water. Shortly after families join the programme, Fonkoze helps them install a pit latrine in their yard.

Before that, few of the families have access to any latrine at all. Of 1,000 families who joined CLM in the south-east in 2020, 635 lacked access to any latrine whatsoever. Of 400 families in Tomond who joined just before them, 339 did. And these numbers are low. The World Bank claimed in 2015 that only 24 per cent of Haitians had access to a toilet (World Bank, 2015), and the CLM team has worked with cohort groups that include hundreds of participants of whom none or almost none had a latrine when we met them.

Obviously, not having access to a latrine doesn't alleviate the need to use one. A standard Haitian euphemism for defecation is '*fè yon bezwen*', which means 'do something necessary', and it captures one of life's simplest truths. People without a latrine go into a field or another hopefully unobtrusive corner and do what they must, with all the risks to their own health, and also their neighbours' health, that doing so can entail.

The CLM team is unwilling, however, to simply give each family a latrine, for three reasons. For one thing, installing a latrine for hundreds of families without the families' contribution would be needlessly expensive. Digging a pit can, in particular, cost a lot. It's hard work. Members take responsibility for the pit, and they provide the water and sand or gravel that gets mixed with the cement. They are responsible for the material they use to enclose their latrine as well. The lumber necessary – if that is what they use – can be costly. Their contributions bring down the cost to the programme.

For another, we believe members are more inclined to see the importance of something that they invest in. We believe this so strongly that the contract we sign with all new members specifies that they must not look at the things we give them as gifts. This statement could be confusing, since they are indeed gifts, however we might ask members to look at them. But we do it anyway just to make a point.

For a third, their participation in latrine construction is part of the education they receive in CLM. Latrine construction is a small project that involves a range of elements: planning, establishing a schedule, mobilizing resources, and following through on plans. Whether a CLM member can master these elements can affect her chance of succeeding in the long term because anything she might choose to undertake in the future will involve the same elements.

Water filters and latrines seem to work. A group of 500 families participating in the 18-month programme in 2022–23 in Savanèt, along the Dominican border, saw a reduction in cases of diarrhea by more than a third over the course of the programme. Other groups have seen similar results.

But almost as importantly, having a filter and, even more so, having a latrine can change the way members feel about themselves. Having a latrine is something graduates frequently cite as having made an important difference in their lives. They no longer face the embarrassment that they connect with having to just find somewhere moderately discreet to do what they need to do.

CHAPTER 14
Building a home

Edner and Merline were living with their four children in an *ajoupa* when the family joined the CLM programme. *Ajoupa* are tent-like structures, shaped like prisms. Often, they are nothing more than two walls of pressed corn or millet stalks, tied together so that they lean against each other. There might be a couple of large, fibrous palm pods lying across the top to help keep the rain out. The triangular front and back of the house are generally made of the same materials as its two sides.

An *ajoupa* tends to be pretty rough and ready, but that doesn't necessarily matter very much to those who sleep in them because they are often just temporary dwellings. A farmer will throw one up in a field that is inconveniently far from home when it's time to till, plant, weed, or harvest. It is a place to sleep for a short time while accomplishing large farming tasks. A home-made tent.

Extremely poor families can, however, find themselves making an *ajoupa* a more permanent home, and that is what happened to Edner and Merline. They had no place of their own, but Edner worked for a wealthier neighbour. He watched some of the man's livestock and did chores in the man's fields. The neighbour allowed the family to live an *ajoupa* by one of those fields. 'It wasn't good, but it was what we had,' Edner explained.

Edner tried to start small businesses several times while he and Merline lived in the *ajoupa*. He would sell kerosene or rum and cigarettes or gasoline: all profitable businesses that require very little investment. A couple of days of fieldwork might earn him enough cash to make at least a small start. But Merline couldn't stay at home all the time, and neither could he. If the kids wandered off while their parents were out and about, Edner's merchandise would disappear. Their home had no secure door and no place to hide anything.

And lost merchandise wasn't all that the *ajoupa* cost the family.

Everything they had was drenched by every downpour. The couple had once owned a bed, but rain rotted out the wood. They had important papers, but no place dry to store them. Edner lost his own birth certificate to rain, and then the certificate of one of the children as well. The other birth certificates in the household were reduced to barely legible pieces that have to be assembled like puzzles to be photocopied or even just read.

***

The most significant of Fonkoze's original adaptations of the BRAC programme concerned members' homes. BRAC would, if appropriate, provide support to participants to enlarge their homes to protect their new livestock at night. If their housing was inadequate, the BRAC staff helped members figure out how to use income from their new business activities to improve it.

Fonkoze's team decided it had to do more.

The team had begun the process of selecting members for the pilot even before staff members went to Bangladesh for their initial training. They had started to organize community meetings for wealth ranking and to visit potential members for preliminary selection.

During these visits, they had been struck by the miserable condition of many families' homes. The families whom the team met were not all living in *ajoupa*, but few of them had adequate roofs. Most of their homes were covered with *tach*, the large, fibrous seed pods from palm trees. In a country subject to tropical downpours, such a roof meant a family was near certain to get drenched. The team heard from women who took their children outside when it rained, out from under their roof, to seek such shelter as they could find under nearby trees. Women would speak of moving their children around the floor of the home, arranging them in whatever dry spots they could find. Their homes simply didn't protect them. Many of the homes' walls were so poorly made, or in such poor repair, that someone standing outside them could see inside – or even reach inside – without difficulty.

For the first part of the training from BRAC, the CLM staff separated into two groups. Each group went to a different part of Bangladesh. They got their introduction to BRAC's programme in different regions, from different BRAC teams. When they came back together after their first experience in the field, they talked about what they were seeing and how it related to what they had seen in Haiti before they left.

The programme's two central priorities were especially on their minds. They knew that they'd have to help members establish small commercial activities, and they knew they'd have to help them stay healthy. And as they thought about the dwellings they had seen while hiking around Boukankare, neither seemed possible.

Families living without protection from wind and rain would have a hard time staying healthy. Their clothes would be wet. Their floors would be muddy. They would have trouble getting good sleep. And anyone would struggle to establish commercial activities without somewhere to secure merchandise. Rural Haiti is not especially subject to theft, but theft happens, and any time a new CLM member had to leave her yard – to do laundry, walk a child to school, work in her fields, or manage her livestock – she would risk losing merchandise unless she had a door that she could close and lock and walls providing at least a semblance of solidity.

The staff of the CLM pilot decided that helping families establish a dry, secure living space had to be part of the programme, and they settled on a modest plan. The team committed to working with members so that, by the end of their 18 months, each would have a nine-by-nine-foot, one-room home with a good tin roof and a cement floor.

The staff knew that they did not want to simply give families these small new homes for all the same reasons that they didn't want to give away latrines, but they also knew that they could not count on the families to build wealth quickly enough to make the necessary investments themselves. Fonkoze would give its members nine sheets of roofing, five sacks of cement, and the nails necessary both to erect the structure and attach the roof. It would also pay stipends to both the builder who put up the walls and the roofer who covered the home.

Fonkoze would be making a big contribution, but it would also be leaving the families themselves with a lot to do. The families had to collect all the lumber they would need. This included the support posts that give the home its structure and the long, narrow slats that the roofer would need to secure the roofing. It also included the planks necessary to custom-make windows, doors, and the corresponding frame for each. They had to haul the water and the sand that would be mixed into the cement. They had to collect the rocks for the walls and the clayey earth that would hold the rocks together.

The size of the task did not, however, keep many families from finishing the job. Of the 150 families who participated in the pilot, over 95 per cent completed their home before graduation, and six months after they graduated, 81 per cent of the families had made further improvements. They were living in homes with cement walls as well as cement floors, even though the programme neither provided the additional cement nor required them to add cement walls (Huda and Simanowitz, 2010a).

But in 2010, a circumstance arose which led to the first change in the programme's approach to housing. Fonkoze had the chance to increase the programme's scale, and the team decided to work more broadly throughout Boukankare. The lower, southern part of the commune had been the site of one-third of the pilot and of a small subsequent cohort of families. As one of the poorest communes in Haiti, Boukankare seemed like an appropriate place to start reaching more families. And though Haiti had other needy communes, the presence in Boukankare of medical facilities supported by Partners in Health would simplify achieving the programme's goals.

The team committed to working with 700 families in the commune. Growing in Boukankare meant spreading out, covering a larger area, moving into the commune's northern half. Much of northern Boukankare is mountainous and hard to access, but the most difficult part is Tit Montay, the commune's north-west corner.

The team was especially motivated by the challenge that Tit Montay presented. Both the pilot and the small cohorts that initially followed it included households that were hard to get to, but the regions they were in were nothing like Tit Montay. Teams led by Bethony Jean François had, however, been visiting the area and seen the extent of the need. The whole staff was anxious to work there.

No roads reach Tit Montay that even a motorcycle can use, much less a car or a truck. Not in 2010, and not in 2024. Getting to Tit Montay takes a long hike from Central Boukankare to reach even its more accessible areas. But about 400 CLM members who were selected to participate in the scale-up lived in the region, so the team had to consider how to make its approach to home repair feasible for them.

The programme had never arranged door-to-door delivery of construction materials. Members would pick up their materials at central drop-off points. Carrying nine sheets of roofing tin was already hard work, but five sacks of cement presented a much more difficult problem – no matter who had to carry them, no matter where they had to get to.

But the distances to even the most convenient possible central drop-off points and the steepness of the paths that members in Tit Montay would have to deal with would make things harder than they had been elsewhere. The CLM families in Tit Montay would have to hike for hours with 2,000 sacks of cement. In the programme's first years, the staff had sometimes been able to mobilize committee members or other local leaders to lend CLM members horses, donkeys, or mules. But sometimes members would just have to put the cement on their heads and carry them one sack at a time or find someone to put a sack on their head for them. Sometimes they would split the sack at the distribution point. This would double the number of trips but make each trip more doable. With the smaller load, even older children could help. They would make as many trips as they needed. For most members in Tit Montay, it do not seem possible that they'd be able to do the job themselves, or that either they or the team would be able to borrow enough animals for 400 families.

So, Fonkoze decided to offer members a choice. They could receive the same materials that the institution had been providing, or they could take additional roofing and nails instead of the cement. Fonkoze calculated how much roofing could be purchased with the money needed to buy five sacks of cement, and it turned out that the extra sheets would enable families to cover a second room. And though carrying it all to their homes across Tit Montay would still be a challenge, it would be nowhere near as difficult as carrying the cement would have been. Almost all the families chose the extra roofing.

Having offered it to the members in Tit Montay, the team decided to offer the same choice throughout the programme, and the decision proved popular. Participating families generally valued a larger home more than a cement floor. They were accustomed to their packed-dirt floors, so the chance to have a bigger home meant more to them than the health benefits of switching to cement did.

But the decision had consequences. For one thing, the initial purpose of home repair assistance was protecting members' health. And though a good tin roof would help by keeping families drier, their dirt floors would leave them exposed to worms. As a health-protecting measure, home repair would lose some of its value. For another, a bigger house would require families to mobilize more of their own resources. Two rooms meant more lumber, more of all the materials that members themselves must provide. Offering them the chance to build a bigger house exposed them to a temptation to incur greater expense at the very moment at which they were struggling to establish any dependable source of income at all.

This latter point would be especially significant as the programme moved from areas where the walls of poor families' homes are typically built of rocks and clayey mud to other areas, with less clay in the soil, where poorer families' homes have walls of palm-wood planks. Even within a region as small as Haiti's Lower Central Plateau, the earth is not uniform, and so customary home construction varies. In areas where rocks and clay are used for construction, members might be able to scavenge what they'd need, but where the soil lacks clay, they would need palm trees and skilled labour to convert the trees into planks.

Giving members even a small measure of choice also slowed the process down. As long as every CLM member built the same home, ordering construction materials was easy. It just involved multiplying the standard package of materials by the number of members in the cohort. The order for the materials for a cohort could be placed with a supplier even before work with the families in a cohort began. Giving members a choice made assembling these orders more complicated. Managers needed to compile reports from case managers, who listed the combination of roofing and cement that each member wanted.

This was still easy enough, however, because the choices were limited. Members just chose the standard mix of roofing and cement, or they maximized one by converting it into the other. Since almost no one chose cement exclusively, in practice there were just two options. Members received either the original package or as many sheets of roofing as Fonkoze could provide with the same funds. Given the choice, very few wanted the cement.

Watching members take advantage of this opportunity over the years led the team to value it for two important but unanticipated reasons. First, building two rooms left members with much more opportunity to personalize their homes. Roofs and the homes beneath them began to have different forms. A few roofs slanted straight downward along the entire length of the house, with the wall on one long side higher than the wall parallel to it and the walls on the home's shorter sides shaped like right trapezoids. More often, roofs slanted downward on both sides of a central spine, the front and back of the home forming pentagons, like the house a child might draw with crayons. Some roofs slanted downward on all four sides, giving them the shape of pyramids sitting on rectangular bases. And there were minor variations. Doors to the outside – Haitian homes always have at least two – were positioned differently. Some homes had windows, in various numbers and variously positioned. Some had smaller rooms so they could have a small, covered entrance, too: something like a front porch. And such entrances sat in different positions relative to the rest of the house: on one of the short sides, in a corner, or somewhere along a long side. Having new, well-made little houses changes members' social status. Their neighbours see them differently, and they see themselves differently as well. And the chance to personalize their home maximized this benefit.

Second, the process of planning and executing a project that is both important and complex became a learning experience for families. It builds capacity and self-confidence. The larger, more complicated homes they could now build posed larger, more complicated challenges. The excitement that members show when they speak of their new homes at graduation ceremonies shows how much they have come to value their achievement.

But the process involves a lot for the team. Supervisors compile the orders for materials, and they pass them along to administrators. Administrators look for suppliers who can both provide a relatively good price and ensure quick delivery. Once delivery dates have been established, the administrator works with the supervisor and the team of case managers to plan the drop-off points where members will gather. Members receive the material they have requested and then sign a distribution list, which functions as a receipt. The members then marshal the team they need, from among family members, neighbours, and friends, to lug their materials home. Even as the team is working to get the members the materials they'll need, it also helps them prepare the construction process. Case managers ask members whether they would like to choose the builder or builders who will work on their home. Almost all of them would. The first step is for the CLM supervisor to meet with the builders whom our members would like to hire. These meetings can be held even before delivery of materials, and they are important because, although the stipend the programme provides for builders has increased considerably over the years, it remains below the market rate. In 2023, the total per member was HTG 6,000, or just over $40. Back in 2010, it was HTG 3,000, which was then worth about $75. Experience has shown that, if members are left to negotiate on their own, they pay more, which can force them to drain funds out of their new enterprises or make it hard for them to complete the construction job. Often, however, meeting with the builders as a group creates a social situation that encourages them to agree to the relatively low rate. And working for the programme can be to their advantage, because jobs can be hard to come by. In rural areas, many are farmers who occasionally earn extra money building a home. Such opportunities can be rare. A cohort of CLM families in their neighbourhood might mean multiple jobs in a short period of time.

The builders sign contracts with Fonkoze, not with CLM members. These contracts stipulate how much we will pay, when the builders can expect an initial payment, and that they will receive the balance owed to them when the CLM member signs a form saying that the work is finished. In regions where the homes are built of stones and mud, the job is divided between two kinds of builders. A *chapant* constructs that home's basic frame and covers it with a roof. Then a *mason* builds its walls. Where the walls are of wood, a *chapant* can do both jobs.

For many members, once they have their materials and their builders, the construction process is straightforward. They have a lot of work to do, a lot of money to mobilize and spend, or both, but they grind away at it, and within a couple of months they have a basic structure with four solid walls and a good roof. The final step involves having doors and windows made and installed. This means buying hardwood and hiring a carpenter. Generally, both doors and windows are custom made.

Given that the programme's graduation rate has been over 95 per cent over the years and that having a dry, secure home has always been a graduation criterion, there is little reason to think that the burden that families take on to build or repair their homes is too much for most of them.

But families do struggle, and some make things harder for themselves than they really need to be. When the CLM team offered families the chance to make two rooms, rather than just one, some decided to go further, planning homes with three or even four rooms instead, much more than the team had intended for them. Since Fonkoze would not provide the additional materials necessary for the larger homes, these decisions committed families to even larger additional expenses, buying additional roofing and nails and whatever material their walls are made of. They would also have to pay the builders for the additional work.

Members would explain their choices in various ways. Some would point to the size of their families. Others would speak of the visitors they hoped to be able to host. And some would just say that they wanted to take advantage of the opportunity while it was before them. The CLM team might try to coach members to carefully consider the increased burden they'd be taking on. As Haitians say, 'koke makout ou kote men w ka rive'. In other words, stay within your means. Some families have been receptive to such advice, but not all. Members work with their case manager to figure out how they will mobilize any extra resources they'll need.

But some of the families struggle not because they have decided to do more, but because they initially have less. Or because something happens that leaves them with less. Members can have trouble finding structural lumber. Edner, for example, needed 14 wooden posts for the one-room home he was planning, and months into the process he had only been able to assemble four. Members might have trouble buying the palmwood planks they need to wall in their home.

And all of this assumes that members know where they will build their home, whatever form it will take and whatever size it might be. Many do. They might have a small plot of land that they purchased when they were better off than when they joined the programme, but most use a plot of family land. It might be where they have already been living. They might have to go to a parent or a grandparent or an in-law to ask for land.

But members can also be landless, for a range of reasons. Some come from families, or branches of families, that have been landless for a long time. Some have been forced to sell the land they once had to pay for a funeral, healthcare, or another emergency. Some are transplants, living for one reason or another in a neighbourhood where they have no roots. Without access to land, a member can build neither a house nor even a latrine. Every family needs a place. And helping landless members gain access to a plot of land can be challenging.

If a member has no land, she and her case manager will try talking to her neighbours, to her fellow programme members, and to the members of her CLM committee. They try to identify someone who might have land that they could make available inexpensively.

Committee members are often the most likely source since they tend to be relatively wealthy and often want to help. They won't often be willing to give land away, but they might be willing to sell a small plot for very little money upfront, allowing a CLM member to owe them a balance. Or they will allow a member to rent land '*sou pri dacha*'. That means the rent paid each year – rent in rural Haiti is usually annual – counts against a purchase price that buyer and seller have agreed to.

Between the generally low price of land in rural Haiti and the mechanisms designed to minimize the up-front cost of the purchase, buying a very small plot of land – maybe just big enough for a house, a latrine, and a small space to cook in – becomes possible for most members. A member might have to borrow the money from her savings and loan association. She might have to sell a harvest or a load of cooking charcoal or an animal. She can choose to build a smaller home than her fellow members do and convert some of the building materials that Fonkoze provides into cash. Whatever she does to assemble the funds she needs, finding a place to build her home will still leave her with a lot to do.

And even members who already have somewhere to build can have trouble getting the job done. Money that they plan to spend could disappear or could fail to materialize. A pig could die. A bean harvest could be lost to drought or to ill-timed rains. A parent could pass away, leaving funeral costs to take care of. Though more than 95 per cent of families over the years have succeeded despite the difficulties they must overcome, some don't. Or look as though they won't. And the team is reluctant to leave a family without a dry and secure home, even if they cannot complete work on it in time to graduate.

So, Fonkoze developed a way to get extra support to especially needy members. When the team initially plans the amount it will spend for each member, it makes sure that there will be at least a small amount left over after the materials have been purchased and transferred to members and after all the builders have been paid. Programme budgets are in dollars, and home repair expenses are in gourds, so managers have to estimate at the start how much they can spend for each member in Haitian gourds based on the exchange rate. They make sure to leave room for additional support for members who need it. If the gourd loses value during the course of a cohort, as it generally has over the years, the amount left over could be significant.

The team has not wanted to provide this additional support too early in the 18-month process. We have preferred to give members every chance to finish the work themselves. But eventually we have to balance that desire against the desire to make sure they have a decent place to live.

Case managers submit a report to their supervisors concerning the families they believe to be unlikely to finish. They explain why each family cannot assemble the materials they need, and they suggest what additional support from the CLM team might help them complete their home. One member might need lumber for doors or windows. Another might need one more palm tree than they can afford. A third might not have the support posts they need to erect the home's basic frame. A member might have the material they need when their family, or someone with a claim to their land, decides to take the land from them. Additional support could go towards their securing a place to build their new home.

Their supervisor goes over the case managers' reports, verifying the explanations and the proposals that the case managers make. Supervisors are familiar with the members. Visiting them regularly, with and without case managers, is an important part of their job. And they know how much funding is available for additional housing support. They are directly responsible for managing the budget for the cohort or cohorts whose teams they lead. They balance members' needs with the resources they have available, and they forward their proposal to the regional director who supervises them. The regional directors make the final determination. Once that happens, the team can give members additional grants.

Even without this additional support, almost all members finish their homes. But the team would not have added support for a secure, dry home to the programme if it had not believed that having such a home would be critical for families trying to build and maintain livelihoods. The difference between seeing 90 per cent finish their homes and seeing 95 per cent or 96 per cent do so might not seem like much, but the stakes are high. When it is a question of whether a very poor family has a decent place where they can live as they struggle to grow, even a few additional successes mean a lot.

Recently, we have moved towards giving members cash so that they can purchase home improvement materials rather than purchasing the materials ourselves and transferring them to our members. This change moves the team in the same direction as we have been moving respecting the asset transfer, and it has similar advantages, but the chance to help members at the very moment when they are ready to use our help is even more valuable in this case.

The loss of sacks of cement was always an issue for some families when they received their cement too soon. It could harden and become unusable. Transferring cash also makes it possible for a family to invest some of their funds in things like lumber, which the programme has not generally purchased over the years, if that is what they need.

***

We got to Clotude's home in Lawa one Tuesday morning. We found eight teenagers sitting in the shade cast by her new house. A couple of gardening tools – hoes and pickaxes – were strewn on the ground next to them. Clotude was in her kitchen, a small straw shack next to her pre-CLM home. She rushed out for a moment to greet us and to explain.

She had hired the team to work in her fields. In Lawa at the time, an adult man was paid 250 gourds for a day of field work. Since the dollar was then worth about 100 gourds, an adult farmworker would earn about $2.50 for a day. Clotude explained that the kids worked for 150 gourds, so that hiring them saved 100 gourds for each of the eight, or 800 gourds total. The guys had just come in from their morning shift, and they were waiting for Clotude to provide their meal. She would feed them large bowls of low-grade white rice with two sauces: one made of pigeon peas and the second a thin tomato sauce seasoned with leeks and garlic and enriched with spaghetti. Then, the team would take a long midday break before heading back into the fields for the second half of their day's work.

Paying 150 gourds each for eight farmhands was still a lot of money for Clotude, but she was happy to spend it. Her part of Lawa had recently had its first rain in six months, and there were signs that the rainy season might be starting. Though Lawa had just had one afternoon's rain so far, neighbouring areas had already had several. So Clotude was in a hurry. If she planted her crops too late, they could fail to develop in time to weather the next dry spell, which is usually in June or July, and that would mean a poor harvest.

Her farming was not the only area of her life where she needed cash at that moment. She had completed construction of her new home, and it had been expensive. The CLM team in Gwomòn had made procedural mistakes that affected her. For one thing, her case manager and the supervisor never held the meeting they were supposed to organize with builders in the area. The occasion slipped through the cracks in the course of transitions between different case managers who worked with her. In Lawa, some families were left to negotiate on their own, and builders charged relatively high fees. Clotude agreed to pay her builder 7,500 gourds, or $75, and she still owed him $45 when we visited.

For another, her case managers did not participate as vigorously as they were supposed to in her planning. The CLM team saw how members relished the chance to build the home they wanted, rather than the standard one that the programme initially offered. But without close coaching from case managers, members can fail to think through all the problems that taking on expenses implies. In their excitement, they sometimes choose to build larger, fancier houses, and though the team wants them to feel free to do so, it is important that they consider carefully other important ways they could use the extra money that a larger home would cost them.

The house Clotude chose to build was larger than the CLM programme was designed to support. Long after the work was completed, she owed a balance on some of the construction materials she purchased: rocks and structural lumber. And because she chose to have the house built with multiple windows and doors, she incurred a lot of extra expense for them, too.

From Clotude's home, we passed to the home of Itana, her nearest neighbour. Itana was excited when she finished building her new home. 'The new home does me good. In my old house, when it rained, I didn't know where to stand.'

The process was, however, difficult and expensive for her, just as it was for Clotude. Itana too ended up spending a lot on construction materials: 7,500 gourds for palm wood planks, 1,700 for nails, 2,000 gourds for wooden support posts. The extra sheets of roofing that she needed to make a home larger than Fonkoze planned cost her 2,100 gourds.

She explained where she got the extra money. 'My son had a small goat he earned by taking care of a grown nanny-goat for a neighbour. I borrowed it from him.' Borrowing his goat means that she sold it. She raised 2,250 gourds from the sale, which was just about enough to pay for the extra tin and to transport it as close to her home as possible. She isn't yet sure how she will repay her boy, but she very much thinks of the transaction as a loan. 'The boy is my child. Everything I have is his.'

And she agreed to pay the builder 9,000 gourds. In all, she added more than 20,000 gourds of her own money to the process, which was about $200 at the time. Fonkoze only budgeted $300 for her, and that included the cost of her latrine, which we are not considering here, and which also involved some expense for her. So, Itana's investment was not much smaller than Fonkoze's, even though she had almost nothing when she joined the programme.

A lot of that money, like what she owed the builder, was debt. Itana's husband began paying the builder 500 gourds at a time whenever he earned money milling cane. For the most part, Itana says that the builder always seemed satisfied.

But this begs an important question. Clotude and Itana were able to access much of what they needed to finish their housing projects by taking on debt. They didn't have to have the money in hand. So, why didn't they do it years sooner? Why did it take CLM to get them started?

Itana had an answer. 'CLM pushed me. I never thought I would be able to build a house until they gave me the roofing tin.'

CHAPTER 15
Healthcare

By any reasonable measure, Clermicile made good use of her time in the CLM programme. When she joined it in 2013, she and her partner were struggling to keep themselves and their two children fed. They were renting a dilapidated room in a small house along the national highway that runs from Pòtoprens, through the Central Plateau, all the way to Okap in the north. Since the birth of her first child, Clermicile had been unable to earn a living. The boy had health issues that both required her constant attention and involved significant expense. The birth of her second son only complicated her life.

When she joined the programme, the four were surviving on what her partner, Jolicoeur, could make as a driver's assistant on trucks that ran between Mibalè and Kwadeboukè. He worked for tips on the days when a driver asked for him. He might collect passengers' fares or manage the merchandise that passengers were shipping to the large markets in Kwadeboukè. The couple did a little better during mango season, when there was plenty of fruit to send off and Jolicoeur could thus stay busy. He was committed to doing any work he could find to support Clermicile and the kids. But the family was often going for a day or more without a meal. Jolicoeur could not earn enough, or earn regularly enough, to cover the family's needs, especially with a child who needed frequent medical care. They lived in a single room that they rented in a two-room shack that was falling apart.

Eighteen months later, everything had changed. They had their own small house on their own small piece of land. The family was eating two meals a day. The couple had received two goats from the programme and had cared for them so well that, by the time Clermicile graduated, they had eight. A note from the staff member who evaluated her for graduation mentions that she had got to the point that she might have had too many goats to manage. She was ready to start her own small commerce and was joining a credit programme run by SFF with the goal of doing so.

And she sustained and even built upon her progress after that. Nine years after her graduation, she and Jolicoeur still kept their livestock. In addition to whatever work he found with drivers, Jolicoeur would also farm small plots of land that they had managed to purchase over the years. Clermicile's business had grown from the small activity she created with her first 3,000-gourd loan to one with 40,000 to 50,000 gourds invested. And she had become a leader in her circles. She was not just an active member of her savings and loan association, but its secretary. She had been elected originally as its president, but she agreed to switch roles with the secretary when she saw that the elected secretary could not do the job.

But for all the changes in her life – economic changes and social changes – if you ask her how the programme affected her, there is a single point that she consistently comes back to. She expresses it in various ways, but it never changes. *'CLM te ban m pitit mwen.'* That means 'CLM gave me my child', and Clermicile means something specific when she says it.

She had spent the first six years of her boy's life making sacrifice after sacrifice to get him the medical care he needed, but she had reached a dead end on her own. He was born unable to defecate, and though she was able to get him the first set of surgeries he needed as a newborn to partially correct the problem, at age six he still depended on a colostomy bag. The hospital that had started the series of procedures he needed had lost his file, and no one she spoke to could tell her how to move forward.

At the initial training she attended as part of the programme, she brought her son's condition up with me. I was responsible for the cohort she was part of. I went to the hospital and talked with a surgeon, who told me to bring the boy and his mother by. He said he'd just start a new file. He planned and executed the additional procedures the boy needed without much trouble. Within a few months, the colostomy bag was gone, and Clermicile's boy was getting healthy.

The story of Clermicile – and in fact the story of Anise, which we shared already – underscore two important points. The first is probably obvious enough. Helping programme members and the members of their families to get the healthcare they need is necessary for at least some of them to move forward in their lives. The programme's emphasis on preventive measures and on coaching families towards healthier lives is sensible, but it is not enough. Some families need healthcare, and we have to help them get it.

The second point is just as important. Thanks to the presence of Zanmi Lasante, the Haitian sister organization of Partners in Health, both Clermicile and Anise lived in a region with relatively easy access to healthcare. Although Clermicile spent what was a lot of money for her and Jolicoeur to get her son to the hospital and stay with him while he was there, the care itself was nearly free of charge. The long-term success of CLM families depends on helping them access the care they need. But it also depends on teaching them to access care themselves whenever they need it. Teaching families when and how to use medical care is a critical part of what we do.

***

Fonkoze's leadership always knew that healthcare would need to be a part of the CLM programme, but meeting members' healthcare needs during the pilot was complicated. Haiti lacks a national system of primary care, and the care available in different areas varies greatly. Fonkoze itself had no thought of becoming a provider. It would need to identify providers it could work with in Lower Lagonav, Twoudinò, and Boukankare, the pilot's three sites.

Boukankare was easy enough. Zanmi Lasante had a small hospital in the centre of the commune, and its larger, original hospital was in Kanj, on the commune's north-eastern edge. And Zanmi Lasante's leadership was committed to the Fonkoze programme from the start. They had been part of the earliest conversations that led to CLM. So, Zanmi Lasante did not hesitate to provide its support. In Twoudinò, an international organization had a close relation with a hospital they were supporting. The organization's leadership agreed to use that partnership to provide healthcare to the CLM members there. On Lagonav, another international organization ran a small clinic in Tamaren, the market community closest to the area where the pilot would be located. Fonkoze signed an agreement with that organization's national office to give CLM members free access to the clinic's services.

The plan in Twoudinò worked well for the most part, though the complexity of the arrangement, which depended on a partner's relationship with the healthcare provider, caused minor problems occasionally. But the setup on Lagonav did not work at all. Fonkoze had contracted directly with the organization's national office for access to care, and when they showed the signed agreement to the clinic's nurse, she began to take care of members. But when her local supervisor found out, he put a stop to her cooperation. There were communications problems between the national and local offices, and the result was that CLM members had only limited access to care.

When medical needs arose on Lagonav, Fonkoze had to take action. When, for example, members were inundated by the types of minor issues common in rural Haiti – skin ailments, minor infections – Fonkoze needed a way to arrange treatment before the issues became more serious. So, it found a team of American nurses willing to offer their services for a mobile clinic. It brought them to Lagonav, and they provided the simple treatments that were mainly needed. They also trained CLM's staff in first aid, and the programme equipped the staff with first aid kits so they could address at least some ailments directly.

But there were a couple of cases too serious for this approach. One pregnant member had been told by a doctor after a first difficult pregnancy that she would need to come to the hospital for any future children she gave birth to. The programme hired a local nurse to check on her regularly and guide her through childbirth. Another pregnant member was showing early signs of pre-eclampsia, a problem related to high blood pressure in pregnant women that can lead to fatal seizures. She was, however, unable to go to the nearest hospital because she still owed money for a previous childbirth there. The programme paid her existing debt and the charges for the new stay to ensure she got the care she needed. In one most serious case, the team crossed the bay with a sick member, bringing her to Zanmi Lasante's hospital in Kanj, when the team could see no other way to help her.

When the pilot was finished, and Fonkoze was thinking about how to continue and grow the programme, one thing was clear: if it wanted to feel confident about its members' access to healthcare, its best bet was to focus on areas served by Zanmi Lasante. The organization had shown both the capacity and the willingness to provide good care to anyone who needed it. In 2009, Fonkoze, Zanmi Lasante, and the Haitian government's Ministry of Public Health signed a three-way agreement guaranteeing CLM members, and the members of their families, free healthcare at the clinics that Zanmi Lasante supports during their 18 months in the programme. Fonkoze determined to continue to build the programme exclusively in areas served by Zanmi Lasante.

The services would have been nearly free of charge even without the agreement. At the time, Zanmi Lasante was charging just 100 gourds for a visit; less than $3. Whatever particular services that the visit called for – lab tests, medications, major surgery – involved no additional charges. But Zanmi Lasante and Fonkoze both realized that even such a trivial-seeming charge might be a barrier for CLM families, who were used to doing without such services, so they agreed to eliminate them.

The system worked reasonably well, despite occasional challenges. Fonkoze made photo-IDs for all CLM members. On the back of the ID card, a member's case manager would write out the names of all the members of the household and they too, and not just the CLM member herself, would be eligible for free care. Members might not, on their own, decide to go to the hospital or to bring a child there. Many were accustomed to waiting and hoping for the best or to seeking help from traditional remedies. But during their weekly visits with their case managers, those managers would encourage them to speak about any health issues in their family. If they thought someone should see a doctor, they would strongly encourage them to do so. CLM budgets included a small fund that staff could use to defray the expenses a programme member would face. That was not for their medical care, but for any costs that might be associated with getting to a clinic or staying there if they had to. For members unfamiliar with the clinics, Fonkoze would try to have a staff member available at the clinic to welcome the sick members there and guide them through the process of getting whatever attention they needed.

The process had flaws in it, though it was possible to fix two major ones.

Two factors contributed to the first flaw. For one thing, our selection process is complex and, more importantly, long. Two to three months can pass between the time we first meet a family and when we can finally integrate them into the programme. For another, people living with the degree of poverty that families face before they enter the programme are fragile. One programme entry criterion is hunger. We ask how often families have gone a day or more without a meal, and many report that they often have. Once in a while, we select someone to invite them to join the programme, but they die before we get the chance to work with them. In one shocking example from 2011, a woman who was selected for the programme in north-eastern Boukankare died in labour giving birth to twins. Her oldest child, a teenage son, left the newborns with Zanmi Lasante for adoption, and the programme worked with his 14-year-old younger sister, the oldest woman in the home, until she graduated.

At the time, Fonkoze's staff could suggest to someone that they should seek medical care, but the team did not feel they could commit a donor's resources to someone who was not yet part of the programme. It is hard to guess whether a more aggressive intervention could have saved someone who died in childbirth, or anyone at all, but a further instance led to change.

In early 2013, programme staff were selecting programme members for a cohort in southern Mibalè. At the time, Hébert was the programme's assistant director. He was in Triyanon with a new member of Fonkoze's central office leadership, a French man named Francis, who wanted to better understand CLM. Francis had come to the Central Plateau with his girlfriend, and Hébert took the couple to meet women at various stages of the programme. That is a typical format for a field visit, because it helps a visitor see the path that CLM families follow. The three also had an American intern named Ange with them. She had returned to spend some months studying CLM after seeing the programme as part of a short tour sponsored by her university the previous year.

One woman whom Hébert and the others spoke with was Osiane Joseph, a widowed mother of four boys, living with her children on her late partner's family's land. She had been selected to join the programme, but she had not started yet. Her initial training was about a week away.

Triyanon is a major community on the road between Pòtoprens and Mibalè. There is an intersection there with a heavily travelled dirt road that leads past a market community called Ti Sèkèy to downtown Sodo, the commune immediately west of Mibalè. Triyanon has a justice of the peace's office. The justices are the lowest level judges in the Haitian legal system, resolving various smaller issues and referring others to higher courts. On Sunday afternoons, Triyanon has a small market. Most importantly, however, Triyanon is home to a Roman Catholic church.

Osiane lived directly across the road from that church. The two-room shack she shared with her boys was falling apart. It had room for a single bed, which was also falling apart. Her older sons were 20 and 14, her others were 5 or 6 and 2. The older son hadn't been to school since his father died. He himself had sent the next younger one to school for a year or two by working in neighbours' fields.

Hébert spoke with Osiane. Or he tried to. He is a trained social worker, and he already had years of experience talking with rural women in the depths of poverty, but he struggled to communicate with Osiane. Haitian children are supposed to disappear when grown-ups are talking, but Osiane's older son Denius stayed near the conversation, answering for his mother when he felt he needed to, avoiding as much as he could any appearance of the lack of respect that his attempts at intervention might seem to imply.

Hébert could see the signs of hunger in the home. Osiane had tied a cloth tightly around her midsection, something rural Haitian women do to suppress the pangs of hunger. It was late in the day, and Osiane was boiling orange leaves in salt water as a sort of tea. She had thrown some cracked wheat into the tea as well. She explained to Hébert that she had nothing else to give her kids. The wheat would provide a small measure of substance.

The staff typically keeps money in their pocket whenever they are visiting the field. Not much. Maybe just enough to buy ingredients for a single meal. The programme does not provide this money, but staff members reach into their own pockets because they cannot feel comfortable walking away from some of the women whom they interview without leaving something behind. But Hébert had no change that day. He had forgotten his wallet back at the programme office. So, he left nothing.

The following week, Hébert saw Denius on the first day of training. When he asked about Osiane, Denius reported that his mother had passed away. The team had invited him to join the programme in his mother's place. Other family members took the two younger boys, but he and his next younger brother had been left on their own.

Hébert was shocked. He had seen the need, but he had done nothing to help Osiane at the time. Hébert travelled to Pòtoprens in a truck with Gauthier for a meeting shortly after that, and he could not keep himself from weeping. The two talked about the problem, and they decided that the programme needed a separate fund for families in crisis who are not yet, or simply are not, part of the programme. Ange raised the initial money for the fund by talking with her family and friends, and in internal conversations, the solution that she and Hébert came up with to the first flaw in the programme's approach to healthcare still carries her name. The team generally calls it 'fòn Anj', or 'the Ange fund'.

The second flaw in the system was becoming increasingly apparent in 2014 as the University Hospital in Mibalè came into use. Zanmi Lasante and its international sister organization, Partners in Health, worked hard to raise the resources to open the hospital and work with the Haitian government to run it. This hospital is a great resource for Haiti and the Central Plateau generally and for the CLM programme in particular. It makes high-quality care available to everyone in the region.

But the demand for that care was great. The hospital was overcrowded every day with patients from all parts of Haiti looking for help. Its size and complexity made getting that care confusing for some people, especially for CLM members. Many were unable to read, unused to big public institutions, and too shy to ask for help. We would encourage members to go to the hospital to seek care, but then we would hear stories of members who went to the big University Hospital, found a place to sit, and returned home without seeing a doctor because they did not know what to do.

In a sense, this problem was easy enough to solve. We would commit to having someone on staff meeting sick programme members at the hospital to guide them through the process. While they were doing so, they would try to ensure that the members whom they guided through the various lines they'd have to wait in were coming to understand how to use the hospital themselves so that they would not need guidance for future visits.

But there were a lot of members who needed the hospital. The days that staff was spending there with sick programme members were impacting the coaching visits members were supposed to receive in their homes every week. Follow-up for a single member could mean that 10 to 14 other members would miss their home visits that day. Sometimes someone from management would go so that the case managers could keep to their schedule of field work, but managers were supposed to be in the field as well. The task of guiding programme members through the process of getting care was too important to slight, but it was getting in the way of other important things.

CLM's leadership discussed the problem with a representative of the programme's oldest and most consistent supporter, the Haitian Timoun Foundation. The team needed a staff member it could specially designate as its patient advocate. That person would help members seek the care they needed without it impacting other members, and with the right training, they could facilitate care more expertly than a generalist on staff could. So, with support from the Haitian Timoun Foundation, it hired a health specialist, who is a licensed nurse. Thanks to the close partnership of Zanmi Lasante, she was able to spend a month in the hospital full-time, learning about each of the services it offers and making connections with its staff.

She quickly took over all the work of facilitating healthcare. Case managers would contact her when someone they were working with needed to see a doctor, and she would meet the person at the hospital and teach them how to navigate the formalities in order to be seen by a doctor. She would take time with them to help ensure any follow-up as well, both coaching them through getting any lab tests that the doctor asked for and making sure that they understood how to use whatever medications were prescribed.

She took on other tasks as well. She reinforces the training concerning health and hygiene that case managers gave programme members. She herself treats members' minor ailments when she encounters them on visits to the field. The CLM team would receive occasional visits from medical teams who would offer mobile clinics, and the health specialist would be in the middle of these clinics, organizing them, receiving patients, creating files for each, and checking and recording their vital signs. When the CLM team added regular screenings for malnutrition to the programme, the responsibility for those screenings fell principally on her.

***

Facilitating healthcare for CLM members and the members of their families remained challenging, but it had become straightforward, at least while the programme worked only in and around the Central Plateau. Programme staff would get someone who needed a doctor to one of the clinics run by Zanmi Lasante, help them through any formalities they did not know how to get through on their own, and let Zanmi Lasante take care of them.

In 2017, an opportunity arose that forced the team to learn an additional approach. Representatives of a congregation of nuns, the Sisters of Mercy, visited Mibalè and went with Fonkoze staff to meet CLM members. At the end of the visit, they said that they would like to sponsor a cohort of families.

There was, however, a catch. They were already active in Haiti, but all the work they sponsored was in Gwomòn, a city well to the north-west of Mibalè and a long way from any clinics run by Zanmi Lasante. The Sisters of Mercy wanted to bring CLM to Gwomòn.

Gauthier, the programme's director, was impressed by the sisters. They showed that they understood what the programme was trying to do. He was reluctant to refuse their offer. At the same time, he was thinking of how much work would go into setting up all the infrastructure that the programme depends upon in another part of Haiti.

So, Gauthier put the problem before the Sisters. He would be happy to establish the programme in a new part of Haiti, but they would have to agree to certain conditions. The most important was that they would need to ensure from the start that they could fund two consecutive cohorts of at least 200 families. Gauthier did not think it made sense to establish a new functioning headquarters in a new region of Haiti only to shut it down after just two years. He thought that the price tag might scare the Sisters off, but they raised all the money for both cohorts – over $600,000 at the time – in less than two months.

But he and his team also had to think about the challenge that ensuring access to healthcare would present. In the Central Plateau, Zanmi Lasante made things easy. In Gwomòn, however, the programme would not be able to count on its services. There was a hospital in Gwomòn, but it lacked the resources and the mission to make healthcare generally and affordably available. It charged patients for any services they needed, and the charges, though reasonable, were beyond what CLM members would be able to afford. For members to receive the same free healthcare that CLM members had always received, Fonkoze negotiated an arrangement through which the hospital would bill the Fonkoze team once a month for services provided to CLM families.

And there was more to the healthcare model that Fonkoze established with the Sisters of Mercy. Fonkoze hired a second nurse to support the programme there. And they arranged check-ups for all the members of all the CLM families at the beginning of their 18 months in the programme as a way to identify problems before they could become serious. For the first cohort the Sisters financed, they also organized check-ups for the families at the end of the cohort as a way to measure changes in their health status.

But learning how to create new partnerships with healthcare providers was the piece of the work in Gwomòn that was most important to the programme's future. It provided a model that Fonkoze could turn to as donors who wanted to finance the CLM programme increasingly pushed the team out of the Central Plateau, into regions well beyond the reach of Zanmi Lasante.

***

As Rose Marie's due date approached, her life became more difficult. She and her partner, Emmanuel, were living in a small shack in Derasin, a rural area of southern Mibalè, off one of its important dirt roads. When she and her family joined CLM, they had two children, but she was also pregnant. The couple and their kids depended on whatever income Emmanuel could earn working for builders, doing chores that were necessary, but which required no skill, like mixing or carrying cement. The only asset the couple owned was a single chicken.

Rose Marie is a tall, strong woman. But she was becoming enormous. Her previous pregnancies had been nothing like this. Her feet and ankles began to swell so much that it became hard to move around at all. And Derasin is far enough off the main road that she would need to walk just to get to where any truck could pick her up to take her to the hospital.

For someone in her circumstances, the options would normally be limited. She and Emmanuel did not have their own means of transportation. They could have tried to get her onto a motorcycle taxi, but it would have been difficult in her condition, even assuming they could have found the cash to pay for one. There was no ambulance service they could call.

Normally, a woman like Rose Marie would have had to risk giving birth at home, perhaps calling on a traditional midwife for help. But pre-eclampsia is a serious threat to the lives of women in rural Haiti, and her case manager kept a close eye on her situation.

The programme had a single solution available. His name is Wilfaut.

He was the CLM team's first driver, and he has been with the team ever since. He is a small, quiet, middle-aged man. When Gauthier retired as the programme's director, Wilfaut became the oldest member of the staff. His coworkers generally call him, '*Pè* Wil'. '*Pè*' comes from the French word for father, and it is not a title that Haitians throw around. The people who use it feel too much respect to feel comfortable calling an older man by his given name. The title suggests more respect than 'Mr' does, but also fondness that neither 'Mr' nor its Creole equivalent imply.

Most of the time, CLM's drivers are transporting staff members to meetings or events. Or they are bringing equipment or supplies to places the team needs to get them to. Sometimes, they help the team distribute livestock or home repair materials to programme members. But with healthcare options limited in the areas where the programme works, they can turn into ambulance drivers as well.

Rose Marie contacted her case manager when she went into labour, and he called Wilfaut. By staying in a room in the CLM team's office residence, Wilfaut could be available any hour of the day or night, at least if he was not driving somewhere. He is accustomed to calls or knocks on his door at any hour, asking him to rush off to pick someone up and drive them to the hospital. All requests receive the same, bored-sounding answer from him: '*nou prale*', or 'we're going'.

When Wilfaut heard about Rose Marie's situation, he rushed to meet her. He could not get all the way to her house, but with his hands on the wheel of one of the programme's very tough Toyota Hilux pick-up trucks, he was able to get close. He forced the truck up a footpath that led towards her home from the main dirt road. He and I then helped Emmanuel support Rose Marie as she struggled along the short, but narrow and winding footpath from the couple's home to Wilfaut's truck. They then rushed Rose Marie to the Mibalè hospital's emergency room. When she got there, it turned out that her labour pains were false, so Wilfaut drove her home. He rushed off to serve as her ambulance driver three more times before she finally gave birth to healthy twins. His quiet, good-humoured manner made it easy for her to call again and again, without ever feeling like a boy crying 'wolf'. And more than 10 years later, Rose Marie always remembers to ask about Wilfaut when we cross paths.

The CLM team's drivers – Wilfaut is just one of them – and its small fleet of Toyotas do the job that should be done by ambulances and paramedics. But ambulances, especially in rural Haiti, are mainly used to bring patients from one hospital to another. The CLM team cannot pretend to facilitate access to care without providing the transportation that access to care depends upon.

***

Right around the time Elsie was graduating from CLM, I visited her home with representatives of the donor who had funded the group of CLM families she was a part of. She and her husband were living in northern Mibalè with three small boys. I asked her about the second son, who was about five at the time. Among the things I wanted to know was how Kervenson was doing at school. Elsie's answer was surprising. She couldn't send Kervenson to school because he suffered from back pain. He couldn't sit on a bench.

I have no medical training, but when I heard that a five-year-old was suffering from chronic back pain, it struck me as odd. I called a physical therapist, who was at the Zanmi Lasante hospital in Mibalè. Jonah was helping the hospital establish a physical therapy clinic. He was surprised at what he heard too, and he suggested that the team bring Elsie and Kervenson to the emergency room.

When Kervenson got there, nurses first took his vital signs, and the staff discovered that he had very little oxygen in his blood. They put an oxygen mask on him, and he came to life.

It turned out that nothing was wrong with Kervenson's back. Elsie had been mistaken. The boy had not been able to explain his problem to her, and she drew incorrect conclusions from what she saw. She had been struck by his inability to sit up straight on a bench, but the problem turned out to be lack of oxygen, not pain. Kervenson had a congenital heart defect. He needed surgery.

But the hospital in Mibalè could not provide heart surgery to a child. It might offer more high-quality services than anywhere else in Haiti, but it does not offer everything. We cannot, however, simply give up when we discover that the hospital we depend on for the most difficult cases cannot help. We have to do whatever we can to see that members with more complicated or less common problems get care as well.

It turned out that Kervenson's case was relatively easy to deal with. Zanmi Lasante had a partner in the States called the Haiti Cardiac Alliance, which was committed to arranging heart surgery for Haitian children. All the CLM team had to do was help Elsie and Kervenson get their passports and visas. Elsie and Kervenson went to New Orleans, where Kervenson got the operation that he needed.

***

Cases like Elsie's and Clermicile's boys are not the norm for the programme. Few members need a lot of medical care, especially that much. But these cases point to an important point. Though the programme's principal goal is and should be teaching prevention, and though its secondary healthcare goal is and should be teaching members when they should use healthcare and how they can access it, the commitment the programme makes to the health of members and of their children is and must be without limit. This is partly to protect its staff from the kind of wound that regret like Hébert's might leave each time we fail to do enough, but it is also part of teaching one of the most important lessons that the programme can teach its members and the communities they live in: each and every person matters beyond any limit.

CHAPTER 16
Graduation

When we have introduced the CLM programme to audiences over the years, we've generally talked about four elements. The first three are selection, economic and social development, and family health. I have described each of these.

International development professionals refer to programmes like CLM and the BRAC programme it is based on as examples of the 'graduation' approach. Programme members are supposed to climb permanently from one socio-economic level to a higher one, and they are supposed to continue to progress, just as students who graduate from elementary school to middle school or from high school to college will not go back. The fourth element of our programme is graduation.

Speaking of 'graduation', however, requires Fonkoze to do at least two things. We must help members mark their transition. In Haiti and in a lot of other places, graduations call for ceremonies. And we must have a way of determining whether a transition has actually taken place. Fonkoze cannot say that someone has graduated without measuring what she has achieved.

In this sense, the ceremony that we hold with members after 18 months is an important part of the programme. The ceremony is a marker, drawing members' attention – and the attention of their friends, family members, and neighbours – to the fact that they have changed. They are big events, and they can seem all the larger when, as is often the case, they take place in communities where big public events are rare.

Most graduations are in churches. There are not many other types of large gathering spaces in rural Haiti. The graduates usually march in singing, wearing matching short-sleeved jerseys. They sit together, either on one side of the church or in its front rows. The CLM team invites community leaders, local government officials, and representatives of other branches of Fonkoze and of the donors who support the programme. The graduating CLM members invite family and friends.

The ceremonies look like a lot of graduations in Haiti. They open and close with prayers. The graduates and their guests listen to speeches by CLM staff, by leaders of the village committees, by local authorities, and sometimes by visitors. In between the speeches, there are songs and, sometimes, dances or skits. The venues tend to get hot, so there is usually one short water break.

The speakers mainly want to congratulate the members for their accomplishments and to offer advice, each from their own perspective, and the sorts of advice they give are easy to imagine. Continue to take good care of your livestock. Manage your small commerce carefully. Keep saving in your VSLA. Remember where you've come from and the work you did to get where you are so that you don't fall back.

One long speech from a member of the CLM management team outlines the programme's history and the steps that the programme follows. By now, none of this is news to the members, and not much of it is news to most of their guests. But if there are local leaders present, it can be helpful to make them understand all the work that Fonkoze put into finding the graduating members and supporting their journey.

The most compelling part of the day consists of speeches by the graduates themselves. A small number are invited to share thoughts about their journey. Each is usually introduced by her case manager, who says a few words explaining why she was chosen. Considering that many of the women who join the programme are unable to even look another adult in the eyes when they begin, much less speak in public, their enthusiasm for the opportunity to speak up is striking.

And their speeches are much more varied than those of the people giving them advice. They talk in moving detail about both the low points of their lives before the programme and the highlights among the things they have achieved. They talk about indignities they have suffered and about misery that they and their children have endured. They talk about owning livestock, living in a house that protects them when it rains, having their own latrine. They talk about accumulated know-how: how they have learned to manage their money, to make and execute plans, to run a business, to write their name, to save. And they talk about their altered social position: about being invited to local events, about being asked to serve as godparents, about being offered or asked for loans. A woman once explained how happy she was that the neighbours passing her home on their way to the market had begun to ask her whether she was going, too. 'People see me.'

Experienced members of the CLM staff pay close attention to the members' speeches. We are listening especially to the way the members talk about what they have achieved. Some graduates will celebrate what CLM did for them, but that is not what we hope to hear. We are always hoping to hear women who talk about what they achieved with the programme's help. The difference may seem small, but it is the difference between those who see themselves as recipients of aid and those who see their own agency at the centre of what they have accomplished.

The final speech used to be delivered by Gauthier, the CLM programme's founding director. When he retired, his successor Hébert took over. As the programme has grown, Hébert hasn't been able to attend every ceremony, so others have sometimes had to do the job. The speech is similar in some ways to the ones given by other staff members and visitors. It includes a lot of advice. But there are two points that set it apart.

The first is its focus on how members live their lives, rather than on what they have accomplished to change their lives. Everything they have undertaken over 18 months – the goats, gardens, and the small commerce they have managed; the home and the latrine they have planned and built – has been in the service of taking better care of their families. Gauthier would talk of his hope that he would continue to cross paths with members. He would always tell them that, if they seek him out whenever they see him, rather than trying to avoid his gaze, he'll know that they are well. He'd promise always to ask them whether their children are in school and whether they feed them breakfast every day before sending them off. He'd say that only then would he ask them about their business activities.

The second point that sets this speech apart concerns the certificate that the graduates receive at the ceremony. Gauthier would tell them to expect to face hard times. Life in Haiti is difficult under the best of circumstances, and no one who has ever been part of the CLM programme has been living under the best of circumstances. Not before CLM, nor even afterwards. Gauthier would tell the graduates that many of them would likely face setbacks. They could easily find themselves in extreme poverty once again. He would tell them to hold onto their graduation certificate. At difficult moments, it would remind them of what they had been able to accomplish. And this is where our members' understanding of their own agency is crucial. Someone who considered that she had lifted her family out of poverty once would have to recognize that she is capable of doing it again if she has to.

The CLM team distributes the certificates and then offers a meal and a drink, serving the graduates first, committee members and honoured guests second, and everyone else after that. Most graduations start at 9:00 in the morning, and they are usually wrapping up by around 1:00.

***

If the graduation ceremony is an important part of the programme, the evaluation processes that Fonkoze undertakes throughout the programme's 18 months are important as well. The programme could not speak of 'graduation' without some evidence of members' success.

According to the notes that Gauthier took in Bangladesh, BRAC had a simple system for determining whether a participant in its programme qualified for graduation. They tracked seven graduation criteria for each member every six months:

1. Households consume two meals a day.
2. Members have three income sources.
3. All members' children attend school.
4. Members have a vegetable garden.
5. Members use some form of family planning.
6. Members have access to a latrine and a tube well. They have access to clean drinking water.
7. Members have improved their housing.

BRAC's team even posted the criteria on members' homes to ensure that the members understood what they needed to accomplish.

Fonkoze worked with similar criteria at the start, but its own criteria emerged through conversations between the CLM team and the organization's monitoring and evaluation staff. A programme document from 2008, in the midst of the pilot, gave an early idea of what Fonkoze was thinking. Members needed to have at least two different types of activities that earned them income: they needed to have shown that they could sustain the value of their business activities, they needed to have a vision to guide them towards their next steps in business, and they needed to have savings. Fonkoze's actual document read as follows:

The following indicators should be considered in determining graduation:

- two sustainable assets – one short term and one long term.
- the total value of their productive assets should be at least 5,400 gourds (the value of their assets at baseline) to ensure their capital base has not decreased.
- If they have a small trade, the value of the small trade should be at least 1,500 gourds (the baseline value).
- a future vision for their enterprises.
- a minimum savings balance.

The CLM team settled on an initial list of criteria similar to the BRAC list, and at first it would also post these criteria on members' homes, just as BRAC would. But in 2011, strange rumours had begun to circulate through Sodo and Boukankare, the two communes the team was working in at the time. People were saying that the homes that members were building would not ultimately be theirs. They would belong instead to Fonkoze when the programme ended. People said that Fonkoze would keep a duplicate key.

These rumours were part of a pattern of falsehoods that were spreading. They seemed to aim at discouraging families from taking advantage of the opportunity CLM offered them. Such falsehoods have been commonplace wherever Fonkoze has implemented CLM. The fact that Fonkoze posted a document on each home's front door was cited as proof of the rumour, regardless of what the posted document actually said. Many of those who saw the posted document would have been unable to read it anyway. So, the team gave up posting it.

Even at the time of the pilot, however, the list of criteria posted on members' homes was not in fact what determined whether a woman qualified for graduation. Fonkoze developed a separate questionnaire that it used to make that determination.

The process of preparing the questionnaire began with a 2009 document that started by defining 'graduating members'.

'Graduating members', it reads, 'have the skills and resources to sustainably provide for the needs of their families, the capacity to manage future economic shocks and are ready, should they choose, to receive their first loan'. The team imagined indicators that would show that a woman could provide for her family sustainably, could manage future shocks, and was ready to receive credit if she wanted it. That same 2009 document proposed criteria to go along with the definition, separating them into absolute criteria and others. A woman would have to meet the first three criteria and then four of the additional six.

- Absolute criteria
    1. No malnourished children.
    2. A viable roof on her house.
    3. Healthy enough to sustain her livelihood.

- Additional criteria – at least 4 of 6
    1. Food secure.
    2. At least two sources of income.
    3. Assets valued at > $150.
    4. An active savings account.
    5. A plan for the future.
    6. Confidence she can provide for her family.

The CLM team has been using some version of this set of criteria ever since, though there have been changes. Some of those changes have merely involved specificity. For example, rather than leaving it for an evaluator to judge whether a family is food secure, they ask the member whether the family eats at least one hot meal every day. An active savings account has been specified to mean a minimum savings balance and a minimum number of transactions over a specified period of time.

But other criteria have changed in other ways. A question asking whether the member's home was covered with a good roof was replaced by a series of questions that together aim to determine whether the home is dry and secure. The question concerning asset value has had to be updated continually due to inflation as the value of assets that the team provides has increased. The question concerning a plan has undergone several revisions, growing from a simple question into a worksheet with multiple parts. A question asking whether the member had planted fruit trees and a vegetable garden was replaced by one asking whether all members of the household had appropriate government IDs. And a question asking the member whether Fonkoze should continue to worry about her disappeared entirely.

But even in 2024, the evaluation survey looks a lot like the one developed for the pilot. Fonkoze initially used it twice during the programme period: once at 12 months, and once at 17. The first survey would give the staff and the programme members a clear sense of how each member was doing. The team could then provide extra attention during the final six months to members who had done poorly at 12. The second survey would determine whether the member qualified for graduation.

***

By 2011, the team was dissatisfied with one aspect of its evaluation process: when and how Fonkoze was evaluating its members. Selection was a first evaluation, but 12 months seemed too late for a first report on the progress members were making. The case managers working with the members knew, of course, how each one was doing. Even though each case manager has 50 families to worry about, they have always been good – remarkably, perhaps – at maintaining a clear sense of each of them. And each team of case managers had regular meetings with their supervisors, where they discussed the progress of individual members. But the Fonkoze staff as a whole felt that a careful look at members' progress would be useful well before the members were 12 months into the programme. They wanted a first indication of how things were going as early as six months in.

But there was a problem. The questions used at 12 and 17 months were not designed to pick up the earliest signs of progress. For example, even under fortunate circumstances, a member's assets could not have been expected to increase much in value, and she would most likely have made very little, if any, progress on building or repairing her home. The team felt that the results of a six-month survey should project a member's tendency to progress, rather than just measuring the progress she had made. But that would mean designing a different set of questions.

At the time, the CLM team had an intern, a recent graduate from Ireland named Barrie Hennebry. Barrie agreed to help the team create the new survey. This discussion of the six-month evaluation is drawn largely from an unpublished programme document written by Barrie, 'Fast and Slow Climber Evaluation Survey Research Project'. The document is undated, but it was written sometime in 2011 or 2012.

Barrie worked primarily with two case managers and their supervisor, Wilson Ozil. The case managers chose 15 of the women they were working with, carefully dividing them into three categories based on how quickly they appeared to be moving forward. They labelled each woman a 'fast climber', a 'slow climber', or a 'slow slow climber'. They then asked themselves a range of questions concerning each of the 15 women. The team went through the questions, working to determine which of them yielded answers that reliably distinguished between the three categories of members they were seeking to define. They ended up choosing 12. Each question included a way to score its answer.

They asked whether the member had been making new friends, whether she talked to and sought advice from the members of her local committee, whether she was making clear and convincing plans, whether she was always at home when her case manager came by for their scheduled visits, and whether she was making use of the advice that her case manager was offering. These seemed to be ways of determining whether she was fully engaged in the process, and the team thought they might be a way to foresee her chances of progressing well. Case managers do not normally ask the member most of these questions. Instead, they fill it out as a worksheet based on what they have observed. The survey is not, in other words, designed to provide information that the CLM team doesn't already have. It is designed instead to give case managers a clear, disciplined way to set down and then share what they already know with their supervisors and with the team generally. The survey's efficacy was eventually validated by Fonkoze's monitoring and evaluation team.

Members who score more than 70 points are rated as 'fast climbers', those who score from 20 to 70 are 'slow climbers', and those who score fewer than 20 points are defined as 'slow slow climbers'. Generally speaking, few members fall into the third group. For example, of 500 families evaluated in Verèt in 2023, just 14, or less than 3 per cent, scored as 'slow slow'. About 56 per cent scored as 'slow', and about 40 per cent as 'fast'.

***

The introduction of the six-month evaluation meant that the team had established the four moments at which it would evaluate all CLM members: at the moment of selection, at six months, at twelve months, and at seventeen months. Case managers fill out the six-month evaluation for the members they worked with. This gives them and their supervisors a snapshot of the members' situation that they can discuss. It helps them ensure that those falling behind are not doing so because of a lack of the team's dedicated attention.

For the twelve-month evaluation, case managers within the same team swap members. Doing so gives evaluators a modicum of distance from the members they evaluate. And here again, teams of case managers and their supervisor have data they can discuss as they work to shape individualized coaching strategies for the programme's final six months.

And for the graduation survey, the staff brings in case managers or other field staff from a different team. The result of this survey determines who qualifies to graduate. Members of Fonkoze's internal monitoring and evaluation department also evaluate about 20 per cent of all members in order to ensure that the CLM staff's evaluations are accurate.

***

Evaluation and graduation are the fourth key element of Fonkoze's programme, and probably of others like it as well. Each plays a role in the long-term transformation that Fonkoze aims to help members achieve. Evaluation helps staff members and the CLM members they are working with see their situation clearly so that they can work on their weaknesses and build on their strengths. The graduation ceremony is valuable as a goal for programme members and an encouraging memory for graduates.

CHAPTER 17
Success

When Claudette joined the CLM programme, she and her husband Franckel had very little. They were living with five children in a single rented room near the Labasti market. Four of the children were theirs, and one was the child of Claudette's brother Mani, who lived nearby. That girl had been living with her aunt and uncle for years. Mani was no longer together with the girl's mother.

The couple struggled to send both their oldest daughter and Mani's girl to school. To pay school tuition and their other expenses, Franckel would make a deal with neighbouring landowners. He would turn wood from their land into charcoal, getting half of the profit from its sale. He sometimes worked in their fields, too, typically earning less than $1 a day to feed the family of seven. Occasionally, he'd get called to join a team for a few days, milling sugarcane in one of the small, ox-driven mills in the area. That would be a windfall. Claudette didn't contribute to the household's income at all. Her hands were more than full with the couple's twin toddlers and the infant boy who followed them.

When they joined CLM, they had no land, and they couldn't afford to buy land to build a home on, so they talked to Franckel's brother. He gave them the use of a small plot that sat downhill from a larger one that he had taken from the two men's half-siblings.

Things weren't easy, and the couple were frustrated when the livestock the programme gave them failed to multiply. They had chosen goats and a pig, and they took good care of the animals. Six months into the programme, their pig was growing, and it would soon have piglets. But the piglets all died. And even at 12 months, their two goats were still just two goats.

So, the two prepared to make a difficult decision. Their baby was no longer breastfeeding, so they decided that Claudette would leave the area to seek work as a maid in Pòtoprens. The work would be poorly paid, but it would be regular income. Franckel would have to manage things at home with the help of the two older children.

But something got in the way. Mani became dangerously sick. At first, Claudette could only watch as his condition deteriorated. One rainy afternoon, seeing Mani in agony, Claudette got him onto a motorcycle taxi in the midst of a rainstorm. She rushed him to the emergency room. Doctors performed surgery right away, and so they saved Mani's life.

He would need at least six months of treatment after he left the hospital, so the couple built a small shack next to their own, and they kept Mani with them. That was the end of Claudette's plan to go to the capital. Mani became a full member of the household, and Claudette became his nurse. She and Franckel helped him get to his follow-up appointments, and they cared for him as he recovered. As he gained strength, he began to help around the house. He had long been a hard-working farmer, but initially he could just manage the smaller chores, like sweeping. He was anxious, however, to do whatever he could.

Meanwhile, the couple's livelihood was undergoing a transformation. They had found a landowner who was willing to let them farm a small plot as sharecroppers. They would do all the work and keep half of any income. Franckel first cultivated the plot for the charcoal he could make out of the wood growing on it, and then he invested the money from charcoal sales into planting a crop of beans.

They also found someone willing to sell them 2,000 gourds' worth of sugarcane on credit. Claudette explained the opportunity: 'Making money from cane is a lot of work. Some people would just as soon take the easy money and be done with it. But Franckel's not like that. If he sees a way to make an extra 50 gourds, he's always willing to make the effort.'

They used the income from that first sale of cane to buy another load. 'Franckel found someone who had a cane field they had already harvested. But Franckel thought it looked like it had a lot of cane still in it, small plants that would grow if they had a little more time. He bought the harvest for 5,000 gourds, and he eventually sold 15,000 gourds worth of cane.'

It was at about this time that their first bean harvest came in, and it was a good one. They sold it off and made good use of the profits. They bought a horse, and they made a down payment on a small plot of land that they could build a house on. They added to the materials the CLM programme provided so they could build a three-room shack. They wanted Mani to have his own room. It wasn't much, but it put a tin roof over their heads, and it was theirs.

They had to sell off their goats to get the house built, however. It was the only way they could think of to buy the construction materials that Fonkoze would not provide. So, they were left with farming as their only economic activity. And with Mani and five children on their hands, things were very tight.

When Claudette graduated from the programme, the couple had their horse and a couple of chickens, but all their other money was in the fields. And Claudette was pregnant with what would be their last child. As Franckel explained at the time, 'We know that our family is already large, but we want one more, and we are sure now that we can support all our kids'.

Their success with sugarcane is what changed their lives. Claudette and Franckel began to buy all the cane they could, and they would rent local mills to turn it into molasses. They'd then sell the molasses to rum distilleries. With each new purchase, they had more to invest. Soon, they were farming sugarcane too, paying five-year leases on plots of land. Eventually, they had over 3 hectares under cultivation and a mill of their own.

As they rolled over the capital that they invested in cane, they invested in the quality of their lives as well. They poured concrete over the packed dirt floor of their home, and they repaired and painted the planking that made up its walls. They re-did its small porch with cinderblocks and cement. They bought the plot in front of the house to plant a garden. Their three younger children joined the two older girls in school.

Many CLM graduates are successful, but few have been as successful as Claudette and Franckel have, and the couple know it. 'Some graduates are willing just to keep the things they have,' Claudette explains, 'but we always are trying new opportunities'.

Each has an explanation for their success, but their explanations converge. Each credits the other. Franckel says that Claudette has two qualities that really help them. 'She works hard with whatever we have, and she never complains when we have nothing.' Ever since she weaned their youngest child, he's made sure that she always has some capital to manage a small commerce. 'Since she manages the house with her business, I can focus on bigger things.'

For Claudette, it's Franckel's willingness to work hard wherever he sees an opportunity. 'He doesn't worry about doing things the easy way. When you are in a difficult situation, if you see a path out of it, you have to be willing to take it.' For both of them, it starts with their willingness to discuss all their decisions and make them together.

And they seem well on their way to continued success. With money from the sale of their sugar mill and 100,000 gourds they borrowed from a local credit union, they made a down payment on another hectare of land. This one they would own. Their next cane harvest enabled them to complete the purchase.

Here, there was a small disagreement between them. Franckel wanted to build a new, larger home on the new plot. Claudette preferred to stay where she was and use the new land for farming. 'We'll have to discuss it,' she said at the time. Her vision eventually won out.

***

Few CLM members have flourished as she and Franckel have since she graduated from the programme. They work as partners. With his support, she keeps up her own business, buying produce and turning it over at a profit at the nearby market. She makes enough to handle most of the family's daily expenses. They each make weekly contributions to a VSLA, accumulating savings and taking out loans when they want credit. They've purchased land that they farm profitably. They buy cane and mill it for the syrup they can sell, also profitably, to rum makers. They send their children to a relatively expensive school in Pòtoprens because they feel that they get a better education there. That involves the considerable expense of making sure the kids have food and enough money to take care of the higher daily expenses they encounter around the capital.

Fonkoze and its partners would have little reason to invest in the programme unless other members were, at least on the whole, making meaningful progress as well. Even if few have achieved on the same scale as Claudette and Franckel. If this book shows anything at all, it is that the programme involves a lot of effort. It is complicated, difficult work. If Fonkoze did not have confidence in its results, the programme would not be worth the trouble.

And though words like 'expensive' are always relative – the programme costs more than some things and less than others – the amount that Fonkoze spends on each CLM family is much more than it spends on any of its other interventions. The programme's per-family cost is something that funders and potential funders like to talk about. Although Fonkoze does not have a precise way to answer someone who asks how much each CLM family costs the institution, in 2024 the cost was something like $2,500–3,000. Fonkoze raises almost all of that money from partners who agree to fund a cohort of families or, occasionally, two. The per-family cost of cohorts varies, but the budget for one cohort launched in 2024 showed a cost per family of $2,800. Whether that is a lot of money to help a family lift itself sustainably out of ultra-poverty is a matter of opinion. It is more, however, than one would want to spend on something that doesn't work.

But there are reasons to think that CLM works.

For those of us directly involved in the programme, the evidence is around us all the time. We are part of the selection process, so we know where the families start. We see them and talk with them at their homes, in the corn and bean fields and along the roads and footpaths near where they live, at local markets, and at training workshops. We see and we hear about their small steps forward even as they are taking them. And we attend their graduations. We are witnesses to the difference that 18 months of their hard work is able to make for them. We continue to cross paths with women like Claudette in the years after their graduation, so we know how they continue to advance.

Convincing those who are not constantly around the programme can be more complicated. Some people find stories of members' success compelling, but others can very reasonably imagine that we are choosing to talk about only the successes and that those stories do not paint the entire picture.

They want to see numbers, and the first number that the team generally talks about is the graduation rate. Of the 150 families who were part of the pilot, 144 met Fonkoze's graduation criteria after 18 months, for a graduation rate of 96 per cent. Of the six members who did not graduate, one passed away before she reached the programme's completion. Just two factors came into play for the other five. They either were unable to complete their home repair, were unable to build up enough in assets, or both. None of the other questions on the survey ended up preventing anyone from graduating.

That 96 per cent became a standard our staff fought to uphold, almost a rallying cry. Neither we nor Fonkoze's management mistook a high graduation rate for the point of the programme. The object was always to help members genuinely improve their lives for the long term. But because families entering the programme were so far from meeting the criteria and because the criteria themselves seemed to reflect elements that very minimally define what someone would need to live a better life, qualifying for graduation can sometimes seem like a reasonable shorthand for the success of an individual programme member and the overall graduation rate as a shorthand for the programme's success.

And the consistently high graduation rate is, at least, encouraging. Among the 44 cohorts from the pilot through about 2022, the average graduation rate remained at 96 per cent. Only eight of those cohorts had rates below 95 per cent, and just one had a rate below 90 per cent.

But two things – the addition of the baseline survey and the introduction of digital data collection and data management – made it easy to look at more than whether CLM members qualify for graduation. It has become easy to measure particular improvements as well.

As an example of what we have learned to see, we can consider results from a 2021 cohort of 500 families that the German government funded in Savanèt, a small commune in central Haiti. We can look, for example, at data about their food security. We tracked three important measures of food security, and there were marked improvements in all areas. As shown in Table 17.1, at the end of the programme, very few families were going without food: the average number of meals they were consuming each day had increased by about 40 per cent, and signs of malnutrition had almost disappeared from the population.

We can also look at changes that concern members' homes. Here the changes are more dramatic because the starting points were so low. Almost none of the families drank treated water before the programme, almost none had access to a latrine, and almost none lived in a home that was dry and secure (Table 17.2). Though 78 per cent as a final result for the condition of members' homes was very low compared to what the programme has generally seen over the years, it still marks a great improvement from the baseline.

Table 17.1 Food insecurity among families in Savanèt, before and after the programme

	The family goes a day or more without a single meal often (%)	Average number of meals per day	The family has children who show signs of malnutrition (%)
Baseline	55	1.43	8
Final	2	2.00	1

Table 17.2 Healthy home environments in Savanèt, before and after the programme

	Families who drink treated water (%)	Families with access to a latrine (%)	Families with dry and secure homes (%)
Baseline	1	1	2
Final	96	96	78

Table 17.3 Household finances for families in Savanèt, before and after the programme

	Members who report having savings (%)	The amount of their savings (HTG)*	Members who own productive assets (%)	The value of their assets (HTG)
Baseline	3	2,683	8	5,750
Final	78	9,352	99	51,300

* HTG, Haitian gourd

Table 17.4 Other changes for programme members in Savanèt

	Are all the family's school-age children in school? (%)	On which step of the staircase does the member place herself?
Baseline	64	0.55
Final	83	2.51

If we look next at some basic financial indicators, we see more signs of improvement. Table 17.3 shows how members' savings increased, and the total value of their productive assets, the wealth that they use to make money, had grown by a lot.

Finally, in Table 17.4 we mention two data points that seem important, even if they are harder to fit into a category.

The data on the left-hand side of Table 17.4 is straightforward. The number of families who were sending all their children to school at the end of the programme was 30 per cent higher than it was at the beginning.

The question in the right-hand column requires some explanation. Fonkoze asks members to imagine their community as a staircase, with each of four steps representing a level of wealth or poverty. Members are asked to place themselves on the staircase relative to the other members of their community, with the lowest step representing the poorest families and the highest one the wealthiest. Members' answers thus provide insight into the way they themselves view their situation.

After 18 months in the programme, members viewed themselves, on average, more than four and a half times higher up the staircase. Women had not, on average, even placed themselves on the first step when they first entered the programme. At the end, they were more than halfway up.

But none of those numbers really measures what the programme is trying to achieve. It is no wonder if families are better off 17 months after they first joined the programme. Fonkoze has been investing material resources and staff time in their well-being all through the period. It would be more surprising if their lives hadn't improved.

The programme's objective is not, however, to put the families who participate in a better place, but to help them set off on a path to a better life.

That means helping them make improvements they can sustain and even build upon on their own.

And the programme's impacts endure.

Here again, for those of us around it all the time the most compelling evidence comes from interactions with programme members after graduation. They like to stay in touch with us, and so we get to see them living their new lives. But there is evidence from research as well, studies that involve finding and evaluating programme members in the years after they graduate.

The best evidence comes from studies of the graduation approach that CLM adopted, but not specifically from Fonkoze's programme or from Haiti. The Fonkoze pilot was one of a set of pilots implemented at the same time. The idea was to determine whether a programme that was working in Bangladesh would work in other places as well. These pilots were studied carefully by a team featuring Nobel prize winners Abhijit Banerjee and Esther Duflo, and the results were clear:

> One year after the end of the intervention, 36 months after the productive asset transfer, 8 out of 10 indices still showed statistically significant gains, and there was very little or no decline in the impact of the program on the key variables (consumption, household assets, and food security). Income and revenues were significantly higher in the treatment group in every country. Household consumption was significantly higher in every country except one (Honduras). In most countries, the (discounted) extra earnings exceeded the program cost (Banerjee et al., 2015).

Fonkoze chose not to participate in that study for various reasons. First, since the programme was new, Fonkoze was reluctant to commit to the level of discipline that a trial seemed to require. It wanted to be able to respond flexibly to situations as they arose. Second, it was unwilling to enrol families in ultra-poverty as a control group, knowing how difficult their lives were, without any guarantee that it would have the resources to work with them even when the study was complete. Third, it was concerned about the negative social impact of choosing randomly to work with some families in ultra-poverty, but not with others, who might even live in the same community or a nearby one.

But in ensuing years, Fonkoze has arranged for independent or partially independent evaluations of CLM families in the years after they complete the programme. The families fall into three groups: those who continue to progress, those who maintain the progress they made during the programme, and those who lose ground relative to where they were at the end of the programme. In studies of CLM, those three groups have been similar in size. In other words, the best evidence we currently have is that roughly two-thirds of members either maintain the progress they made while they were part of the programme, or they build on it. Table 17.5 summarizes the results of three studies.

Table 17.5 CLM members after they graduate: summary of evaluation results

Study and year	Families made further progress (%)	Families sustained their progress (%)	Families lost progress (%)
Concern Worldwide and Fonkoze (2014)	31	39	30
Shoaf and Simanowitz (2019)	31	41	29
Mercy Focus on Haiti 1 (2021)*	27	31	43

* Unpublished document entitled 'Post-graduation evaluation: Mercy Focus on Haiti Cohort #1', August 2021.

A recent study of two cohorts about two and four years after graduation was less encouraging, suggesting that Haiti's current socio-political upheaval is having a negative impact on the families' ability to sustain their progress.

We worry about the families who do not sustain their progress, persistently tinkering with what we do, hoping to achieve more. One basic question about them is how far back they slip. Fonkoze has very little data to answer the question with, but we do have some. Those whom we have evaluated have still been, on average, better off than they had been when they started, most of them by a lot.

But even as we struggle to improve our work, hoping that we can help our members accomplish more and accomplish more enduringly, we must remember to celebrate our members' success. The numbers – such as we have – tell a largely positive story. Families who live in some of the direst poverty that the world knows are, on the whole, making and sustaining progress along the path toward a better life.

CHAPTER 18
Changed lives

The VSLA for former CLM members in Lawa meets in a small structure that community members built especially for their VSLAs. More than three years after graduation, the association that the CLM programme established there still meets on Wednesday afternoons. Three other VSLAs meet on other days. These others were founded by community leaders who learned the VSLA approach by being drawn into assisting Fonkoze's staff in creating a VSLA for CLM members, and they found it useful enough to want more.

The members of all four VSLAs contributed to the building's construction. Its rectangular frame is made of rough-hewn wooden support posts, and the corrugated metal of its roof still has much of its original shine. That same metal roofing material was used for its four walls and its doors as well. The packed dirt floor takes a heavy sweeping before every meeting. Rough wooden benches line the two walls on its long sides. Two more benches are available just inside of the front entrance. A wooden table and a couple of chairs are arranged in front of the back wall. That's where the VSLA's management committee sits during meetings. They take in people's savings and loan repayments, they pay out all the loans, and they record each transaction in the group's notebook and in the appropriate member's booklet as well. The official counters sit there too. They are the ones who actually handle the money.

***

It is worth taking some time to think about the value of the CLM programme's work and the impact of Fonkoze's investment of money, time, and effort into the programme and the families it serves.

I started writing this book with an axe to grind. Years into my experience with the CLM programme, I need nothing to convince me of its value and importance. I wanted to write something about it that would be convincing but also detailed.

The argument for the programme's importance depends on two claims. The first claim is easy to make. There are human beings who live with a degree of poverty that should be unacceptable to everyone. In a sense, the UN's first Millennium Development Goal makes that claim for us, at least formally. But descriptions of the families whom Fonkoze's team meets during the selection process makes the case concretely, vividly. Looking back at Hébert's description of the families he met in Lawa can and maybe should generate the sort of outrage he carries with him all the time.

The second claim is more complicated. Agreeing that there is a problem is one thing, but agreeing about a solution is another.

I have shared data that I find convincing. About 95 per cent of families meet simple graduation criteria after 18 months. Two-thirds of families who complete the programme either sustain their success or build upon it in the years that follow. And the limited evidence available suggests that most of the one-third of the families who lose ground are still a long way ahead of where they were when they started.

But my finding the data convincing says very little. I was already convinced.

I have shared stories of women like Clermicile, Lucienne, and Claudette, who have made spectacular progress, and those stories will always impress some readers. But other readers might suspect, very reasonably, that these stories were cherry-picked, selected precisely because of how striking they are. And their suspicion would be true. That is exactly why I chose to share them.

I think that one of the strongest arguments for the programme is the positive transformation it helps women make even when it has not quite worked as well as we would like it to. Women, after graduation, who might even want to talk about their losses, who are probably part of that unfortunate third, but who still show the signs that their lives remain changed for the better. Searching for such women, I went back to Lawa.

***

By June 2024, the three women from Lawa whom Hébert had met during his final verification visit – Jeanna, Itana, and Clotude – had been programme graduates for over three and a half years. They were still attending their regular VSLA meetings and, halfway through the association's 12-month cycle, each had savings. None had been able to purchase shares every week. All three women's savings books showed lines traced with pens across some of the spaces that should have shown the star-shaped mark with which the VSLA's secretary records each share that a VSLA member buys. But after about six months, they all had over 3,500 gourds saved. That's not a lot. It's less than $30. But it is about half of what the team hopes a programme member will save during their first cycle. And during that first cycle, members have six months of regular cash stipends and case managers encouraging them. So, all three retained a savings habit that none of them had before they joined CLM.

Jeanna looks great. She comes to the meeting with her hair carefully done and her dress clean and pressed, despite the rough hike from her home to the meeting. She and her husband have eight children now, and they have only been able to send two of them to school all through this past year, but in the past they were often unable to send any child to school at all. Jeanna still goes occasionally to Senmak to stay with her sister and earn money through small commerce, but she's moved from selling drinking water and kerosene, which might earn 300 or 400 gourds on a very good day, to selling cooking oil, which earns her twice as much on an average day. Her husband Nelso still farms, and Jeanna works with him closely when she's not in Senmak, but their farming has changed in one important way. They were able to buy their own farmland, so Nelso is no longer restricted to sharecropping. He, his wife, and their children are entitled to everything they can produce.

Jeanna is unhappy that she has had very little luck with her livestock. Her goats and her pigs have all died. But the one animal she's been able to keep healthy is an important one. Since her time in the programme, she had wanted a pack animal. With a pack animal, she could dream of giving up her trips to Senmak entirely and of running a business without leaving her family. Without a pack animal, it would be hard to carry enough product to downtown Gwomòn, where she would like to sell. So, she is very pleased with the young donkey she was finally able to buy this year. She hasn't started her new business yet. She needs more capital to get it going. But having a donkey is a first step, and the next step no longer seems far away.

Clotude has 5,000 gourds of savings, which puts her well ahead of the two other women. She invests most of her money in her farming, planting mainly beans and sugarcane. All three of the children who now live with her are in school, though as the end of the school year approaches, she still has debts she needs to clear with the school's principal.

When I first met her, she explained to me patiently that there was no way to do commerce in Lawa. People would buy on credit, and then they wouldn't pay. She did not think of herself as the kind of person capable of insisting that people pay her what they owe. Now small commerce is her main source of income. The home she built with the programme's help has become something like a grocery store. She sells food staples – rice, oil, corn meal, seasoning, spaghetti, and the like – but also laundry supplies and other basics.

She talks about the difference that the advice she got from Fonkoze's staff has made for her. 'I used to see something I needed to do and ignore it. I would always say I would get around to things later. They taught me to get things done right away when I can. That way I accomplish more.'

Like Jeanna, she has had bad luck with some of her livestock, but she's anxious to start investing in livestock again. 'When I get my VSLA money in November, I want to buy a goat or a pig or a sheep, whatever looks good in the market.' Until then, she will manage her fields and her commerce, and she'll continue to save.

In some ways, Itana's progress has been less striking than that of the other two women from Lawa. Like the other two, she's had trouble keeping livestock. Unlike the other two, she has not built a single clear strategy for earning, even if she has been able to save more than 4,000 gourds.

But the first time I spoke with her she talked of how she wished she could have afforded to keep her children with her. Several of them had moved out to live with wealthier family members, but some of those have now come back. The country's deteriorating social situation left them feeling unsafe where they were, and she was excited to be able to welcome them home.

She is no longer the only earner in her household because, though her husband still struggles to stay healthy and do his part, she now has older children living with her who can lend a hand. Either she or one of the kids will buy a load of sugarcane or charcoal or beans or whatever is available in the neighbourhood, and they will lug it to where they can sell it. The small lumps of income that they earn enable them to manage the household together. Between her, her husband, and their various children and grandchildren, they are now nine. Her home has become a lively place.

She puts things clearly, 'We have lost ground. The country is full of problems. There have been no harvests because of drought. The animals died. Things cost too much. But we aren't discouraged. We have our plans. We know what to do.'

***

The changes that the three women in Lawa have experienced have been unspectacular, but they've been positive and important. Their lives have improved. Each woman lives in a dry, secure home that she is proud of, each is able to take care of her family better than she once could, and each is accumulating savings that she'll be able to draw on if she runs into trouble or will be able to invest to help her take a new step forward.

But the first person I wrote about at the beginning of this book was Lucienne, another woman from Gwomòn, but from a different part of the commune. In 2024, she still lived in the house she built when she was a member of the programme, overlooking the river in Ravin Gwomòn. I found her sitting on a low chair on her front porch, cleaning a bowl of cherries that she was preparing to make juice for her children when they came home from school. A young boy was sitting with her, watching her anxiously. She introduced me to him, her nephew. Her sister, who lives in a neighbouring town, was struggling to take care of the boy, so Lucienne invited him to stay with her. He came in May. By then he had lost the current school year, but Lucienne will send him to school in Gwomòn in September.

Lucienne graduated from the CLM programme a few months before the women in Lawa joined it. It had been about five years since her graduation when I went to see her in June 2024. She was pregnant. Her baby would be her second child with the partner who joined her and her three older children back when she was part of the programme. 'We did not want another child. Children are expensive. They set you back. But once a child arrives, it is yours for good.'

Lucienne juggles a couple of different income sources to support her family. Most of the time, she buys and sells at the downtown marketplace, which is not far from her home. She buys sacks of produce and divides them up for retail sales. It is the same business that she managed before the programme, but she no longer depends on credit. She buys her merchandise with cash, which allows her to let her business decisions depend on what seems best, rather than what seems possible. She belongs to three different VSLAs, and she makes deposits in all three every week.

When she misses a day in the market, it is no longer because she cannot get her hands on anything she could sell. She has to stay home sometimes to work the land she has purchased with income from her business. She now owns two fields planted with sugarcane, and she is sometimes drawn away from the market to supervise fieldwork or the milling of her harvest to make molasses. She is happy to have a partner helping her with all the farming, but she very much thinks of the cane fields as belonging to her, not to them.

Lucienne smiled shyly as she explained that the next time I come by her neighbourhood, I probably won't find her. She had managed to save up 50,000 gourds from the sale of her cane, and she had bought a small plot in downtown Gwomòn. She was getting ready to build a new home there. She would be closer to the market, and her children – including her nephew – would be closer to better schools. She was living in that new home by the beginning of 2025.

Five years after graduation, Lucienne is one of the spectacular successes. And I ask her whether she can explain.

> 'Lucienne, you know the women who were in the programme with you. You know that a lot of them have made progress, but there are not many who have made the progress you've made.'
> 'Really? You think so?' she answered with a grin.
> 'Come on. Let's be serious. You know that better than I do.'
> 'I guess it's true. It's because of where I started. When I started in the programme, I wasn't even human. Now I am someone. People see me.'

She goes on to talk about the humiliations she once knew. Abandoned with her three children, she lacked her own house, and she could not even afford to rent a room in someone else's. She depended on a homeowners' not always gracious willingness to let her sleep rent-free with her children in a decaying shack they no longer needed. She fed herself and those children with a business that depended on always finding people willing to sell her produce on credit. Like the space she lived in, her income depended on a life of constantly asking people favours. For Lucienne, that memory keeps her moving forward.

Of course, there is more to Lucienne's success than that. The humiliations she remembers might be a strong, an important spur to her success but she has been smart and, probably, fortunate too. She does not herself mention either her good judgement or her good luck. Years ago, she spoke of how important her case manager's encouragement had been, but that was no longer foremost on her mind by 2024.

But there is a simple truth that lies behind all her success, just as it lies behind the less dramatic successes of the women in Lawa and the thousands of women who have been through the programme. Lucienne and the other women were stuck in ultra-poverty because they lacked the tools they needed to work their way out: know-how, perhaps, but also resources to invest and the materials and the strategies they needed for their health. The CLM programme gave them those tools and helped them see how to use the tools well. Its staff then stayed by their side as they took their first steps forward. It provided them with an opportunity to flourish that is their right.

CHAPTER 19
Perspectives

I had originally wanted to end the book with what I was able to say about Lucienne and the three women from Lawa. I imagined it as a case for a certain approach to extreme poverty, with a detailed account of that approach. But I have come to think that it needs a last few words about the programme's perspectives for the future.

I hope that these pages have made it clear that the programme has evolved over the years. I have written about various pieces of it that have changed since it was first piloted. Members select the assets they will receive for businesses differently than they once did, and Fonkoze provides the assets differently as well. Fonkoze has altered the way it supports members through home repair and construction. Individuals with disabilities have been added as an explicit focus of the programme. The promotion of savings has shifted from a focus on savings accounts to a focus on village savings and loan associations. These are just a few important examples, and I could go on. But Fonkoze is in the process of changing the programme in two fundamental ways, and it is worth talking about each: we are trying to bring services to a broader population of families in extreme poverty and to sharpen our focus on building up women's agency, and not just wealth.

The approach that Fonkoze's programme grew out of was created by BRAC to reach the very poorest families, those living in ultra-poverty. Fonkoze adopted the approach with that same goal in mind. We have always invested significant time and energy into identifying the families in the deepest poverty in each community we pass through. Selecting only those families is one of the programme's basic elements.

But we saw a problem early on. There were always families who did not quite qualify for the programme. Their poverty might be deep, but as Hébert wrote of one of the families he rejected for CLM in Lawa, 'Things might be hard for them, but they have a minimum'. Originally, Fonkoze could serve such families by offering a programme called *Ti Kredi*, which ran parallel with CLM, but Fonkoze was not consistently able to offer the two programmes together, and we eventually stopped offering *Ti Kredi* at all. This left a gap in our programming between the services we can offer to families in ultra-poverty and the solidarity-group credit that our sister organization can offer to families who, while still far from wealthy, were much better off.

Framing this issue in jargon, calling it 'a gap in programming', risks making it sound less serious than it is. For years, we have been leaving behind families whose poverty is deep because their poverty is not quite deep enough for CLM. The least serious consequence of doing so – though not an insignificant matter – is the weight of frustration that the staff making selection decisions carries with them. For one thing, these decisions are painful for the staff. For another, the weight of them may lead us to loosen the standards for admittance to the programme. Saying 'No' gets hard.

The more serious consequence of doing so relates to the families themselves. Hébert wrote that they 'have a minimum'. But the CLM programme works with many families who once had a minimum, or even much more than a minimum. Livelihoods in Haiti are fragile. People get sick, and livelihoods disappear to pay for treatment. People die, and livelihoods disappear to pay for funerals. And those are just two common, obvious examples. Families grow and expenses grow with them. If the expenses grow beyond the family's income, the family's livelihood is doomed. And under ordinary circumstances, the CLM team would not plan to pass back through a community a second time. A family who falls into ultra-poverty after we pass through their community may never get another opportunity.

In 2014, Fonkoze collaborated with Concern Worldwide to evaluate families who had been part of the pilot. The study found, among other things, that 70 per cent of the families it interviewed had either sustained the progress they made during the programme or made additional progress four years later (Concern Worldwide and Fonkoze, 2014). There was, however, nothing to compare the families to, so it was difficult to interpret the results.

In the absence of a control group, Fonkoze sent evaluators to interview some of the CLM graduates' neighbours, families who had been too wealthy to join the programme when the members of the pilot had been selected. The evaluation report was never published, but we can share its results. Fonkoze's team found that the former CLM members were well ahead of the formerly wealthier neighbours across a range of indicators:

> [O]ur data show that the CLM graduates are better off than the control group even though the control group started off doing better than the CLM members. For example, 91.11% own farmland compared to only 56.67% for the control group. And such land ownership can do a lot for both food security and income-generation. 28.89% own at least two large animals compared to 6.67% for the control group, and 55.55% have goats and poultry whereas only 16.67% of the control group do.

> We see similar differences when it comes to their children's education. 71.11% of CLM graduates send all their children to school whereas only 23.33% of the control group do. No CLM graduates fail to send any children to school, but 46.66% of the control group do.

> Finally, the data for food security reveals a big difference between their levels of poverty. 60% of the CLM graduates are food insecure

but without hunger and a small number, 2.22%, are food secure. Here we see the consequences of the data concerning ownership of farmland. Only 37.78% of the CLM graduates are hungry, whereas 100% of the control group is.

These once-wealthier families lacked productive assets, including land; they struggled to send their children to school; and scored as hungry on the food security survey they were given. All this is exactly what would have qualified them for CLM.

Fonkoze's team decided it needed a another approach it could offer such families, not so much because of their immediate need, though their need was compelling enough, but to help them make themselves less likely to fall into ultra-poverty. The new approach involves less intense coaching and smaller transfers of resources, and it lasts for less time. It is built around helping people invest in their existing sources of income and organizing them into savings and loan associations. Eventually, Fonkoze would like to offer this programme in parallel with its standard graduation programme everywhere it works.

***

The second fundamental change the programme is undergoing involves its very goal. The programme always framed its goal in terms of helping families lift themselves out of ultra-poverty, and doing so centred on helping them build income they would be able to sustain.

From 2018 to 2022, Fonkoze organized independent studies of the programme. The studies drew important conclusions about CLM's impact on gender equity. Two studies by two different experts underscored the programme's positive effects, and both also suggested ways CLM could do more.

The first study, unpublished work by Haitian feminist Sandra Jean-Gilles, documented how the programme's success at increasing women's economic empowerment encountered resistance both from partners and, sometimes, from the wider community. The second, by Dutch development expert Keetie Roelen, showed how the way women bear an excessive portion of the caregiving tasks in their homes hindered the progress they might otherwise make through CLM (Roelen and Saha, 2019).

Fonkoze began to look beyond the simple but important question of the means that the women it works with have at their disposal to the larger question of the degree to which the women are empowered to manage and to improve their lives. Over the course of four years, a Fonkoze team in Haiti's south-east, funded by the Swiss embassy, piloted a series of new or adapted CLM measures designed to make the empowerment of women the focal point and, second, to integrate training aimed at transforming masculinities into its work with members and their partners.

The effort to make women's empowerment the focus of the CLM programme was led by Nathalie Lamaute-Brisson, a Haitian economist and expert in social promotion and protection. She led the design of the pilot through which we experimented with changes in the programme, oversaw evaluations of the pilot, and led the thinking about how to integrate its lessons.

Putting women's empowerment at the centre of the graduation approach meant, first and foremost, extensive retraining of staff. But it also meant redesigning programme measures to increase flexibility and, so, to maximize the field within which members are making choices. It meant reorganizing and redesigning one of the training modules the programme offers its members – called 'confidence-building training' – to place a focus on developing critical consciousness into the earlier stages of the programme's 18 months. And it meant establishing indicators of empowerment that it would be able to follow.

Introducing sessions aimed at transforming masculinities meant, first of all, doing more from the start to help members' partners feel as though they are part of the programme. Over the years, they have too often looked at the programme as something just for their wives. It meant, in addition, engaging the men in conversations about masculinities both during individual coaching sessions and during workshops. It also meant developing protocols that integrate work with couples into the schedule of the individual coaching each member receives.

The studies by Jean-Gilles and Roelen and Fonkoze's experimentation in the south-east have given the CLM programme a new understanding of its work. The programme has come to see that building a sustainable livelihood is merely a means – though a central means – towards a greater end: helping its members – especially the women – take the control of their own lives that they are entitled to.

References

Andrews, C., de Montesquiou, A., Arevalo Sanchez, I., Dutta, P. V., Paul, B. V., Samaranayake, S., Heisey, J., Clay, T., Chaudhary, S. (2021). *The State of Economic Inclusion Report 2021: The Potential to Scale*. Washington, DC: World Bank. Available at https://openknowledge.worldbank.org/handle/10986/34917

Archibald, E. with Alfers, L., Cabot-Venton, C., Andrews, C., de Montesquiou, A., and Datta, P.V. (2020). *The Potential Role of Economic Inclusion Programmes to Respond to Those Affected by COVID-19*. SPACE and the Partnership for Economic Inclusion. FCDO. Available at https://socialprotection.org/sites/default/files/publications_files/SPACE_~2_0.PDF'.

Artus, H. (2019). Gros-Morne, Habitation Lawa: le Cris de Désarroi d'une Communauté en Détresse. [Lawa, a Neighborhood of Gros-Morne: The Troubled Cry of a Community in Distress]. Available at https://www.apprenticeshipineducation.com/lawa-a-neighborhood-of-gros-morne-the-troubled-cry-of-a-community-in-distress/

Banerjee, A., Duflo, E., Goldberg, N., Karlan, D., Osei, R., Parienté, W., Shapiro, J., Thuysbaert, B., and Udry, C. (2015). A Multifaceted Program Causes Lasting Progress for the Very Poor: Evidence from Six Countries. *Science* 348 (6236). https://doi.org/10.1126/science.1260799

Banque de la Republique d'Haiti (2025). Indice des prix à la consummation [Consumer price index]. Available at https://www.brh.ht/wp-content/uploads/ipc.pdf

BRAC (2014). *Targeting the Ultra Poor Programme Brief: Challenging the Frontiers of Poverty*. Available at https://www.brac.net/images/index/tup/brac_TUP-briefNote-Jun17.pdf

Chemen Lavi Miyò Team (2018). *Evaluating a Graduation Program for Persons with Disabilities: Fonkoze's Experience*. Fonkoze. Available at https://fonkoze.org/wp-content/uploads/2023/05/tech_clmd-evaluation-addendum_1.pdf

CIA (2022). Haiti. *The World Factbook* [online]. Available at https://www.cia.gov/the-world-factbook/countries/haiti/#people-and-society

Concern Worldwide and Fonkoze (2014). *Sustaining Graduation: A Review of the CLM Programme in Haiti*. Available at https://fonkoze.org/assets/tech_sustaining-graduation.pdf

De Montesquiou, A., Ayoubi, Z., Hashemi, S., and Heisey, J. (2017). *Building Resilience through the Graduation Approach: Economic Inclusion of the Poorest Refugees*. United Nations High Commission on Refugees, Trickle Up, and CGAP, March.

The Economist (2015). Leaving It Behind: How to Rescue People from Deep Poverty—and Why the Best Methods Work. *The Economist*, 12 December. Available at https://www.economist.com/international/2015/12/12/leaving-it-behind

Elliott, D. and Werlin, S. (2016). *Final Evaluation: Chemen Lavi Miyò for Persons with Disabilities (CLMD)*. Available at https://fonkoze.org/wp-content/uploads/2023/05/tech_final-report-clmd.pdf

Fonkoze (1995). Propositions de Statuts de Fondation Kole Zepòl (Fonkoze), Modifiés et Votés le 23 janvier 1995.

Fonkoze (2023). Strengthening VSLAs for their CLM Members [online]. Available at https://fonkoze.org/wp-content/uploads/2024/07/CLM-Insights-Maintaining-CLM-Graduates-in-VSLAs.pdf

Greeley, M. (2019). *Targeting the Ultra-Poor: Lessons from Fonkoze's Graduation Programme in Haiti.* IDS Learning Brief. Available at https://fonkoze.org/assets/who-are-the-ultra-poor_learning-brief_jan-22,-2019.pdf

Huda, K. and Simanowitz, A. (2008). Chemin Lavi Miyò – Midterm Evaluation (Unpublished).

Huda, K. and Simanowitz, A. (2010a). *Chemin Lavi Miyò – Final Evaluation (24 Months).* Concern Worldwide and CGAP. Available at https://fonkoze.org/wp-content/uploads/2023/05/tech_clm-24-month-evaluation.pdf

Huda, K. and Simanowitz, A. (2010b). Haiti's Graduation Pilot Final Evaluation, Promising Results [blog], 25 June. CGAP. Available at https://www.cgap.org/blog/haitis-graduation-pilot-final-evaluationpromising-results

International Action (n.d.) Why Clean Water? Haiti Water. Available at: https://haitiwater.org/why/why-clean-water/

Innovations for Poverty Action (2016). Measuring the Fight Against Global Poverty: 10 Years Later [blog], 7 September. Available at https://poverty-action.org/blog/measuring-fight-against-global-poverty-10-years-later

Mullainathan, S. and Shafir, E. (2013). *Scarcity: Why Having Too Little Means So Much.* Times Books/Henry Holt and Co.

Oxford Poverty and Human Development Initiative (2024). What is the Global MPI? [online] Available at https://ophi.org.uk/what-global-mpi

Reed, L., Tardif, J.F., Brown, V., Hastings, A., Marsden, J., and Puri, S. (2017). *The Global State of Ultra-Poverty 2017.* Uplift and RESULTS. Available at https://www.boma.ngo/wp-content/uploads/2019/02/Global-State-of-Ultra-Poverty-2017.pdf

Roelen, K. and Saha, A. (2019). *Fonkoze's CLM Ultra Poverty Programme: Understanding and Improving Child Development and Child Wellbeing.* Institute of Development Studies and Centre for Social Protection. Available at https://fonkoze.org/wp-content/uploads/2023/05/fonkoze-clm-children-s-research-endline-report-final-13-oct-19-.pdf

Shoaf, E. and Simanowitz, A. (2019). *Pathways to Sustained Exit from Extreme Poverty: Evidence from Fonkoze's Extreme Poverty 'Graduation' Programme.* Institute of Development Studies and Fonkoze. Available at https://fonkoze.org/assets/fonkoze_pathway-report_march-2019.pdf

Sulaiman, M., Goldberg, N., Karlan, D., and de Montesquiou, A. (2016). *Eliminating Extreme Poverty: Comparing the Cost-Effectiveness of Livelihood, Cash Transfer, and Graduation Approaches.* Forum. Washington, DC: CGAP.

United Nations (UN) (2023). Nearly Half of Haiti Going Hungry, New Food Security Report Warns. UN News, 30 May. Available at https://news.un.org/en/story/2023/05/1137152

United Nations Department of Economic and Social Affairs (UNDESA) (2013). *The Millennium Development Goals Report 2013.* Available at https://www.un.org/en/development/desa/publications/mdgs-report-2013.html

Werlin, S. (2016). *To Fool the Rain: Haiti's Poor and their Pathway to a Better Life.* Washington, DC: Ti Koze Press.

World Bank (1990). *World Development Report 1990: Poverty.* Available at http://hdl.handle.net/10986/5973

World Bank (2015). 5 Things You Need to Know About Water in Haiti. News, 27 May. Available at https://www.worldbank.org/en/news/feature/2015/05/27/five-things-you-need-to-know-about-water-in-haiti

World Bank and Observatoire National de la Pauvreté et de l'Exclusion Sociale (2014). *Investing in People to Fight Poverty in Haiti, Reflections for Evidence-Based Policy Making.* Washington, DC: World Bank.

www.ingramcontent.com/pod-product-compliance
Lightning Source LLC
Chambersburg PA
CBHW051257020426
42333CB00026B/3250